MW01064263

Welcoming
The
Children

Welcoming The Children

History and Programs of Arizona Baptist

Children's Services 1960-2002

Second Edition

C. Truett Baker

In collaboration with
present and former staff and trustees
of Arizona Baptist Children's Services

i

To order additional copies of this book, contact:
Xlibris Corporation
1-888-795-4274
www.Xlibris.com
Orders@Xlibris.com
80073

TABLE OF CONTENTS

PART I: BACKGROUND

PART II: BEGINNINGS OF ARIZONA BAPTIST CHILDREN'S SERVICES

PART III: FROM GIVING A HOME TO PROVIDING SERVICES

PART IV: FROM SERVICES TO CHILDREN— TO STATEWIDE FAMILY-BASED SERVICES

PART V: TRANSITIONS, CHALLENGES, A BRIGHT FUTURE

Dedication

In appreciation to
the founders and early supporters of ABCS

Mr. and Mrs. J. B. Carnes
***
Mr. and Mrs. Lester Jennings Sr.
***
Rev. and Mrs. George Wilson
and to the

ABCS Baker-Scott Trust for providing the fund for the revised edition.
This trust was established to honor the parents of the author and his wife,
Rev. and Mrs. W. D. Baker
Mr. and Mrs. R. G. Scott

In memoriam

Donna Jakes

1948-2006

**The wife of former president David Jakes who shared
her husband's vision for "welcoming the children" in Jesus' name**

One can see . . . how immensely powerful the belief in and love for a supernatural and noble character and Friend is upon such wild natures; how it inspires to nobleness, restraint, low passions, changes bad habits, and transforms base hearts; how the thoughts of this supernatural Friend can accompany a child of the street and make his daily hard life an offering of loving service . . . whoever has had this experience . . . will begin to understand that Christ must lead reform as well as charity, and that without Him, the worst diseases of modern society can never be cured.

Charles Loring Brace,
The Dangerous Classes of New York

If nothing else, it is the children who cry out for our personal involvement. It's their vulnerability that calls us to start by doing something, not our own sense of readiness.

Jim Wallis,
Faith Works

Foreword

The history of child welfare in the United States rests virtually entirely on the actions of women and men of religious groups and communities who had a heart for children. Long before there was any vision that government had responsibilities for the smallest and youngest and most vulnerable members of communities, people of faith were folding children into their own homes and, when their homes were no longer adequate to the need, creating systems of care that in their day were innovative and compassionate. That history is as old as the nation and as recent as yesterday. People of faith are still on the front line of concern for children. This narrative account of the history of Arizona Baptist Children's Services (ABCS) is unique in the detail and critique from within one such thread of compassion. ABCS is one of the younger religiously affiliated organizations that exist in this country, and yet it is almost forty years old. Long before the "faith-based initiative" was a gleam in any politician's eye, ABCS and other such organizations had been expressing the concern of religious people for vulnerable, troubled, and troubling children who seem to be expendable, discarded by our society using means perhaps more sophisticated but no less devastating than the abandonment of newborns more than two thousand years ago.

Truett Baker tells this story as a passionate insider of ABCS, giving us the advantage of his commentary on and critique of this heritage of care. Because he brings his own knowledge as a former leader of this organization, he can relate this narrative in a way no other can. The result is a rich mine of information about the development, struggles, defeats, and successes of ABCS, illustrated by all the twists and turns of caring for children in a changing society. In a time when "faith-based organizations" are being described with a broad brush that ignores the intricacies of differences and development over time, *Welcoming the Children* highlights the multiple dimensions and complexities that any such organization represents. For example, it tells the story of collaborating with government to provide services in ways that recognize the challenges and compromises, as well as the advantages, that such collaboration represents for religiously affiliated organizations.

Finally, in many respects, *Welcoming the Children* actually tells a multitude of stories, stories of individuals who gave their lives as maintenance personnel, child-care workers, board members, donors, presidents, chaplains, nurses, and secretaries in this organization. Ultimately, every organization is a compendium of such stories, but we rarely are able to glimpse the complexity and diversity of people with their complex motivations and commitments and their shared passion for a mission that Truett Baker highlights in *Welcoming the Children*. He has given the gift of memory to Arizona Baptists, a memory of what they have been able to do when they committed themselves together and trusted in God to work through them. Beyond Arizona and Baptists, the fields of child welfare and church social work will be enriched by the lessons learned and illustrated about taking the deep compassion of faithful people, adding to it professional competence, and then seeking collaborations that can create hope for those with no hope.

Diana Garland
Dean, Baylor School of Social Work   July 8, 2006

Acknowledgments

History has been a hobby of mine since college days when it was my degree minor. In later years, I have added to that interest biography, family history, and the history of Christian ministry to children and families. As president of Arizona Baptist Children's Services, I hoped for years to write the history of this ministry that I dearly love. When my successor, President David Jakes, approached me about the subject, I tried to act as surprised as I was thrilled, since I had started writing the history *two years earlier*! Unknown to Mr. Jakes at the time of his request, the board had suggested in a strategic planning session in 1986 that I write such a book following a brief history that I had presented. The minutes of that board meeting read:

> A very informative, enlightening history of the Arizona Southern Baptist Convention, its involvement in childcare support (dating from at least 1925), and of the Baptist Children's Home, was then presented by Truett, reflecting the extensive historical research he has conducted on this subject. The board expressed hope that information will be made available in some form prior to Truett having the time *to develop it fully into a book* . . . (Minutes, Arizona Baptist Children's Services, Board of Trustees Strategic Planning Session, May 6, 1986)

I employed David Jakes as a consultant in business management and planning during my presidency and quickly developed a friendship with and affection for him and his lovely wife, Donna. When the board selected him as my successor, I couldn't have been more pleased. I am grateful for his friendship, and his request of me and that of the board to write this history of which I am a part.

I am grateful for the 2002 ABCS Board of Trustees who approved, supported, and encouraged this project. They shared the belief, which many of us have, that this is a history that must be preserved for generations of Arizona Baptists to come and for all those interested in Christian family ministry development.

2002 ARIZONA BAPTIST CHILDREN'S SERVICES BOARD OF TRUSTEES

This project was a group effort. There was no way I could do it alone. There are not enough words to adequately express my delight and appreciation for the team of past and present staff and board members who provided information and editing. Simply to list their names seems a small gesture for the giant task they preformed. My eternal thanks to them and appreciation for them!

THE EDITING COMMITTEE

Rev. David Jakes, president of Arizona Baptist Children's Services

Mrs. Shirley Cravens, director of Resource Development, ABCS, and agency guide in the publishing process

Mrs. Diana Browning, the president's executive assistant for fifteen years and relentless catcher of errors. Diana was one of two committee members who read and edited the entire manuscript.

Ron Willcoxon, PhD Psychologist, executive vice president, ABCS

Rev. Steve Hanna, developer and director of the Southern Regional Office of ABCS. Steve is also director of Regional Operations, ABCS.

Mr. Jack Willis, retired, former trustee, former interim executive director, former director of Finance and Administration

Mr. Bob Garrett, former director and developer of the Wrangler Program and current director of Admissions

Mr. Les Jennings, former trustee and former director of Maintenance. His parents were part of the group that founded ABCS. Les also read the entire manuscript. The writer is especially indebted to him for access to the wealth of information that he has gathered and written about ABCS.

Mr. Archie Stephens, present and former trustee, and former director of AZCARE, an Employee Assistance Program (EAP) earlier owned by ABCS

Rev. Glen Crotts, retired, member and president of the first Board of Trustees of ABCS

Rev. Don Cain, retired and the second executive director (president) of ABCS who was responsible for the transition of ABCS from a children's home to a family-multiservice agency.

Dr. Dan Stringer, retired and former executive director/treasurer, Arizona Southern Baptist Convention and former executive director of at least two other State Baptist Conventions.

They include the Arizona Southern Baptist Convention Staff with special thanks to *Nelda Kent* and the Arizona Baptist Historical Society. Mrs. Kent spent hours making copies of minutes that saved my Phoenix time for research in other areas of ABCS history.

My cousin *Mrs. Noreene Doss* of Springfield, Missouri, read every word of this book and put her former experience as an administrative assistant for the superintendent of schools and the board of the Springfield school system into editing the book for spelling, grammar, and syntax. She also looked at the book with fresh eyes and helped with wording that was clear to me but may be unclear to others. My eternal thanks to this dear lady.

My greatest fan, my beloved wife *Carolyn*, deserves much credit and my thanks for her support and patience during those months when she was a "writer-widow." She did editing, ran errands, and kept the details of everyday living from crashing in on me to allow time for this project.

Acknowledgments would not be complete with expressing appreciation for the patient guidance of Xlibris, the publisher. Special thanks to Jake Mama and and Jem Adams who were untiring in their efforts to please.

C. Truett Baker

Introduction

Jesus had left Caesarea Philippi earlier with his disciples. He set his course to Jerusalem for the last time. He was going there to die. While the disciples didn't understand all that Jesus said, they understood enough that a pale of uncertainty and apprehension overshadowed the weary travelers by the time they reached Capernaum, his base of ministry. The cross was on his mind, but personal greatness was on their minds. To teach them about humility, he sat down and took a child on his lap and said to them, "Anyone who welcomes a little child like this in my name is welcoming me, and anyone who welcomes me is welcoming my Father who sent me" (Mark 9:36-37 *The Living Bible*).

The following day he left for Judea. Arriving there, he was met by the crowds who responded to his growing popularity. As was the custom, the women brought their children out to be blessed by the young rabbi. The disciples tried to protect Jesus from unnecessary interruptions as they journeyed toward Jerusalem. However, to Jesus, the children were not an interruption. They were always welcomed. He rebuked the disciples with a reminder, "Let the children come to me, for the Kingdom of God belongs to such as they. Don't send them away! I tell you as seriously as I know how that anyone who refuses to come to God as a little child will never be allowed into his Kingdom. Then he took the children into his arms and placed his hands on their heads and he blessed them" (Mark 10:14-16 TLB).

On these two occasions and many others, Jesus forever established the principle that children are to be valued and loved. Every generation since then has had to decide how to flesh out that tender principle. The eternal ideal is that children will be raised, loved, and nurtured by a family. Nevertheless, families become crippled and are even taken by death. The people of God are left to decide their fate. Every generation since Jesus has passionately embraced his challenge to "welcome the children" and "care for the least of these . . ."

This story is about how people of faith, with the major focus upon Arizona Southern Baptists, have responded to the mandate of Jesus to "welcome the children" whose families have been crippled or absent. To tell that story, the writer has chosen to go back in time to create a context of historical connection. What Southern Baptists and Arizona Baptist Children's Services (ABCS) are doing in the year of the Lord 2006 is little different than the experience of how the church responded to the needs of children in the first, fifth, or eighteenth centuries. Only the methods have changed.

Part I: Background

Chapter 1

Early Beginning In Child Care

The Early Church and the Children

Imagine that you are standing on the outskirts of Rome in the year AD 50. You are at the city dump. Fires burn to destroy the refuse of the hordes of people who live in that crowded city. The smell is almost overwhelming. The bodies of dead animals are brought there, as well as trash and garbage of every description. The smoke, flies, smell of spoiled food all mingle together. This is like the *Gehenna* of Jerusalem of which Christ spoke when he described it as a place where the "fire is not quenched" (Mark 9:46).

Your attention is soon turned from the smell to the sounds of the place. You hear the cracking noise of the fire and the occasional shuffle of rats as they scurry about, and then you hear a sound that is not consistent with the morbid character of this place. It is the low whimper of a baby. It is not the sharp cry of hunger or discomfort but the whimper of a baby who has cried herself hoarse and hasn't the energy to make the sharp, shrill sounds of healthy infancy. As your eyes search the hazy surface of the litter, you see a small cloth-wrapped bundle move. You believe, at first, that it may be a wounded animal that someone has disposed of here at the place where unwanted things are left. As you move closer and carefully pull back the wrapping, you discover a baby that could not be more than a few hours old. A baby has been left to die at the city dump.

1

If you were born during the century before or the century after Christ in the Greco-Roman world, you could have been that baby. Greek and Roman families who had birthed handicapped children, or for any reason didn't want their newborn children, could abandon them in this fashion. Aristotle and Plato approved of this, and it was a common, accepted practice in the Greek and Roman civilizations. Life was cheap, and children were often considered a burden or nuisance.

Evil men would collect these abandoned babies and raise them as slaves, beggars, and prostitutes. The early church in Rome, Athens, and other great cities would also go to the city dumps and rescue these children and place them in the homes of the widows in the church. The church was then known to care for orphans and widows (Acts 7). This, together with Paul's collection for the needy saints in Jerusalem, were the first acts of benevolence by the New Testament Church (Brace 1872).

In this culture, the unwanted children included those who were illegitimate, deformed, children of incestuous relationships, and twins. The gradual spread and acceptance of the Christian ethic changed this pattern of dealing with children. As rejection of children through infanticide, abandonment, or the other measures became less acceptable to society, alternate means of care for these unwanted children came into practice.

Child-care ministry as an institution can be dated as early as AD 325 with the Council of Nicea. This first universal church council was called following the conversion to Christianity of the Roman Emperor Constantine. The council was called to address the doctrinal issue of the nature of Christ; however, one of the mandates to come out of the council was a decree that a Xenodocheion, or shelter for the needy, should be established in every Christian village. This included the care of destitute, abandoned, as well as ill children who were cared for together with the elderly and disabled (Kadushin 1974).

The Middle Ages

The care of children became fully institutionalized during the Middle Ages. Life was organized around the manor, and dependent children were often cared for within the larger common "family" of the manor. The manor as a social institution supported the integrity of the family unit. Nevertheless, mortality among children was high. Estimates were made that as many as two-thirds of all children died before reaching the age of four.

The medieval church was an integral part of that social structure. The great monasteries of Europe provided refuge for orphan children when the manor system proved insufficient. The care provided by the monasteries, abbeys, and convents was supplemented and later replaced by the hotels de Dieu (hospitals), which were supported by the Church.

In AD 600 at the Council of Rouen, priests were instructed to inform their congregations that women could leave unwanted children at the door of the local church and provision would be made for them.

Datheus, the archbishop of Milan, established a hospital for foundlings in the 700s. Other Christian asylums for deserted children were established in Treves in the sixth century, Angiers in the seventh century, and in Milan in AD 787.

The Secularization of Relief: A New Role for Government

A shift in responsibility for needy children came following the decline of the manor. This occurred at the beginning of the Industrial Revolution and the onset of the Protestant Reformation. The Protestant leaders, Luther and Zwingli, urged that contributions be made for the needy through local government authorities; however, the church wardens played the leading role in relief administration. This represented the first cooperation between church and state in charity work and established a model that would be followed for hundreds of years.

In 1572, Queen Elizabeth signed the Acts of Parliament, which created a tax to provide care for the needy. The statute of 1572 marked the first recognition that government was responsible for providing aid to people who could not maintain themselves. Interestingly, the law provided that the church wardens and four homeowners would oversee the dispensing of the funds (Friedlander 1955). The early leaders of the

Charity Organization Society (1869) and the Settlement House movement in England were ministers.

There are perhaps several explanations for the shift from total church responsibility to joint church-state support of charity. Only three will be mentioned here. First, with the collapse of the manor system and the beginning of the Industrial Revolution, the impact upon the family system was devastating. The church simply could not handle the magnitude of the social fallout caused by the Industrial Revolution. In addition, dwindling revenues to the church resulted from the collapse of feudalism and the beginning of the Reformation. Second, the church was reeling under the impact of the Reformation and turned its energies inward, redefining and crystallizing its theology. Church leaders, including the reformers, believed that the needy should be cared for but did not believe that the care necessarily had to be provided by the church. Therefore the church leaders became strong advocates for providing care through the local government.

Third, separation of church and state were understood to involve issues of spiritual authority, not benevolence. This would change following the Great Awakening in the colonies as the number of dissenters grew. Dissent, which began as an expression of soul freedom in the context of the established church, would spread to include dissent against everything that connected the church with the state. As persecution increased, the dissenters (primarily Quakers, Baptists, Mennonites, and Dunkers) determined to have nothing to do with the state. Furthermore, they mistrusted those church bodies who had any ties whatsoever with the established Church of England. That distrust of government by some conservative religious groups continues to the present.

As the church gave less attention to direct care of children during this period, the state began to take a more active role in their care, but there was a difference in the motivation involving state care, as well as a difference in methods of care. The church had followed a tradition of providing care because of the love of Christ, which motivated love for all people. This affected the type of care provided by the church. The state's motive was different resulting in different methods of care. The idea of the "public good" came later in the history of the American Republic.

The Early American Period and Social Control

In Europe and the early colonial period, children were cared for as a means for social control. As the new world was being settled, English authorities would remove homeless street children and ship them to the colonies. This solved two problems. It removed the beggar children who were creating a social problem on the streets of London and, at the same time, provided cheap labor for the colonies. Charles Dickens wrote about those children in *Oliver Twist*, his nineteenth century novel about English workhouses.

From 1619 to 1620, the Virginia Company of London recruited in the almshouses and among the poor of London to increase the settlement population in the new world. A hundred children over the age of twelve were shipped the first year. Many died during the long and difficult trip. "Transportation of idle and needy children from crowded England to labor-starved Virginia was regarded not only as a boon to the Virginia planters but as a service to king and country and a kindness to the children. From the early days of the colony, children were sent to Virginia as servants or apprentices" (Kingsbury 1970, 1:6-7).

The English New Light evangelist George Whitfield came to America on a ship carrying such children. He was burdened as he thought of what would happen to them in the new world. With the help and encouragement of Benjamin Franklin, he started the first Protestant orphanage in America at Savannah, Georgia, in 1740. He named it Bethesda, "House of Mercy." Whitfield lit the fires of the Great Awakening in the American colonies. He also stirred the hearts of the colonists for helping needy children. After each service he would take up a freewill offering for "his" children at Bethesda (ibid.).

Dr. Marshall B. Jones, a scholar of the orphanage movement, writes, "His Bethesda Orphan House was not a response to need; after 20 years it ran out of sufficient orphans to justify its existence. Bethesda was inspired by a religious ideal . . ." (Jones 1993, 12). There is certainly a basis for arguing about Rev. Whitfield's motive, but many orphanages experienced a sharp decline in their populations after twenty years.

That did not mean they were unneeded at their beginning. What cannot be disputed was the loving heart the evangelist had for children. This tradition of caring for the helpless was a part of the "works by faith" that would characterize the Christian tradition throughout history. When the evangelist was twenty-five years old, the state of Georgia gave him five hundred acres for the site of his orphanage. The following excerpts from Whitfield's journal describe both his love for children and commitment to the Gospel of Christ. In Whitfield's mind and heart, these two could not be separated:

January 24, 1740 Went this morning and took possession of my lot. I called it Bethesda, that is, the House of Mercy, for I hope many acts of mercy will be shewn here, and that many will be stirred up to praise the Lord, as a God whose mercy endureth forever.

Tuesday, January 29, 1740 Took in three German orphans, the most pitiful objects I think I ever saw . . . they have been used to exceedingly hard labor . . . Were all the money I ever collected, to be spent in freeing these three children from slavery, it would be well laid out. I have also in my house nearly twenty more, who in all probability, if not taken in, would be ignorant of God and Christ . . . continue this and all other blessings to them, for thy mercies sake, O Lord.

Wednesday, January 30, 1740 . . . I trust before my return to England, I shall see the children and family quite settled. I find it will be an expensive work; but it is for the Lord Christ. He will take care to defray all charges . . . Whatever is done for God, ought to be done speedily, as well as with all our might.

Monday, February 1, 1740 Took in four fresh orphans, and set out with two friends to Frederica, in order to pay my respects to General Oglethorpe, and to fetch the orphans in the southern parts of the colony. ((Bremner 1970, 1:272).

The first orphanage in America was started in 1727 by seven Ursuline nuns who came to New Orleans to operate a hospital and school for the East India Company. The care of orphans was added to their responsibility following the Natchez massacre. The East India Company paid the sisters 150 liras per year for each orphan. In 1732, the French government contributed an annual subsidy of 4,500 liras to the orphanage. This was the first example of government purchase of care in the New World.

In 1790, the Charleston (S. C.) Orphan House was opened. This was the first public-supported orphanage in America. In 1798 the St. Joseph Female Orphan Asylum was opened in Philadelphia (Eckhard 1970). St. Paul's Orphanage opened the following year in Baltimore, Maryland.

It is important to note that each of these early beginnings came about as a direct result of need. (See arguments to the contrary as stated elsewhere in this chapter). This need was often expressed in different and unusual ways. The Hebrew Orphan Asylum in New York was started in 1822. When the first group of Portuguese Jews arrived 167 years earlier in what was then New Amsterdam, they were allowed to remain on the condition that they would always take care of their own. Their cultural and religious roots would have demanded that of them anyway without the mandate of the city fathers. Catholic orphanages developed because of the belief that Protestants would proselytize Catholic children (Jones 1993). A perceived need that could not be appropriately met by others has been the basis for the church's interest and involvement in children's work from the beginning to the present day.

The Era of the Great Orphanages

Modern residential child care resulted from several historical streams. The Jewish child-care movement has already been mentioned. This movement began in New York as the Hebrew Benevolent Society in 1822. It was the nature of the Jewish community to take care of its children, but it was also true that those Jewish children were not welcomed in the early non-Jewish child-care institution. Having been forced early to get into the child-care service, they became very creative in their methods. They were the first to do away with the large warehouse-type institutions. They were conducting programs in the 1930s that others called progressive in the 1960s! They were the first to do children's residential treatment, day treatment, specialized foster care, and treatment group homes. Jacqueline Bernard wrote a history of this movement for their 150th anniversary called *The Children You Gave Us* (1973). It describes the process that took the Jewish Child Care Association from orphanages to a style of continuum of care, offering the specialized services described above.

The second major stream in the development of modern child care was the orphanage movement following the Civil War. The great orphanages of the South, which were developed in the aftermath of the Civil War, were primarily church sponsored. The notable exception was the Charleston Orphan House founded in Charleston, South Carolina, in 1790. (The development of the Baptist orphanages will be described in the next chapter.)

There were also orphanages in the north, but they were funded primarily by the states. One of the largest private orphanages was the New York Catholic Protectory, which housed two thousand children at one time in1891. In addition to the needs of the orphans of the Civil War soldiers, epidemics such as influenza (1918-19), cholera (1832, 1849, 1866), yellow fever (1797, 1805), and small pox orphaned many children in the eighteenth and nineteenth centuries (Jones 1993). The growth of the great cities and urban poverty that accompanied the growth further contributed to the rise in the orphanage population.

Mentioned earlier, Marshall B. Jones, chairman of behavioral science at the Pennsylvania State University College of Medicine in Hershey, isn't convinced that the "vicissitudes of hardship" resulted in the origins of the American orphanage (ibid.). His rationale follows: Most reform movements were led by women, following the Enlightenment and the Revolution. While having little political involvement or power, as their husbands had, the Revolution (as do most wars) forced many women into leadership roles unknown to them before the war. Already possessing the strong nurturing role in the family, they now had to assume all of the leadership in the family in the absence of their soldier husbands. This newfound power would find expression in the drive for social reform, which included the orphanage movement. Mary Beth Norton said it well, "The rhetoric of the revolution found its way even into domestic relations" (1980, 223-224).

It was Professor Jones's belief that this maternal and family instinct, coupled with women's newfound power, was behind the development of the American orphanage. "With few exceptions, orphanages were managed by women and usually owned by them. The women directors were well positioned in society and often from the very top" (1994, 14).

The care of children was not confined to orphanages and almshouses. The practice of placing needy children in private homes (foster care) gradually developed.

The first and perhaps most famous organized "placing-out" was done by the New York Children's Aid Society founded in 1853. Its director, the Reverend Charles Loring Brace, was a thirty-seven year-old missionary in New York's notorious Five Points District (Trattner 1974). Brace believed there was no better place for children to be raised than on the farm, and he developed a plan for the vagrant street children of New York to be sent by train to farms in the Midwest. The "orphan trains" carried over 150,000 children, between 1854 and 1930, to their new homes in the West (Cook 1955). This was not an altogether satisfactory experience for many of the children, but it represented an innovative way to care for needy children and rid the streets of New York of what Brace called *The Dangerous Classes of New York* described in his book (1872). Trattner points out that Brace had a conviction about the importance of family life, but he overlooked the child's own family as the first family of choice in placing children (Trattner 1974).

Children Can't Be Beat . . . or Abused

Prior to 1875, children could be treated just about in any way a parent desired. There were no laws to protect them. In that year, New

York State became the first state to pass legislation protecting children. It came about in a strange way. Mary Ellen Wilson was a nine-year-old girl indentured to Francis and Mary Connolly. She was beaten, stabbed with scissors, and tied to her bed. Neighbors reported the mistreatment, but authorities could do nothing because there were no laws forbidding this or provision for removing an abused child from such a home. Etta Wheeler, a church worker, contacted Henry Bergh of the Society for the Prevention of Cruelty to Animals (SPCA). Based upon the fact that Mary Ellen was an "animal," the SPCA obtained a writ of habeas corpus to remove Mary Ellen from the home. On April 9, 1874, her case was tried before the New York State Supreme Court, and Mrs. Connolly was sentenced to one year in prison, and Mary Ellen was placed in a new home. In April of the following year, the New York Society for the Prevention of Cruelty to Children was established (Bergh 1971).

Other states would follow the example of New York State and establish their own societies. In the wake of this development, a growing concern for the rights of children developed. Near the close of the nineteenth century, Charles Birtwell, a minister, worked out a system for providing care for at-risk children. His unique contribution to the development of child welfare was individualizing the needs of children. His goal was "in each instance to suit the action to the real need, heeding the teachings of experience, still to study the conditions with a freedom from assumption and a directness and freshness of view as complete as though the case in hand stood absolutely alone" (Kadushin 1974, 396). Assessing and addressing the needs peculiar to each child would be embraced at the First White Conference on Children in 1909 and become a standard principle in the child-welfare practice and culture.

Toward the end of the nineteenth century, agencies developed better methods of placing-out[1] children who could not live with their own families. This involved more careful studies of prospective foster parents, understanding the needs of children, and giving individual treatment to children. Few adoptions were carried out because this had not been a

---

[1]   An early term for foster care.

measure provided for in English common law (Trattner 1994). A turning point in the care for children in this country took place during the First White House Conference on the Care of Dependent Children in 1909. The conference was called by President Theodore Roosevelt in response to nine prominent child-welfare people, which included Homer Folks, the best known social worker of that period (Proceedings etc. 1971). Several principles regarding the care of dependent children resulted from this First White House Conference on Children attended by child-care professionals from all over the country. To name only three are as follows:

** Children of worthy parents, as a rule, should be kept with their parents at home.
** Children should not be removed from their home because of poverty alone.
** Homeless and neglected children, if normal, should be cared for in families, where practicable (ibid., 357).

This was the beginning of the deinstitutionalization of orphanages and children's homes, but it was not until the Title IV amendment to the Social Security Act in 1935 that Aid to Dependent Children (ADC) legislation was passed. This would make it possible for children to remain in their own home rather than enter an orphanage or children's home due to poverty. At that time, most children had at least one living parent, and poverty was no longer a reason for removing children from their homes for placement in orphanages. In fact, the use of the term "orphanage" has been a misnomer since the 1920s. Only about 10 percent of all children in orphanages in 1933 were true orphans (Smith 1995). By this time, eighteen of the twenty-three state Baptist child care programs were in place; and the children's home, earlier called the orphanage, was a solid part of the Southern culture.

From Orphanage to Children's Home and More

Following World War II, the needs of children and families would again change. The war had a tremendously negative impact upon the family. The men went away to war, and many never returned. Those who did return were changed forever, and their ability to resume their roles as fathers and husbands was grossly compromised. The women had worked in the factories, and they too experienced change. Their "wounds" of loneliness, despair, and excessive responsibility were often as great as the physical wounds suffered by their men from the battlefields around the world. The children were left with older family members, and many were left alone. The children experienced the most damage, and children's homes that had been in the process of closing because of fewer orphans and poor children were now beginning to fill up with the "orphans of the living." These were the children of divorce and mental illness. Families were so wounded by the war that parenting skills were diminished or damaged. These unbonded and scarred children would grow up, marry (several times), and have damaged children of their own who would find their way into our treatment centers, substance-abuse programs, and our jails and psychiatric hospitals.

This brief review of early care of children would not be complete without mention of "kinship care." This form of care involved placement of children with members of their immediate or extended family when they could not remain with their parents. A study completed by the U.S. Health and Human Services reported that more than 31 percent of all children in state custody were placed with family members in a twenty-nine-state study (U.S. Dept. of Health and Human Services 1992). That number is actually low as most states will report 50 percent or higher placement with relatives. Today, this has become the placement of choice when children must live away from their parents (ibid.).

Having established some antecedents for Christian child care in general, the remainder of the book is about how the challenge of "welcoming the children" has been met by faith-based child and family agencies in general, and by the Arizona Baptist Children's Services in particular.

References

Bergh, Henry. *The Case of Little Mary Ellen. New York Times.* 1874. Quoted in R. H. Bremner, ed., *Children and Youth in America* (Cambridge: Harvard University Press, 1971) 187-189.

Bernard, J. 1973. *The Children You Gave Us.* New York: Bloch Publishing Company.

Brace, C. L. 1872. *The Dangerous Classes of New York.* New York: Wynkoop & Hallenbeck. Repr. Washington, D.C.:1950

Bremner, R. H., ed. 1970. *Transportation of Poor Children from London to Virginia, 1619-1620.* Vol 1 of *Children and Youth in America.* Cambridge: Harvard University Press.

Cook, Jeanne F. January/February 1955. A History of Placing-Out: The Orphan Trains. *Child Welfare* January-February:181-197.

Eckhard, George B. 1844. An Ordinance for the establishment of an orphan house in the City of Charleston, A Digest of the ordinance of the City Council of Charleston, from the year 1783 to October 1844 (1844), 188-189. Quoted in Robert H. Bremner, *Children and Youth in American: A Documentary History,* vol. 1, 1600-1865. (Cambridge: Harvard University Press, 1970) 275-276.

Freidlander, Walter A. 1955. *Introduction to Social Welfare,* 2nd ed., Englewood Cliffs: Prentice-Hall, Inc.

Jones, Marshall B. 1993. The Antebellum American Orphanage. *Caring,* Spring. "Caring" is the journal of the National Association of Homes and Services for Children. It was published in the Spring issue of the journal in 1993.

_____. 1994. Correction, Not Charity. *Caring*, Spring.

Kadushin, A. 1974. Substitute Care: Foster Family Care. *Child Welfare Services,* New York: Macmillan Publishing Co. Inc. 1974.

Kingsbury, Susan M., ed. 1906. *The Records of the Virginia Company of London. The Court Book, from the Manuscript in the Library of Congress* 1: 270-271. Quoted in Robert H. Bremner, *Children and Youth in America: A Documentary History*, vol. 1 (Cambridge: Harvard University Press, 1970).

Norton, Mary Beth. 1980. *Liberty's Daughters*. Glenview, ILL: Scott, Foresman and Co.

Proceedings of the Conference on the Care of Dependent Children 1909:17-18. Quoted in R. H. Bremner, *Children and Youth in America: A Documentary History*, vol. 2 (Cambridge: Harvard University Press, 1971), 357-369.

Smith, Eve. 1995. Bring Back the Orphanages, etc. *Child Welfare*. January-February.

U.S. Department of Health and Human Services, Office of the Inspector General. 1992. *State Practices in Using Relatives for Foster Care*. Washington, DC: U.S. Government Printing Office.

Trattner, Walter I. 1974. *From Poor Law to Welfare State*. New York: The Free Press.

Chapter 2

A Short History of Southern Baptist Child Care [1]

There is a paucity of information available on the beginnings of child care among Southern Baptists, except through the histories of the individual states and the Baptist institutions in those states. It is interesting that the words "children," "homes for children," "orphanage," or other related terms are not found in the index of W. W. Barnes's book, *The Southern Baptist Convention 1845-1953* (1954); however, other Baptist institutions were frequently mentioned. The same was true in Robert Torbet's book, *A History of the Baptists* (1959). In the *Baptist History and Heritage* series of monographs produced by the Southern Baptist Convention (SBC), the venerable James L. Sullivan wrote an article, "Baptist Laymen as Denominational Leaders: A Historical Perspective" (1978). The article lists laypersons of renown in many areas of Southern Baptist life including Sunday school leadership, other church organizations, publications, universities, and hospitals. No mention is made of the leaders in children' home work. The kindest explanation for this omission would be that the Baptist children's agencies were a product of the state conventions and not the national convention.

Beginnings as a Result of the Civil War

Baptist child care began in the latter part of the nineteenth century as this country struggled with the inadequacy of the almshouse (early institutions for orphans and dependent adults) as a resource for dependent children. The system itself was bad enough, but the misery of the system was compounded by overcrowding, which resulted from the Civil War. In 1880, approximately nine thousand children under fifteen years of age were in almshouses (Bremner 1971, 2:247). Several of the northern states—Pennsylvania, Illinois, Kansas, Minnesota, Ohio, Indiana, Iowa, and Wisconsin—established special institutions for these children. They first placed the children who were in almshouses and orphaned by the war in the new institutions (Torbet, 1959). The Southern states, whose resources were ravaged by the war, were unable to make similar provision for their children. It would be the religious denominations that would largely respond to this need, and the denominational orphanage would become an intrinsic part of southern culture extending to the present.[2]

Southern Baptist child care is clearly recorded in the histories of the individual Baptist state conventions and their agencies. The following are examples.

** It is an honorable history beginning with the first Southern Baptist children's home work, the Louisville Baptist Orphans Home, which began in 1869. This was the outcome of the compassion of a group of women from the Walnut Street Baptist Church in Louisville to minister to the needs of children orphaned by the Civil War. Other states would soon follow the example of Kentucky Baptists. Earl Joiner states in his book on the history of Florida Baptist Children's Home that the first orphanage effort among Southern Baptists was made by the Mississippi Southern Baptist in 1864. That work was closed in 1875. Mississippi Baptists would later begin a work in 1894 that continues into the present. The Kentucky Baptist program holds the record of being the earliest to begin and maintain continuous operation to the present (Joiner 1995).

** A group of deacons in Paris, Texas, was organized into a convention in 1879 by a pastor who was also the editor of *The Texas Baptist*, Rev. R. C. Buckner. That evening they discussed the duties and responsibilities of the deacon. They also approved a resolution to organize an orphan's home. Buckner was appointed the general superintendent, and several other ministers were named to assist him including B. H. Carroll, the founder of Southwestern Baptist Seminary. Under the shade of a spreading oak tree near the meeting house, Rev. Buckner took out a dollar bill and laid it upon his knee and said, "Brethren, to give this thing a start, here is my dollar." B. H. Carroll followed his example. Twenty-seven dollars were raised (Bullock 1993, 44).

** On November 11, 1885, the Thomasville Baptist Orphanage opened in North Carolina. It would later be named the Mills Home after the founder and first general manager, John Mills. Even later, the Mills Home would become the flagship of the North Carolina Baptist Homes for Children (Grant 1958).

** In 1863, two years before the Civil War ended, Alabama Baptists passed a resolution at their annual meeting in Marion to start an orphanage. By the end of the Civil War, $140,000 had been raised . . . in Confederate money, and it was worthless (Wise 1961, 1). It was almost thirty years before the dream of starting an Alabama orphanage would be realized. It was started through the efforts of Rev. John Stewart, pastor of the Twenty-first Avenue Baptist Church in Birmingham, and a benefactor, Mrs. Mariah Louise Woodson, who deeded her estate to Alabama Baptists for this purpose. The town of Evergreen and the Evergreen Baptist Church, where Rev. Stewart was pastor, opened its arms to this needed ministry and gave the orphanage its first home in 1891.

Baptists in other states[3] would respond to the needs of the orphaned children by establishing special institutions, but a new war against children was emerging on the social horizon that would continue to require special homes for other needy children.

Beginnings as a Result of Poverty and Family Breakdown

From 1869 to 1903, there was a steady development of Baptist children's homes in twelve southern states. The early need grew out of the devastation of the Civil War and Reconstruction. At the turn of the century,

17

poverty and illness continued to hurt families and create a continuing need for child care, although the need for orphan care was diminishing. Many children placed in the orphanages during the early years of the past century had one or both living parents, but the parents placed their children as an alternative to starvation. The First White House Conference addressed this issue about the importance of assistance being given to mothers to prevent placement but "indicated a preference for private charity rather than public relief as the means of supporting dependent children in their own homes" (Bremner 1971, 2:369). One of the Baptist agencies, Buckner Baptist Benevolences, provided such assistance, which they first called "Mother's Aid" and later "Family Aid." Bullock notes in her history of Buckners that the Mother's Aid Program cared for forty-six children in April of 1959 (Bullock 1993). The writer's brother Bill Baker started this program for Buckners. Virginia Baptist Children's Home had a similar program as did other denominational child-care institutions.

Poverty and divorce in the early twentieth century would continue to make increasing demands upon those institutions caring for needy children. These same agencies would begin developing programs more suited to this new generation of out-of-home children and their families. Mother's Aid, as already mentioned, was only one of those programs. Baptists in several other states would respond to this new growing needs of children. The following exemplified the homes started in this era.[4]

** While Rev. James Allen Scott made the motion before the Oklahoma Baptist State Convention in 1902, the vision of an orphanage had been that of his wife. Scott was pastor of the Washington Avenue Baptist Church in Oklahoma City and eventually became the first superintendent of the orphanage. The home first opened in 1903 with three girls. It operated as a local institution until 1915 when indebtedness led to acquisition by the Oklahoma Baptist Convention (Gaskin 1978).

** The New Mexico Baptist Orphanage was founded in 1918 by the First Baptist Church of Portales and was transferred to the New Mexico Baptist Convention the following year (Winters 1958). More will be said of this agency in the next chapter because of its relationship with Arizona Southern Baptists.

** The Baptist Family and Children's Services of Maryland Inc. has undergone several name and program changes since its beginning in 1921. It was known earlier as the Baptist Children's Home of Maryland. In 1961 the agency returned its child-placing license due to lack of need for residential services and focused upon in-home services, counseling, and referral services. In 1989, the agency again obtained a child-placing license and began therapeutic foster care (Parry 1995).

Beginnings as a Result of World War II and Public Policy

The damage inflicted by World War II extended much further than the terrible loss of life and property to the world. The heart of the American family was ripped apart by diminished resources, stress, and long separation from loved ones. Denominational agencies, along with other private agencies, would respond to the increased need for children's services, and additional agencies would be born. Those already in existence would expand their services and tailor their programs to meet the needs of the "orphans of the living." This would be a time when agencies would rethink their mission since the new population of children needed more services. Since almost all of these children had families, the agencies had to consider what their role would be with the families. Public child-welfare policy was changing, and more federal dollars were available for children's services. With that money, however, came service requirements that would mandate that certain guidelines be followed. Fewer dollars were available for residential care and more for family services, including foster family care.

A new vocabulary would include such terms as "permanency," "prevention," "family reunification," "family preservation," and "home-based services." Gradually, Baptist agencies that once provided only residential care began to shift their programming to provide a variety of family support services. Also, increasing regulations would require program adjustments, increased accountability, and increased costs. Some agencies would not survive these demands. Agencies would begin to focus on special populations. The following new agencies within the Baptist community would reflect the arrival of this new era in child and family services:

** The Mexican Baptist Children's Home in San Antonio opened its doors to Hispanic children in 1944. The name was later changed to the San Antonio Children's Home, and then later to Baptist Children's Home Ministries. The scope has been enlarged to include children of all ethnic backgrounds and a much broader mission.

** The openings of the Texas Baptist Children's Home in Round Rock in 1950 and the South Texas Children's Home in Beeville in 1952 were made possible by gifts from Baptist families who wanted to do something for children in their areas. Unlike the earlier orphanages, these programs were started as children's homes to care for dependent-neglected and delinquent children who had one or both living parents but, for many reasons, could not live with their parents.

** The Sunny Crest Children's Home in California was opened in 1951. Marvin Mouser gave one dollar to start a fund (Carroll 1958). It began under the private auspices of the Child Care Board directed by Ed Brown. The board was later received under the umbrella of the California Baptist Convention and supported with funds from the Southern Baptist Convention Home Mission Board. The home was moved to Bakersfield in 1955 and was closed in 1965 due to stringent state-licensure requirements that made it impossible for the agency to find qualified staff. California Baptists today have no child-family services program.

** The minutes of the Ohio Baptist Convention indicated that the executive board set up a fund for construction of a Baptist children's home in 1955 (Cottrell 1958). The funds that were raised were eventually transferred to the Ohio Baptist Foundation where they were used for convention children and youth programs. There was never a champion to promote a children's home work in Ohio, and consequently, one was never developed (Pollard 1999).

** Arizona Baptist Children's Services began as a children's home in 1960. The details of this ministry are the primary focus of this book and will be discussed in greater depth in subsequent chapters.

** Baptist child-care work in Alaska began with the establishment of the Turnagain Children's Home in 1948 by Rev. B. Clarence Evans, executive secretary of the convention. The cost of upgrades to meet state standards proved too much, and the home was closed in 1972. The convention opened a new program called the Alaska Baptist Family Services two years later. The cost of the new facility was funded from the proceeds of the sale of a portion of the original children's home property.

An Analysis of Southern Baptist Child-Care Beginnings

The lack of coordination in the spawning of Baptist orphanages may be explained by Baptist polity, which advocates local church autonomy and the subsequent disdain for an ecclesiastical hierarchy. As a result, there was often lack of technical expertise and capitalization for the individual state programs, but there was no limit to the desire, determination, and love for children that motivated these early pioneers. The following statements are an analysis of Baptist child-care beginnings.

(1) The various state conventions generally were receptive to the establishing of a Baptist orphanage in their state with the exception of Florida and Arizona. Those two state conventions have since embraced the work they were reluctant to support in the beginning.

(2) All of the Baptist child-care programs began with a residential model that remains the flagship program today for most of the programs. In a presentation by Dr. Alan Keith-Lucas to the Child Care Executives of Southern Baptists in 1984, he commented on the outstanding contribution Baptists have made to the field of residential group care (Keith-Lucas 1984).

(3) The Baptist orphanages of the South are part of the Southern culture and way of life. This is not just true of Baptists but other church-related orphanages as well in the South. Of the thirty-five Southern Baptist state conventions, twenty have residential children's agencies. Of the thirteen state conventions in the South, all thirteen have residential programs for children. Of the twenty-two other state conventions in the Southern Baptist Convention, only seven have children's residential programs. This may be due to the fact that those nonsouthern state conventions were started later, and the need for services for children were being met by other sources by the time those later state conventions were organized.

(4) There had been little or no cooperation among the various state convention children's agencies. However, Child Care Executives of Southern Baptists, organized in 1949, met a need for fellowship, inspiration, and exchange of information among the executive staffs of the Southern Baptist agencies. They continue their annual meetings to the present day.

(5) Unlike missions and evangelism, child care has been started outside of the state-convention staff offices by interested individuals and groups. Only Alaska has been an exception. Child-care beginning occurred at a Deacon's Convention in the matter of Buckner Baptist Benevolences in Texas; a wealthy couple in Missouri; private institutions already in existence in Georgia and North Carolina; a layperson in Alabama; pastors in Louisiana and Oklahoma; a church in New Mexico; an association in Florida; and a small group of interested laypersons and WMU members in Arizona. In other words, the work of benevolence has not been on the agenda of the national or state-convention staffs as have church planting, missions, and evangelism. There are probably several reasons for this, but only two will be offered. First, it has simply not been an important matter in light of other priorities for Southern Baptists. W. W. Barnes said it well in his classic volume on the 1845-1958 history of the Southern Baptist Convention.

During the last decade of the nineteenth century and the first years of the twentieth, the Convention was occupied in the task of rethinking its own character and objectives. Several controversies—mission methods, theological education, young people's work, Sunday school work, women's work, sources and bases of representation in the Convention—gave neither time nor opportunity for consideration of social problems. (Barnes 1954, 246)

I believe the second is a more compelling reason. Southern Baptists have historically identified the social aspects of ministry with "liberal" theology. Caring for needy and troubled children is a social ministry and involves the services of professional social workers. This has contributed to the reluctance of the denomination to embrace children and family ministries. The word "social" has frequently been deleted in Southern Baptist program terminology for the more desirable term "Christian Life" to describe the work of benevolence and child advocacy.

(6) Each children's agency was expected to raise money for capital needs and most of the operational needs, which were generally true of the state convention's educational institutions, hospitals, and senior adult programs. Yet the state conventions have maintained tight control over their agencies while sometimes financially supporting them very little. Most, if not all of the children's agencies, receive a portion of their budget from the Cooperative Program, the Southern Baptist plan for financing missions. In most instances, that portion represents a small percentage of the agencies' total budget. Several of the Southern Baptist hospitals and universities have separated themselves from their state conventions because of funding, liability, and accreditation issues. Accepting government funds or loans in any form has been viewed by some as a violation of church-state separation, and yet those institutions believed they could not survive without contract income through purchase of care or government

loans. Accepting purchase of care and practicing nondiscrimination in hiring have also been viewed by Baptist institutions as necessary to meet contract and accreditation requirements. In order to do this, some of those institutions had to alter their denominational ties.

Cutting ties with their state convention has involved another issue frequently overlooked by those who would like to see their institutions controlled and accountable to the state convention. This is the matter of ascending and descending liability. This was dramatically illustrated by the bankruptcy of the Baptist Foundation of Arizona (BFA). While not compelled by a court judgment, the Arizona Southern Baptist Convention (ASBC) reached an agreement with the bankruptcy court to pay a settlement fee because of their structural relationship to the BFA Liquidation Trust. In a worst-case scenario, the court could have attempted to attach the assets of all the Southern Baptist institutions in Arizona because of their common relationship to the ASBC. By "cutting the cord" of ownership, that liability potential is diminished or eliminated.

(7) Communities have often wanted to be a part of starting a children's home with the Baptists. They saw the benefits in terms of resources for their local children and perhaps some economic benefit to the community.

(8) The beginning of all Baptist homes for children involved struggle and sacrifice. The Georgia home did close for a time. California closed their home, and Ohio was never able to start their children's home program. The Baptist homes did not begin with endowments as did others, such as Thornwell in South Carolina and Casey Family Homes of Seattle, Washington. While there were some large cash gifts and bequests, the rank and file of support came from Baptist laypersons who loved children and believed that they were acting under divine initiatives in supporting these ministries.

The people who started these homes were not professional child-care people. They were farmers, pastors, storekeepers, teachers, and people whose only qualification was that they loved children and refused to stand idly by when children were abused, homeless, and needy. Many learned about "social work" for the first time when talking to state welfare workers. They didn't understand about licensing, child placement, family attachment, and the many other matters involved in caring for out-of-home children. They did learn about the need for specialized resources for children who could not live in their own homes. They loved children, but they loved God more, and many saw this as a ministry to which God had called them.

ENDNOTES

1. This paper was originally given by the author as the closing address to the Fifty-first Annual Meeting of the Child Care Executives of Southern Baptists in Richmond, Virginia, April 22, 1999. It was later published in *Family Ministry*, vol. 14, number 2, summer, 2000, pages 39-52 and used here by permission from the editor of the journal.

2. The term "orphanage" would be dropped in the 1940s and 50s for the more appropriate term "children's home"; however, the function and purpose would remain much the same. With the permanency movement in the 1970s, efforts would be made to find permanent homes for the residents of these institutions rather than focus upon raising the children in the institution.

3. While not listed in the text, Baptists in these states would also open orphanages for children orphaned by the Civil War:

   Georgia—1872 (Newton 1958, 538)
   Missouri—1886 (Ray 1986, 27)
   Virginia—1890 (Pugh 1983, 1-4)
   South Carolina—1891 (Keith-Lucas 1991, 3)
   Tennessee—-1894 (Byrd 1991, 10)
   Arkansas—1894 (Biggs 1978, 1)
   Mississippi—1894 (Cathey 1958, 895)
   Louisiana—1899 (Keith-Lucas 1986, 1-2)

4. It is interesting to note that all of the Baptist agencies, which started as a result of the Civil War, were in the South. Those agencies, which started

years later as a result of poverty, war, and family breakdown, were both in the North, South, and West. The following were started but are not listed in the text:

Florida—1904 (Joiner 1995, 20)
Washington, D.C.—1914
Illinois—1917 (Murrie 1958, 668)

References

Barnes, W.W. 1954. *The Southern Baptist Convention 1845-1953*. Nashville: Broadman Press.

Bremner, R. H., ed. 1971. *Children and Youth In America*. Vol. 2. Cambridge: Harvard University Press.

Bullock, K. O. 1993. *Homeward Bound: The Heart and Heritage of Buckner.* Dallas: Buckner Baptist Benevolences.

Carroll, J.E. 1958. *Sunny Crest Baptist Children's Home*. Vol 2 of *Encyclopedia of Southern Baptists*. Nashville: Broadman Press.

Cottrell, N. T. 1958. *State Convention of Baptists*. Vol. 2 of *Encyclopedia of Southern Baptists*. Nashville: Broadman Press.

Grant, J. M. 1958. *Mills Home*. Vol. 2 of *Encyclopedia of Southern Baptists*. Nashville: Broadman Press.

Gaskin, J. M. Spring 1978. The Child Care Ministry of Oklahoma Baptists. *The Oklahoma Baptist Chronicle*. Child Care ed, 21, (1): 1-110.

Joiner, E. E. 1995. *Florida Baptist Children's Homes: A History of Caring*. Lakeland: Florida Baptist Family Ministries.

Keith-Lucas, Alan. 1984. *Baptist Contributions to Child Care : Proceedings of Thirty-Sixth Annual Meeting of the Child Care Executives of Southern Baptist*. Williamsburg, VA. Child Care Executives of Southern Baptists.

Parry, P. 1995. *The Least of These—75 Years of Ministry 1920-1995*. Columbia: Baptist Family and Children's Services of Maryland Inc.

Pollard, Will. 1999. Correspondence by the writer with Will Pollard who was a staff member for the Ohio Baptist Convention, March 29.

Sullivan, James L. "Baptist Laymen as Denominational Leaders: A Historical Perspective," Baptist History and Heritage Series, 13:1, Nashville: Baptist Historical Commission, January, 1978, 4-16.

Tolbert, Robert G. A History of the Baptists, Philadelphia: The Judson Press, 1959

Wise, C.A. 1961. *The Alabama Baptist Children's Home*. Montgomery: Brown Printing Co.

Winters, D. 1958. *New Mexico Baptist Children's Home*. Vol. 2 of *Encyclopedia of Southern Baptists*. Nashville: Broadman Press. 1958.

Chapter 3

A Dream And A Resolve

The Period Before 1960

The birth of Arizona Baptist Children's Home (as it was then called) was not a timely one. The convention could not afford to support it. Yet a small group of Arizona Southern Baptists would not let their dream die and pledged their resources to keep it alive; therefore, it came stumbling into existence, struggling to keep its balance. While not a good time for beginning new things by man's history clock, it was God's time for the fledgling agency to begin.

Roots in the New Mexico Baptist Convention

The history of the Arizona Southern Baptist Convention has its roots in the formation of the first Southern Baptist church in Arizona organized in 1921. By August 1925, there were eight Southern Baptist churches in the state, and they organized into the Gambrell Memorial Baptist Association affiliated with the New Mexico Baptist Convention. J. O. Willett served as the first president; and C. M. Rock, pastor of Phoenix First Southern Baptist Church, served as vice president. As part of the New Mexico Baptist Convention, the new Arizona association supported the New Mexico Baptist Convention agencies, which included the Baptist college at Montezuma, the Baptist hospital, and the Baptist orphanage in Portales.

At the Fourth Annual Meeting of the Gambrell Memorial Association held in 1928, the Arizona group voted to constitute the Baptist General Convention of Arizona, forerunner of the Arizona Southern Baptist Convention. Messengers from ten churches first met at Globe on September 9, 1928, and adjourned to meet again in Phoenix December 6, 1928, to complete the organization (Annual 1928).

At the second annual meeting of the newly formed convention, the report on the New Mexico Baptist institutions was given by S. T. Hayes and Thomas B. Hart of Calvary (now First Southern) Baptist Church in Glendale. The meeting was held October 24, 1929, at the First Baptist Church in Chandler. The following report appeared in the convention proceedings:

> When the Baptists of Arizona organized the Baptist General Convention of Arizona, they saw fit to adopt Montezuma college, the orphan's home, and the hospital of New Mexico until such time that Arizona may have institutions of this kind of her own. Believing that God has willed that we should foster such institutions, we have done our best for them. In the past year our convention contributed regularly to the Montezuma college, the orphan's home, and to the hospital. In addition to this, many of the WMUs of our state have aided in caring for some of the children of the home . . . The hearts of all go out to the child that has no parents. We, as Baptists of New Mexico and Arizona, are doing our best for children of that kind through our home at Portales. At this time there are 44 homeless children cared for at the home. We recommend to the Baptist General Convention of Arizona that a percentage of the gross income derived from the Unified Program of Arizona be given to Montezuma college, the orphan's home, and the hospital of New Mexico. We further recommend that we of Arizona support the above named institutions in every way possible. (Annual 1929, 17)

The New Mexico Baptist Orphanage, later to be called the New Mexico Baptist Children's Home (NMBCH), was established by the First Baptist Church in Portales in 1918 and taken over by the New Mexico

Baptist Convention in 1919, as noted in the previous chapter. They cared for forty boys and girls. The program provided a home-like atmosphere for homeless children.

In 1928, 15 percent of the new Arizona convention budget went to support the New Mexico Baptist Convention agencies. Four percent of that went to the children's home. This was in addition to the gifts of individuals. That year, Rev. and Mrs. Grant were in charge of the NMBCH where thirty-eight children were provided care. There was a $1,600 debt, some of which represented unpaid salaries. In 1931, $69.72 was given to the orphanage by the Arizona churches and convention (Annual 1931). In 1932, $134.41 was given, and in 1934, $173.71 was given (Annual 1934, 4). In 1935, the Arizona WMU "adopted" two children, which involved paying $50.00 per month for their care (Annual 1934). The following year, the WMU would "adopt" two additional children, and the Arizona convention would give $347.50 (Annual 1936).

The example was established. The seeds had been planted. Arizona Southern Baptists committed themselves to follow the tradition of generations of Christian churches to "welcome the children" in Jesus' name. They began by supporting the only children's work within their reach. Sixty-nine dollars and seventy-two cents was given at the fourth annual session in 1931 (Annual 1931). In 1933 and 1938, $210.85 and $244.00 respectively were given. Minutes of the 1938 annual meeting of the convention indicated that two churches, Phoenix First Southern Baptist Church and Phoenix Central Baptist Church, sent regular amounts each month, while other churches set aside their birthday offerings (Annual 1938). Two hundred and sixty-four dollars and eighteen cents was given in 1942, the last year for formal support from the Arizona convention. That would be the year that Arizona Southern Baptists would begin a fund for their own children's home. Nevertheless, the Arizona WMU continued their support of the New Mexico orphanage for an additional period of time. Whatever other good the NMBCH may have done, which was considerable, perhaps one of its greatest contributions to Christian child care in Arizona was the example they set, which undoubtedly influenced their Baptist neighbors to the west.

A new superintendent for the NMBCH was appointed in 1937, and he spoke at the newly formed Arizona Baptist General Convention annual meeting. He brought along one of the young residents of the home who sang for the audience (Annual 1937). Using dependent children in this manner seems inappropriate today, but it was a common practice at that time.

A Dream That Would Not Die

When Arizona Southern Baptists formed their own convention in 1928, many believed that someday they would have a home of their own for needy children. No one at the time had any idea of how that could be done. Such a project was expensive, and the new convention was struggling to meet the challenges of missions, evangelism, and later, education.

The fourteenth annual meeting of the convention was held October 29-30, 1942, at the First Southern Baptist Church in Phoenix. In the children's home report, which previously reported on the work of the New Mexico program, the following statement was made.

> In the case of a children's home, it has been on the minds and hearts of some for quite some time, we recommend that we begin a fund with the regular offerings that come into the state mission's treasury, for the beginning, just as soon as it seems wise in the providence of God, of a children's home in Arizona. (Annual 1942, 15).

The report was approved. The president of the convention that year was Dr. C. Vaughan Rock, pastor of the Phoenix First Southern Baptist Church, and the vice president was Rev. George Wilson, pastor of First Southern Baptist Church in Tucson. Little progress was made toward realizing the dream until 1945. Less than a thousand dollars had been raised. In that year, a gift of forty acres of Salt River bottomland had been placed in a will to be used for the children's home (Annual 1943). Also a house had been offered for this use, but the offer was later withdrawn due to the donor's unexpected illness. The convention elected trustees to manage the funds that were being collected for the new children's home that year. Paul Vercher was elected chairman. Other members were Andrew J. Priest and Cyril Pate (Annual 1945). As interest increased in the proposed Baptist home in Arizona, fewer funds were sent to the NMBCH.

Support from the Arizona Southern Baptist Women's Missionary Union (WMU)

From the beginning of interest in a children's home, the Arizona WMU had been in favor of establishing a home for children, and that interest continued until the home became a reality. Their interest has continued to the present day. This comes as no surprise as women took the lead in all national reform movements in this country, including the orphanage movement. "But nothing more perfectly extended women's role within the home to the world outside it than the orphanage. An orphanage, after all, was another kind of 'home'" (Jones 1993, 1:15).

In 1946, the Arizona WMU supported resolutions that encouraged prayer, fund-raising, gathering of linens, and establishing an annual Children's Home offering on Mother's Day. The minutes of the fourth annual meeting of the Central Baptist Association reported that

in the past, we have bought four $1,000 bonds and set them aside for the home. We have a small sum of cash now on hand for that purpose. Each year, $100.00 per month is set aside from Cooperative Program funds for the home. A designated offering on Mother's Day has been recommended by the WMU. Our birthday offerings have been placed in this fund also . . . We are so sure that the home will be reality soon that the ladies of WMU are even now making bedding, etc. for the day of realization. The First Southern Baptist Church in Tucson has a large store room and has graciously offered to store packages sent them for the home. Moth balls were placed in boxes and they were tied securely and marked "FOR CHILDREN'S HOME" and sent to Tucson. (Central Baptist Association 1947, 17)

The opening of the home was due to the determination of a relatively small number of laypersons including the WMU. Today, ABCS has the full support of the convention and Arizona Southern Baptists. In fairness, it needs to be said that this predominance of lay support was present in the formation of every other state convention child-care work with the exception of Alaska.

It would be the WMU who would encourage the giving of birthday offerings and taking an offering on Mother's Day for the proposed children's home (ibid.). The same report also recommended that the convention be urged to pursue obtaining a license to establish a child-care institution. On December 11, 1945, the convention's executive secretary was authorized to apply for the license. This would not be done at that time.

When the Baptist General Convention of Arizona approved building a children's home in Arizona in 1942, some of the WMUs were continuing to support the New Mexico Baptist Children's Home (Annual 1942). Eventually this support would go to the Arizona program. The same was true of the Arizona Baptist churches. In 1946, the annual reported that only $27.52 was sent to the New Mexico Baptist children's ministry (Annual 1946). While neither home received much, the New Mexico orphanage received support from eleven Arizona churches, while the proposed Arizona children's home fund received support from five. The new proposed home received a boost in support when the WMU designated Mother's Day as a time for an annual offering for the home.

With the birth of Grand Canyon College in 1949, support for the children's home temporarily declined but was not forgotten. In 1960, once again WMU would take a leadership role in preparing for the children's home by making plans to furnish the new cottage as well as provide linens (Baptist Beacon 1960). A year later, WMU presidents were asked to encourage support of birthday offerings as one means of helping the new home (Flint 1986).

Efforts Are Delayed

Finances were a challenge for the new college, and support waned for the proposed children's home project. The college was in debt, and Arizona Southern Baptists focused all their available resources upon support for the college. In 1950, the convention took a position that no other institutions would be established until the college was on solid financial ground (Annual 1950).

By 1951, the children's home fund had grown to $9,547.19, and the Baptist Foundation of Arizona trustees were given the responsibility of holding the children's home funds. Assets at that time consisted of $10,000.00 in bonds and $387.84 in cash. By 1955, the cash had grown to $1,038.98 (Annual 1956).

There is no record of activity toward establishing the home to be found in the 1952 through 1954 convention annuals. Some of the earlier momentum generated by supporting the New Mexico work was being lost. People support a work that is in operation or whose establishment is eminent more than one that is being proposed, particularly when the plans extend over a long period of time as did the plans for the Arizona child-care program. The vision began in earnest in 1942, and twelve years later, the vision was beginning to weaken. Coupled with this was the convention's concern for the stability of Grand Canyon College and the uncertainty as to whether the small convention could support two rather large institutions. Convention leaders were cautious in their support of a children's home, but the issue was kept alive by interested laypeople and the WMU whose hearts God had burdened for this ministry. The dream would not die.

A Reluctant Convention

Historically, missions, evangelism, and sometimes Christian education have been the priorities of Baptist state conventions. It has been Baptist laypeople who have pushed for programs for needy children in almost every state of the Southern Baptist Convention.

The beginning of a children's home was never a priority on the Baptist General Convention of Arizona's early agenda. To its credit, it must be recognized that the convention approved establishing a children's home fund in 1941, and for a time it appeared that one hundred dollars per month was put into the fund by the convention. (Annual 1942). Some money was raised by individuals and churches in the following years, and reports of those gifts would be made at the annual meeting, but little else happened.

Dr. C. L. Pair, in his book *A History of the Arizona Southern Baptist Convention,* points out that the messengers to the 1947 convention approved a five-year plan, which included ten very challenging goals. This included new work and establishing "a Christian college with an enrollment of 500 students and a physical plant valued at one million dollars" (Pair 1989, 136). There is no mention of establishing a children's home although the convention had approved such a move as recorded in the 1942 Annual.

Those who carefully read the history of the Arizona Southern Baptist Convention have paused to question the implementation of that 1928 convention resolution: "When the Baptists of Arizona organized the Baptist General Convention of Arizona, they saw fit to adopt Montezuma college, the orphan's home, and the hospital of New Mexico, *until such time that Arizona may have institutions of this kind of her own*" (Annual 1929, 17). It is doubtful that the children's ministry would have started when it did were it not for that small group of interested Baptists who relentlessly pushed this agenda upon a reluctant convention.

Two Major Gifts and the Baptist Children's Home Is Born

On recommendation of the executive board, the 1955 Baptist General Convention of Arizona unanimously approved a motion, for the second time, to establish the children's home (Annual 1955). In reporting on this action, the state's official publication, the *Baptist Beacon,* reported the following resolution made by the convention's executive secretary-treasurer, Dr. Willis J. Ray:

Since four individuals have approached us the past year offering substantial support for a children's home, and since our attorney, Milburn N. Cooper, has secured a go sign from the Child Welfare Association for opening of a home, and proving a need and ability to operate, and since people will give to a children's home above the regular tithes; therefore be it resolved that the Executive Board be authorized to receive gifts, secure property and open a children's home—as money, children, and property are available. (*Baptist Beacon* 1955, 1)

The convention appointed two study committees in 1956 (Annual 1956). In 1958, specific steps were approved by the convention to start a children's home (Annual 1958). The convention approved, for a third time, the beginning of the children's home in its 1960 session held at Winslow, November 16-18 (Annual 1960). The motion to approve came with this caveat: "Interested people must respond with gifts to the home or the operation will be curtailed." This made it clear that, unlike the college, support would have to come from sources outside the convention budget. Later, the convention would help in the home's support, but this would not be for several years, and even then, it would be very minimal.

Mrs. Alma Carnes

At that time the funds for the children's home had reached $14,157.04. The following year, 1956, a gift of twenty thousand dollars was given by Mr. and Mrs. J. B. Carnes of Yuma, Arizona. The Carnes had been ranching in Texas but moved to Yuma when they retired. They became one of the Arizona Baptist families who wanted to see the birth of a children's home. They had no children of their own and believed that this ministry would give them the satisfaction for children they never had. Alma Carnes was active in one of the Yuma Baptist churches and played the organ for a time. Following Mr. Carnes' death, Mrs. Carnes moved to Blanket, Texas, where she lived until her death at the age of 105.

After President Baker came to the Children's Services in 1984, she notified the administration through a trusted relative that she had left her entire estate to ABCS. The president visited her in her home during the year she celebrated her one hundredth birthday. She remained in her home, taking care of her own needs until she was 103, at which time she entered a nursing home. The proceeds from her estate went to the ABCS endowment fund following her death.

The convention executive board made it clear that the program could begin when there were sufficient funds to build and operate the home for one year. Great caution had been taken to be sure that the new program would not put added financial burdens on the convention. By the November 1956 meeting of the convention, the children's home fund had reached $34,927.07.

A second major gift was made that would insure the beginning of a Baptist home for children in Arizona. Baptist Children's Home of Arizona (BCHA) Board member L. E. Jennings, Sr., of Laveen, Arizona, along with his wife Marie, had been one of the "interested families" that had kept the dream alive for a children's home in Arizona. The details of the gift were somewhat complex but explained to the writer in a letter from their son Les Jennings, Jr.

> I know from what Dad told me that at one time he had offered the ten acres of citrus land we owned at the corner of Lateral 16 (43rd Ave) and Carver Road, to the convention as a site for the children's home. The convention personnel looked at this site, rejected it for that purpose but agreed to accept title, sell the land and place the funds in the children's home account. Dad and Mom rejected that proposal and withdrew their offer . . . So, according to the minutes of the BCHA trustees meeting of September 7, 1959, the motion was made and carried to purchase 2 ½ acres of land offered by the Trust and Memorial Fund committee of the convention for $4,000 per acre, with a $4,000 cash down payment (presumably from the home's account then on deposit), and the balance of $6,000 to be paid in 90 days, from the proceeds of the sale of the Jennings property . . . What I can assume . . . was that Dad and Mom

had again offered this ten acres to the convention—not as a home site, but as a funding source . . . (Jennings 2005)

The gift was made in 1958 according to a letter written by the children's home attorney, Milburn N. Cooper, to the Jennings couple.

Lester Jennings, Sr

About a year ago, you and your wife made a very generous and kind offer to the trustees of the Baptist Children's Home of Arizona, offering 10 acres of your land as a site for a home, or for said 10 acres to be sold and the proceeds there from used to purchase a site or erect a home for said children's home, as our records indicate. (Cooper 1959, 1).

Mr. Jennings served on the board as president for seven years and remained as an honorary board member until his death in 1982. His son Lester Jennings, Jr., has also served on the board and the staff of the children's services. This is the only known family who has been actively involved with the children's services from its inception to the present day; however, Archie Stephens, a Baptist layman in Phoenix, has served on the board during the tenure of the four ABCS administrations. At one time, he was director of an ABCS subsidiary corporation.

The Board: Strong and Committed but Uncertain

Starting a children's home was new territory for these interested and committed pioneers. Similar beginnings in other states were always characterized by the idealism of "child saving." This desire to help the less fortunate is endemic to religion and part of the underpinning of civilization. There is nothing wrong with this desire. Like many other areas of life, desire and motive are not enough to bring about success, but it is doubtful that there would be success without them.

These energetic leaders knew little about starting a children's home, but they pooled their limited knowledge and knew some things for certain.

They would need property; a building; staff; and hopefully, the blessing of the Baptist General Convention of Arizona. They would later learn of their need for a license and for people with specific qualifications. Learning took place step by step and sometimes by trial and error. They would need to organize to consolidate their strengths and knowledge.

Two committees were appointed by the 1956 convention to implement the establishment of the children's home. The first committee chaired by Mr. Jack Maben, pastor of First Southern Baptist Church of Glendale, was charged with the responsibility of making a study to determine the type of home that was needed. The second committee composed of Mr. Ed Packwood and Dr. Willis J. Ray was assigned the task of receiving property and selecting a site for the home. Neither committee was able to make any recommendations during that year.

A third committee was established by the executive board at the November 1957 meeting of the convention (Packwood 1958). The chairman was Rev. George Wilson, pastor of the Phoenix Central Baptist Church and a leader in the Baptist General Convention of Arizona. The committee was asked to serve as interim trustees of the children's home until the convention could elect trustees at the regular meeting of the convention.

Additional members of the newly formed interim board were Jack Maben, Glendale; Keith Hart, Casa Grande; W. A. Risinger, Yuma; Mrs. George Nagel, Winslow; Bob Ethington, Casa Grande; James Ray, Glendale; L. F. Rucker, Chandler; L. E. Jennings, Sr., Laveen; Glenn Crotts, Tucson; Mrs. Wiley Henton, Globe; and Milburn N. Cooper, Phoenix, who was also board secretary. A former ASBC convention staff member told this writer that part of the delay in launching the children's home was the "limited interest," which some of the board had in the children's home, and this was a "major factor in slowing the process."

The board was eventually elected by the convention. Rev. George Wilson later went off the board to become the first superintendent. This fully constituted authority had little idea about the magnitude of their job. They were elected by the convention to carry out a purpose that the convention could not finance; nevertheless, the convention would hold this new board accountable for doing their job and at times would give them specific instructions for doing it. Gradually, the convention began to accept some responsibility for supporting its "new child." To the present day, financial support has never been more than 3 percent of the agency's budget, but the convention has encouraged support of the Mother's Day offering and, on occasion, has included the Baptist Children's Home in its State Mission Offering. At a later time, when the convention was financially stronger, the children's home would be included in its annual budget.

Articles of Incorporation were filed with the Arizona Corporation Commission on May 5, 1958, and on May 9 a Certificate of Incorporation was issued. The incorporators were Charles Hood; C. Vaughn Rock, pastor of Phoenix First Southern Baptist Church; James R. Staples, pastor of North Phoenix Baptist Church; Irvin M. Reed; Jack Maben, statutory agent and pastor of Glendale First Southern Baptist Church (Jennings 1997). The first bylaws set forth the purpose of the new ministry. They stated as follows:

> The object and purpose of this corporation is to carry out the purpose and actions of the Baptist General Convention of Arizona providing for the establishment and operation of homes for the care and training of orphan and needy children and the placement and adoption of children when proper and authorized as set forth in the Articles of Incorporation (Cain 1979).

On March 4, 1958, the executive board authorized that all funds held by the convention be released to the children's home trustees for the purpose of establishing the children's home.

Land Is Purchased

On September 7, 1959, the children's home board purchased two and one-half acres of land at the corner of Thirty-first Avenue and West Missouri in Phoenix from the trust and memorial fund of the Baptist

General Convention of Arizona. (This was a committee appointed by executive board chairman Jack Maben, who later served on the children's home board, to study the matter of a rotating fund for purchasing sites for future churches). The purchase was made with the option of later adding two and one-half acres of adjacent property, which it did. The board paid four thousand dollars per acre for the first parcel and five thousand dollars per acre for the second. The organization received a 501 (c)(3) tax status from the Internal Revenue Service September 7, 1959. The dream was unfolding, and Arizona Southern Baptists would have their children's home, thirty-two years after the founding of the convention and eighteen years after the decision was made to begin such a home. (Baptist Beacon 1960) Simmons speculated on the long delay in getting the program started.

Many people no doubt have wondered why those who have delegated responsibility have been so slow in activating this institution authorized by the convention, the Baptist Children's Home of Arizona. In spite of all the seeming tardiness, the idea has developed with a great deal of soul searching, and we believe with wisdom that will give the institution security. We know that board action, committee recommendations, *Beacon* headlines, dreams and hopes, postponement and discouragement seems to be the history of the children's home on the surface, but to find the answer to the entire process that has faced the board of trustees of the home, you must go much deeper. The board faced the fact that in spite of money in the bank, given by donors several years ago that would afford a beginning in capital needs, operating expenses were not in sight, and it would be folly to build an institution so important without some practical plan for sustaining it through the years. Arizona Baptists had seen the struggle to maintain a college with budget limitations characteristic of a pioneer area and it therefore taught them that another institution could not depend on the convention budget for its sole support. Therefore, the slow pace and precautionary steps that seem to some as dragging feet"

were but the measured and calculated, though slow, process of a group of men and women who were headed toward an ultimate goal of certain security for our orphaned and underprivileged children. The board now is ready to act, and the Home is a reality. (Simmons 1960, 4).

All was in readiness for the construction of the first cottage on the campus at 3101 W Missouri in Phoenix.

Reference

Baptist General Convention of Arizona and First Baptist Church. 1928. *Annual*. September 9.

_____. 1929. BGCA, First Baptist Church, Chandler, AZ. October 25.

_____. 1931. BGCA, Grace Baptist Church, Phoenix, AZ. October 23.

_____. 1934. BGCA, First Baptist Church, Chandler, AZ. October 10.

_____. 1935. BGCA, First Southern Baptist Church, Tucson, AZ. October 24-25.

_____. 1936. BGCA, Calvary Baptist Church, Glendale, AZ. October 22.

_____. 1937. BGCA, First Southern Baptist Church, Phoenix, AZ. October 19-22.

_____. 1938. BGCA, Calvary Baptist Church, Phoenix, AZ. October 18-21.

_____. 1942. BGCA, First Southern Baptist Church, Phoenix, AZ. October 29-30.

_____. 1943. BGCA, Central Baptist Church, Phoenix, AZ. November 11-12.

_____. 1945. BGCA, First Southern Baptist Church, Phoenix, AZ. October 31-November 1.

_____. 1946. BGCA, Calvary Baptist Church, Glendale, AZ. October 28-31.

_____. 1950. BGCA, First Southern Baptist Church, Tucson, AZ. October24-25.

_____. 1955. BGCA, Central Baptist Church, Phoenix, AZ. November 8-10.

_____. 1956. BGCA, First Southern Baptist Church, Yuma, AZ. November 14-16.

_____. 1958. BGCA, First Southern Baptist Church, Tucson, AZ. November 12-14.

_____. 1960. BGCA, First Baptist Church, Winslow, AZ. November 16-18.

Baptist Beacon. 1955. Way Cleared for Children's Home. November 24.

Baptist Beacon. 1960. Progress is Made on Children's Home. August 18.

Cain, Don. 1979. Letter dated February 21 to Grady Gamage. The material is an attachment to the letter and located in the Archives of Arizona Baptist Children's Services.

Cooper, Milburn N. 1959. Letter to Mr. L. E. Jennings dated September 9, 1. Filed in ABCS correspondence archives.

Flint, Gerald David. February 1986. The building blocks of the ABCS: the Arizona Baptist Children's Services. An independent research project conducted through the Department of History, Grand Canyon College, Phoenix, AZ, 36. Filed in the ABCS Archives.

Jennings, Lester, Jr. 1997. Early beginnings & growth of Arizona Baptist Children's Services. Unpublished paper delivered at the Historical Society of the Arizona Southern Baptist Convention in March and filed in the Archives of Arizona Baptist Children's Services.

Jones, Marshall B. 1993. The Antebellum American Orphanage, Part I: America's History of Caring for Children in Need. *Caring*, Spring: 10-14.

Central Baptist Association WMU. 1945. Minutes of the second annual session held at FBC, Tolleson, AZ. October 8- 9.

_____. 1947. Minutes of the fourth annual session held at Eastside Baptist Church, Phoenix, Arizona. October 6-7.

Packwood, Ed. 1958. Children's Home Meets at Casa Grande. *Baptist Beacon*, January 9.

Pair, C. L. 1989. A history of the Arizona Southern Baptist Convention. Commissioned by the executive board of the Arizona Southern Baptist Convention, Phoenix, AZ.

Simmons, J. Kelly. 1960. You Can Help a Child. *Baptist Beacon,* February18.

Chapter 4

A Ministry To Dependent Children

The Period 1960-1970:
"The Wilson Years"

With some exceptions, this chapter will cover the period from the beginning of Rev. George Wilson's administration in 1960 until his retirement in 1970. The stage was set for the birth of the children's home by having a board, financing, property, authorization from the Baptist General Convention of Arizona and many hours of planning and prayer. While early supporters of a children's ministry thought in terms of an orphanage, later leaders decided upon a community-based, homelike program, which would be called a children's home.

Never an Orphanage

The era of the "great orphanages" was drawing to a close in the late 1950s, and the newly appointed board of the Baptist Children's Home of Arizona was wise enough to recognize the changing needs. Countless children had earlier been orphaned by the Civil War. In both the North and the South, between 1830 and 1860, orphan asylums became the nation's predominant method of caring for dependent children (Hacsi 1995). This need would be met in the south primarily by individuals and faith-based groups. The birth of the privately supported orphanage would be a part of southern reconstruction and remain for the following years as a component of Southern culture. While family preservation, home-based services, family foster care, and adoption would later be accepted as "best practice" in services for dependent, neglected, and orphaned children, remnants of institutional care in the form of group homes and children's campuses kept the tradition of congregate care alive in the southern states.

Culturally embedded paradigms in society are difficult to overcome, and nearly all references to the residential service for children in Arizona in the 1940s and 50s were to the "orphanage." This confusion in titles for children's residences is clearly seen in the Central Baptist Association Book of Reports, which uses "orphanage" and "children's home" interchangeably, perhaps without recognizing their different natures (*Book of Reports* 1945, 14-15). Board member Rev. Glen Crotts, former pastor of FSBC Tucson, wrote in a letter dated June 26, 1959,

> (Crotts) reported to the board the results of a survey he had conducted in which he found that only three percent of children in Baptist care across the Southern Baptist Convention were orphans, and the other ninety-seven percent came from broken homes. (Jennings 1997, 4)

On March 10, 1961, Superintendent Wilson presented to the executive committee of the board a statement of purpose and six eligibility criteria for admitting children to the home. The primary purpose of the home was to give short-term care to children in a group and familial atmosphere. Six factors would be considered in admission of children were as follows:

1. Children from broken homes
2. The need for training of those children in family living before placement in foster care or adoption
3. The need for association with peers, which was unavailable in foster care
4. The need for restoration of confidence in adults
5. Disciplinary problems, which can be addressed through a group home atmosphere

6. The necessity of being removed from a home situation in which the child would feel too threatened by the family closeness of family foster care (Minutes. BCHA Board, March 1961, 1)

The ultimate goal of the home was to prepare children for return to their own homes or progress to more individualized permanent care (ibid., 2). The general public understood orphanage placement as the treatment of choice for all children unable to live in their own homes. The "orphanage idea" has been slow to die if in fact it has truly died. As late as the 1990s, a member of Congress was promoting a "back to the orphanage" movement as the need for out-of-home placements increased, coupled with an unwillingness of the government to pay the high cost of residential behavioral health treatment.

Children continued to need out-of-home care, but there were better models. This whole orphanage issue did bring to the attention of the American public a new awareness of the needs of so many children for out-of-home care.

The First Leadership: Rev. George Wilson

The simpler the culture, the less skill that is required in many areas of that culture, including the appropriate care for people. In the early church, the unwanted and abandoned children were placed in the homes of widows. The widows reared the children, and the church cared for the needs of the widows—a simple but effective system. The care for dependent children in the United States in the 1950s and 60s was far more complex, but many still thought that the first-century church method would work. Not so. These latter-day children needed more than room, board, clothing, education, and religious training.

Since the 1950s, the children in out-of-home placement have primarily been children who had one or both parents living but who could not live with those parents for a variety of reasons. The orphan could accept his/her circumstance because of the finality of death. The "orphans of the living" in the present age do not have that finality or closure. They are trapped within the limbo of what they want and what they need. Caring for these complex children requires understanding and skill. In addition, a unique personality for caregivers is necessary, characterized by unconditional acceptance, tolerance for aberrant behavior, and a love that reaches out in spite of rejection. Being a successful parent with one's own children does not qualify one to care for the children of others. While being a committed Christian is right up there at the top of desirable qualities, it does not guarantee success in working with troubled children any more than such godliness would qualify people to be a doctor, lawyer, or a schoolteacher. The new staff members at the Baptist Children's Home of Arizona (BCHA) were soon to discover this truth.

The first leadership position to be filled at BCHA was that of the superintendent. He would then be responsible for recruiting and hiring the additional leadership. There seemed to be little question among Arizona Baptists as to who was the most qualified person to fill that first important position.

Rev. George Wilson was appointed superintendent by the Baptist Children's Home of Arizona Board on February 29, 1960, and assumed his duties on June 1. Rev. Wilson was the popular Pastor of Central Baptist Church in Phoenix. He had been the chairman of the Children's Home Study

Rev. & Mrs. George Wilson

Committee of the BGCA Executive Board and chairman of the first children's home trustees. No one had worked more tirelessly to begin the home. Mrs. Wilson was also a vital part of this ministry her husband would lead. Glen Crotts, who succeeded Wilson as president of the children's home board, had this to say about him: "In order to do a job like this, one must have a special unction (calling, empowerment) from the Holy Spirit, and we believe George Wilson has manifested evidence of such" (1960, 1).

Rev. Wilson was a graduate of Oklahoma Baptist University and Southwestern Baptist Theological Seminary. He also served as a chaplain in the military. Rev. Wilson had pastored churches in Texas and

Arkansas, as well as the First Southern Baptist of Tucson. He was active in denominational affairs in the states where he served and was a member of the Foreign Mission Board of the Southern Baptist Convention, serving as vice president for one year.

The Wilsons had no experience in rearing children other than their own children. They had no experience in children's home administration or in fund-raising other than what a pastor would do in encouraging good stewardship on the part of church members. They did love people and could communicate their love to the children. That would make up for some of their lack of training and experience.

Building on the New Campus

The original cottage on campus was a brick house at 3101 W Missouri, which was built in 1960. The architect was William A Lockhart, AIA of Phoenix. The 3,434 square-foot cottage was constructed by Claude Reel at a cost of twenty-six thousand dollars. The building would provide housing for fifteen children and a "live-in" couple who would supervise them. Groundbreaking services were held on the new site August 29, 1960. The Woman's Missionary Union (WMU) took on the responsibility of furnishing the house and providing linens.

A happy group is quickly assembled to turn the first spade of dirt for the first unit of the Children's Home. From left to right are: W. D. Lawes, John Sullivan, Almarine Brown, Mrs. W. I. Moseley, Lester Jennings, Claude Reel, George Wilson, Lee Jackson and Ed Packwood.

With construction and furnishing completed, an open house was held on December 9, 1960. The home for fifteen children was debt free, and this was cause for much rejoicing. Special guests honored at the gathering were the two major benefactors, Mr. and Mrs. J. B. Carnes and Mr. and Mrs. L. E. Jennings, Sr., whose gifts were largely responsible for the opening of the new facility (Pair 1989).

A number of modifications and uses of the building would be made over the next forty years. In 1965, the patio was enclosed, creating another

51

room. In 1971, one of the large bedrooms for boys was divided into two bedrooms. A wall was built in 1974 in the dining area to separate the kitchen and dining area from the remainder of the house. In 1977, the rear patio was enlarged, enclosed, and made into a classroom.

It was enclosed, except for a covered concrete slab area used as a children's play area. This play area was enclosed in 1971 and used for a commissary to store food. Five years later it would be used for a classroom, while an off-site storage area would be rented for the commissary (Cain 1979, 2).

Other Staff Are Now Added

One of the first actions of the new superintendent would be to employ houseparents who had the responsibility for the daily care of the children. These would need to be special people because the care and safety of vulnerable children would depend upon them. In addition, their stewardship in child caring would be a reflection upon the convention for good or for ill. Mr. and Mrs. Otis (Lucille) Dickson from Tucson were selected and would move into the home on December 1, 1960. They would help make final preparations to receive children and were presented to the executive committee of the board March 10, 1961. Their annual salary was four thousand eight hundred with a sixty-dollar monthly car

Otis and Lucille Dickson

allowance. They had no previous experience in this type of work, except for rearing their own children. They would later attend workshops for houseparents to gain the technical skills that were needed.

Early Social Workers and Social Services

In the course of the licensing process, Mrs. Elaine Eddy, the state child-welfare worker, informed the new superintendent that the home would need social services to meet licensing requirements. Social workers are trained to evaluate children as to the appropriateness of placement and to work with the family toward return of their child to the home. When that was not possible, the social worker would assist in either a foster home or adoption placement following the children's home placement. One of the stated purposes of the new children's home was to keep children only on a temporary basis and prepare them to return home or to another form of permanent care.

The first time that Rev. Wilson heard the term "social worker" was probably from the state worker who pointed out that agencies licensed to place and care for children were required to have a social worker on staff. In the 1950s, states were beginning to recognize that regulations were needed to protect children who are in out-of-home care. Part of that protection was to have people who were trained in the social work profession on the staff or available to do case studies and make decisions about placements. The Baptist Children's Home developed job descriptions and policies to insure that children in the Baptist home would have the professional services they needed.

These early, simple policies would be an example of the complex, numerous policies that would later be required. The later policies would reflect the complexity of the society and that of the children's problems, the omnipresent liability for those who work with children, and the thoroughness of Joint Commission Accreditation requirements.

Mrs. Mayola Miltenberger was employed as a social worker on a part-time basis and would later move to half time. Mrs. Miltenberger announced her resignation in May 1962 but agreed to remain on the staff until her replacement could be found. Her plans were to begin a children's program for her church, but she was most complimentary of the work being done by the Baptist home and particularly the houseparents. In her final words to the board, she emphasized the importance of well-trained administrators and the desire that the board assume more responsibility for the financial security of the home.

The new social worker, Bill Johnson, was introduced to the board during their meeting on August 24, 1962. At the September 28, 1965, meeting of the executive board, Mr. Johnson reported to the committee the need for an additional cottage to allow for separation of the older from the younger children. He also noted that finding suitable foster homes was a problem, and many children had been turned down due to lack of space at this time. At the recommendation of Mr. Johnson, the executive committee began an investigation as to the possibility for opening a home for unwed mothers (Flint 1986).

Bill Johnson resigned his social work position, and this position was filled in August, 1969, by Ms. Phyllis Faye McFarland. With the exception of two educational leaves and a brief time spent in private practice, Dr. McFarland would spend the next twenty-seven years with the children's services. She would play a major role in its success with troubled children and with program development. In those early years, she had no office for counseling and would frequently use the laundry room or a tree stump as a counseling site.

Not Enough Space

Things had gone well during the first two years, but it was soon apparent that additional facilities were needed. During 1962, eight boys and two girls were denied admission due to lack of space. Rev. Wilson recognized there was a need for expansion, and the executive board gave him permission to raise fifty thousand dollars during the next year to construct

another cottage for twelve more children (Annual 1963, 60). A year later, at the next meeting of the convention, three thousand one hundred dollars had been raised. An emotional appeal was made to the convention by Rev. Wilson: "We continue to receive requests for placing children in the home which cannot be met for lack of space. What difference

Religious life has always been a focal point of the ABCS program. Here, girls at the original Children's Home prepare for Sunday morning worship. Residents attended local churches until 1975, when a chaplain was hired and on-campus services became an option. Children of all faiths are admitted into the ABCS programs, and many make commitments to Christ through ABCS' ministry.

can we make in the lives of those we turn away? Will it be another blow to their sense of worth as they reason, 'I am so bad they wouldn't even take me there,' when the truth was, that we did not have room. A child does not always understand things as an adult and especially when this is just another in a long series of rejections" (Annual 1964, 62).

Policy for Admission of Children and Operation of the Home

The Baptist home did not have a policy manual, as such, but various policies and procedures appeared in undocumented historical files in the archives. The following represent all that has been found in the way of policies and procedures. An article in the state Baptist paper described the first policy.

Children from any section of Arizona may be received into the home, following proper investigation as to their need and suitability for group care in a Christian home. The children will be required to take a physical examination before being received. They need not be Baptist, but they would be expected to attend Sunday school and worship services in area Baptist churches.

Parents or other relatives may contribute toward the cost of care and the clothing expenses of the children where possible. They may remain in the home until circumstances of parents or relatives are such as to permit their return. Investigation of all cases will be made by a competent social worker. The children will attend near-by public schools. Concerned and dedicated houseparents will supervise them in the home, under the direction of the superintendent. The children will receive Christian guidance and prayerful help in all of their problems. (*Baptist Beacon* 1961, 1).

The above admission policy and the following policies were necessary and reflect the desire of the board and administration to develop a sound and beneficial environment for the children. The policies are based upon state licensing requirements. It is to the credit of these early leaders that they respected licensing regulations rather than circumvent them on the grounds of church-state separation. This will be dealt with in greater detail in chapter nine. It was not at all uncommon for leaders of other faith-based programs in the past and present to object to these licensing requirements. They asked for concessions, such as permission to spank, which was not permitted in licensed agencies. Many hide, then and now, behind the position that their status as a faith-based organization should give them the right to treat children in any way they chose.

All children admitted to the Baptist home would be under the immediate care and supervision of the houseparents. It would be the duty of houseparents to formulate, under direction of the superintendent, and carry out whatever "house rules" may be needed. These would include hours for mealtime, bedtime, wake-up, and play. The policy would include safety rules and chores that were expected to be done. Parent visitation, clothing arrangements, and other personal matters would be worked out with the staff and legal guardian.

It was the responsibility of houseparents to report any illness or accidents immediately to the superintendent or, in his absence, to the Baptist home physician. The houseparents had responsibility for keeping such records as the home required to help evaluate the child's progress and his readiness to leave the institution. They would, on request, attend staff conferences and participate in the planning for each child (Procedures, 1960-1970).

Licensing and Partnership with State Child Welfare

 Before any group can care for children on a twenty-four-hour basis, in all of the states, they must have a state "child-caring license." The name of this license will vary from state to state and vary with the nature of the child-welfare program. Early on, the children's home board recognized the necessity for licensure and made application to the Arizona Department of Welfare. A study was completed by the department, which

included inspecting the facility; studying its policies and procedures; reviewing its governance and finances, personnel, and other areas.

On January 12, 1961, a license was issued to care for nine children between the ages of six and fourteen (*Baptist Beacon* 1961, 1). The license would be effective for six months, which is the usual time for an organization's first license. Following that initial "trial" period, the license would be issued on an annual basis, provided standards were met. In September, the license was increased to fourteen children.

The Arizona State Child Welfare worker Mrs. Eddy was always available to provide consultation on licensing and best practices. She assisted the children's home staff in determining the criteria that would be established for admission of children. One of the early temptations in residential child care was to accept every child based strictly upon their dependency status. Social work technology helped the early leaders of the Baptist home to focus their help on children who they believed could be helped with the resources provided by the Baptist home. Even still, children too troubled for the Baptist home's level of care would occasionally be admitted, only to be discharged shortly after admission. This was always sad.

Technical assistance from the state was a mutually beneficial process. The state had the responsibility of caring for needy children such as the Baptist home could provide. In addition, state child-welfare staff were willing to help the home's staff provide state-of-the-art care. This mutually beneficial working relationship would continue to the present day.

The Arizona Department of Public Welfare (DPW) was very pleased with this new child-care program and the willingness of the staff to gain technical skills in working with children. The licensing representative for the Children's Agencies and Institutions for DPW, Glen Richard, wrote to Superintendent Wilson, "I am pleased to report that the Baptist Children's Home is one of the best child-care facilities we have . . . to my knowledge, the Baptist Children's Home is the only children's institution in Arizona providing their houseparents the advantage of attending a national workshop for the training of child-care staff . . ." (1962, 2).

A Temporary Home for Children: The Primary Goal

The decision was made early in the study process that an orphanage would not be built. Closely related to that was the decision to provide short-term care until the child could be returned to a permanent home. In other words, unlike the orphanage, the Baptist home would not be rearing children but providing care until they could return to their own home or another form of permanent care. To the credit of these early leaders, there was the recognition that the Arizona Baptist Children's Home was not a permanent home for children; however, they were not yet ready to accept the responsibility for family rehabilitation, which is necessary for the return of children to their own home.

One cannot help but wonder how they thought the family would make sufficient improvement for the children to be returned to their home without serious help. One explanation for this reasoning was the belief that the problems always lay with the child. The belief was that an out-of-home placement would be for the purpose of "fixing" the child so that he/she could later return to their own home when they were "repaired." The focus would be upon custodial care and not treatment, which would later replace custodial care. During these early years, children who were placed were primarily dependent and in need of custodial care. Children were provided with adequate and appropriate activities, spiritual care, nutrition and health care, and education and recreational opportunities.

The First Children Admitted to the Home

Everything was ready for the home's opening, and the first child was admitted in January 1961. One month later, there were five children in the home—four boys and one six-year-old girl. The capacity of the home was for fifteen children, but the initial license only permitted nine residents. Because of the need, a request was made to the Arizona Department of Welfare to increase the

"Red and yellow, black and white, they are precious in his sight."

licensed capacity to twelve, and this was granted. By September 1961, Superintendent Wilson reported that the new capacity of twelve had been reached. Several children were turned away that year. From the period of 1961 to 1974, the average age was twelve, and the average number of children cared for per month was ten (Cain 1979). They attended public schools and churches in the community. Considerable support was received from church groups who donated supplies and provided hours of volunteer service.

On several occasions throughout the history of ABCS, attempts were made to start programs that never materialized. Others were started and later were closed. The administration, trustees, and ASBC Executive Board were constantly attempting to determine and meet current needs, which were always changing. This demanded regular evaluation of the programs and attempting newer relevant programs for children. As an example, during the September 5, 1961, meeting of the BCHA Board, Mrs. Miltonberger, the children's home social worker, warned about the high cost of operating an adoption agency. Superintendent Wilson, Mrs. Miltonberger, state child-welfare worker Mrs. Eddy all met with a national child-welfare worker, Ms. Hines, to discuss the children's home interest in adoption. The results were discouraging because of the high costs, lack of need at the time, and the many problems, including legal issues, that resulted from having such a program.

The board agreed to further study the feasibility of beginning an adoption program (Minutes. BCHA Board, September, 1961, 2). By 1962, ASBC Board member Bob Ethington made a motion in a board meeting: "We the executive board recommend that the Arizona Southern Baptist Convention determine whether the Baptist Children's Home will continue to operate a children's home of the type presently operated; or terminate the present operation and commence the operation of an adoption agency, receiving only adoptable children; or operate some other type of children's home" (Annual 1962, 55).

Later, in another meeting with the ASBC Executive Board, Mr. Johnson suggested they consider opening a home for unwed mothers (Flint 1986). The suggestion was appropriate and needed in the state at the time, but it did not move past the level of believing it to be a good thing. Both programs were in keeping with the home's simple mission, but they would require a level of expertise and funding that were beyond the reach of the children's home at that time.

The Ongoing Search for Adequate Funding

From the earliest years of interest in a children's home, church leaders were aware of the financial burden, which such a venture could bring to the convention. At the very onset of the home's beginning, convention leaders made it clear that the funding for this new venture must come from "interested individuals" rather than through the official funding sources of the convention (Annual 1960). Because of this, a pale of reluctance and uncertainty hung over the Baptist General Convention of Arizona in regard to starting a children's home. These doubts were further intensified by the financial strain, which was created by the new Grand Canyon College, which opened in 1949. The messengers (delegates) of the 1950 annual meeting of the Baptist General Convention of Arizona approved a resolution that "no other institution [be] started until Grand Canyon College was on its feet" (Annual 1950, 19).

The message was clear that leaders of the new children's home would be expected to raise all capital and operational costs for the home; nevertheless, there was an uneasy ambivalence about this by convention leaders, which would ultimately lead to providing some support through convention funding sources. In the

BAPTIST CHILDREN'S HOME OF ARIZONA

Original Building

early years of the children's home, Mrs. Wilson the bookkeeper and Superintendent Wilson's wife reported that $4,993.54 had been received from the convention as its share of the recent State Missions Offering (Minutes. BCHA Board 1961). The support from the convention was encouraging, but it was sporadic and minimal. This search for funding began in earnest after George Wilson took office as superintendent on June

1, 1960. He traveled throughout the Arizona Southern Baptist Convention territory speaking eighty-nine times in his first year as superintendent.

The early financial needs of the Baptist home were twofold. The first was to pay off the debt for the additional property at Thirty-first Avenue and Missouri. The final payment on the property of two thousand five hundred dollars was made on May 27, 1963.

The second financial need the home faced was for operations. No help was received from the convention at first, as earlier noted. Only gifts from churches and individuals supported the ministry. Reimbursement for the care of state wards would soon be accepted, and this probably saved the day for the children's home ministry at that time. This purchase-of-care money from the state would eventually become the mainstay of financial support for the children's home. The record is clear about the board's position on accepting purchase of care from the state.

One of the matters referred to the board by the executive committee was to decide whether or not we would accept state reimbursement for children referred or sent to our home by the welfare department. Motion by Cooper, seconded by Carroll, and carried with all present voting except Ethington and Mauldin who voted in the negative; that our policy be and that we accept allowance or reimbursement from the welfare department and other agencies for expenses for the care or maintenance of children placed with us or in our home by the welfare department, but not to exceed the amount of costs or expense to us to care for the child; but with not more that 50% of the capacity of our home be such children at any one time" (Minutes, BCHA Board, September 1962, 1).

The issue of purchase of care was again raised by board member Ed Packwood at the May 27, 1963, meeting of the board. The board minutes reported:

"Ed Packwood stated that he wanted it known that he objects to our children's home receiving any compensation or reimbursement from the

State Welfare Department in regard to children placed there by the welfare department, but he did not make any motion in regards to the previous action of the board" (Minutes, BCHA Board, 1963, 1). This issue would surface from time to time throughout the ABCS history, but it was never a problem for those responsible for providing resources for the children needing care. (This will be discussed in more detail in chapter 9.)

While there is no available evidence to support this theory, this writer believes that neither Superintendent Wilson nor the early children's home board had any notion that the work would be supported other than by donations or perhaps fees from parents and sponsors. When approached by state workers about accepting state children, Wilson at first accepted the children with no thought of reimbursement. The April 6, 1961, board minutes reported, "The welfare department is pleased with our group and will pay $50 per month for the care of each child" (Minutes, BCHA Board Executive Committee, April

Birthday envelop used in the churches

1961, 1). The early budgets list an income source as "subsistence," which is believed to include some support from parents and sponsors, as well as payment for children in state custody. This line item accounted for slightly more than 5 percent of the first year's annual income. Even with this $1,125.60 "subsistence," the children's home still ended the year with a deficit.

The financial report for 1961 was grim showing receipts of $18,814.68 and expenses of $19,619.30, leaving a deficit of $804.62. However, the good news was that $905.22 had been earned from their reserves to offset the loss (Dupree and Walmsley 1961). This led to a special called meeting of the board on September 29, 1961, to approve a one-thousand-dollar withdrawal from their reserves in the trust and memorial fund to pay salaries.

Superintendent Wilson had not expected financial problems this early in the home's history, and his appeals to Arizona Baptists became more intense and widespread. The Arizona Woman's Missionary Union

(WMU) wanted to help in a tangible way, and the associational WMUs throughout the state were encouraged to promote birthday offerings for the home. At first, the suggestion was for each individual to give one dollar on their birthday to the children's home. That was later changed to one dollar for each year being celebrated. The latter suggestion was never fully accepted, and people generally gave what they felt like giving.

For the first eighteen months, there were few, if any, plans for fund-raising. This urgency was put on hold possibly because the board knew they had reserves to cover the first year of operating costs. The minutes contain no treasurer's reports until July 1961. Even with a major deficit after the first operating year, it is not addressed in the board minutes. The first glimmer that some kind of plan needed to be developed was reported at a semiannual board meeting in 1961 when the superintendent asked for permission to "experiment" with a pledge system. He had designed a pledge card that gave people the option of pledging one dollar per week or per month (Minutes, BCHA Board, June 1961). Approval was given for his request, but little is reported regarding the results of this "experiment." Wilson made several appeals through the *Baptist Beacon* for churches to sponsor a child by providing clothing and allowance, and remembering the child on special days.

A month later, Superintendent Wilson reported that it had been suggested to him that he might be able to secure additional financial help by making a trip through Texas. He requested and was given permission by the Board to seek support for the home outside of Arizona (Flint 1986). This followed the poor response to the pledge program, which had not yielded the results Rev. Wilson expected. No information is available regarding the success of this last request. At that same meeting, a financial report was handed out to each member (Minutes, Executive Committee, ABCS Board, July 1961).

At the December 1961 meeting of the board, the first serious suggestion was made that churches be encouraged to put the children's home in their budget. This emphasis would continue until the convention decided to include the children's home in its annual budget (Minutes, BCHA Board, December 1961).

Mr. Wendell Newell, director of Arizona Boy's Ranch, made a presentation to the November 24, 1964, meeting of the children's home board, urging that a statewide organization of children's agencies be formed to advocate for state funding for children (Minutes, ABCS Board, November, 1964). The board authorized Superintendent Wilson to explore this type of advocacy. This appeared to be a further affirmation of the board's willingness to embrace the concept of accepting purchase of care. The Baptist Children's Home would later become one of the founding members of the statewide association of children's agencies. There was some concern at that time that this might violate the principle of separation of church and state.

It appears that there was little, if any, recognition on the part of the early board for its responsibility in developing resources for the children's home. This, coupled with the fact that no organized plan was ever put in place, made adequate fund-raising difficult, if not impossible, to do.

At the August 26, 1963, meeting of the board, the matter of a fund-raising campaign was discussed for the purpose of raising fifty thousand dollars for a new cottage and staff to supervise the cottage. The Baptist Children's Home Board approved the campaign as did the convention board, and a date of February 14, 1964, was set as the kickoff date. A brochure was developed, and personal letters were sent out to every one on the *Baptist Beacon* mailing list (Flint 1986). The campaign died after five months, and apparently only about three thousand dollars was raised. The campaign was in conflict with another convention fund-raising activity (ibid.). The campaign was never mentioned again in the board minutes after May 28, 1964.

Property located near Castle Hot Springs, Arizona, was suggested as a possible site for the children's home in March, 1964, but the idea was not pursued due to the limited finances of the home. Mr. Jennings visited the site and determined that it would not meet the needs of the new children's home, and the matter was dropped.

Finances during the mid to late 1960s continued to be a concern, but interest by the churches in the home had increased, and there was more visibility for the home because of the birthday offerings and the State Mission's Offering. Local Baptist women volunteered to help with the ironing, and readers of *Love In Action*, a children's home publication, were encouraged to save their Gold Bond Stamps and Green Stamps to help in purchasing another vehicle for the home (Flint 1986). As a result, another station wagon was purchased in late 1966 for $3,015.14.

The building fund had been growing yearly since the disappointing campaign of 1963 and 1964. By 1969, the fund had reached $17,537. The fund had been helped by some generous gifts from Texas Baptist friends. Talks about constructing additional facilities for the children began again, but those plans were put on hold as some dramatic changes in personnel would be made that year. In 1969 and 1970, there would be a change both in administrator and houseparents. The good news was that all bills had been paid, and there was no debt. By the time of the actual change in leadership, the building fund had reached eighteen thousand dollars.

In 1969, the expenses for the children's home were $40,638.75. These included "administrative" and "home expenses." The projected budget for 1970-71 was $45,986.00 or $3832.17 per month (Minutes, Executive Committee ABCS Board, September 1970).

The same report pointed out that the Baptist Children's Home was receiving $100 per month per child from the state for its children, while similar homes in Arizona were receiving $75 to $560 per month per child. A new rate was negotiated with the state increasing its per diem to two hundred dollars per month for each child (*ibid.*). The following chart illustrates the children's home finances for selected years from 1961-1969:*

	1961	1967	1969
Income	$21,121	$34,242	$51,890
Expenses	58,731	38,702	$43,384
Profit/loss	($37,610)	($4,460)	$ 8,506
Fixed Assets	$53,925	$65,243	$66,189

·   Taken from board minutes during those selected years.

Programs and Activities

In the beginning, the program was simple and basically involved school, church, chores, and playtime. At one point the home owned horses that were donated, and beef cattle were raised to provide meat for their table. The children attended the Maryvale and later Cordova Elementary Schools and Love Baptist Church, all of which were near the Thirty-first Avenue  campus. An enclosed playroom was constructed soon after the home was opened. In time, as the neighbor children became acquainted and played with the children from the home, the neighbors would invite the residents to use their swimming pools. This amicable relationship continued until the needs and the behaviors of the children became more complex and difficult. In addition, the City of Phoenix provided free use of the city swimming pool across the street from the children's home. Play was unstructured, and the children were able to have their own toys.

Little is recorded about the interaction between the children and the staff although a social worker was the first professional staff member to work in the home. This would not have taken place, except that licensing standards required admission screening and evaluation by a social worker. Records indicated that the children participated in trips to theme parks and visits to local public entertainment.

Early plans for Expansion

It must not go unnoticed that the early leaders were mindful of the essential needs of children and used the "best practice" knowledge of that time very effectively. Foster care and adoption were both programs that were discussed, and foster care was added to residential care soon after the opening of the home. The trustees and superintendent recognized that not all children would do well in a group setting. They applied to the

State Welfare Department for a child-placement license for six children, which they were awarded January 23, 1963 (Richard 1962).

Those early foster-care records have been lost, but board minutes indicated that social worker Bill Johnson had found recruiting suitable foster homes to be a problem (Johnson 1965).

It would be many years before the home could support an adoption program, but it was to their credit that the early leaders were aware of the value of this service in meeting the needs of children. This awareness came perhaps as a result of the State Welfare Department staff who assisted the children's home personnel in the licensing process.

Future planning and goal setting were quite simple in those early years of the children's home. This was before the "strategic planning" and corporate management technology of the 1980s and 1990s. But that is not to say that there was no planning. The Executive Committee of the Baptist Children's Home Board met February 28, 1966, to discuss an earlier request made by the convention. The children's home was asked to develop a list of goals for the next seven years. After some study, the committee came up with the following goals:

(1) A new cottage should be built for twelve more children on the campus.
(2) The home should expand its social work program to include family counseling.
(3) Foster home services should be increased.
(4) A program should be developed to serve unmarried mothers and establish adoption services.
(5) The children's home should be included in the convention's Cooperation Program budget.
(6) The children's home should be promoted through the pastor's conferences. (Minutes, Executive Committee BCHA Board, 1966, 1).

Little progress was made toward these goals until the 1970s when a new emphasis was made on long-range planning, which later resulted in the evolvement of the "strategic planning" process.

Tireless Worker

The executive director-treasurer of the Arizona Southern Baptist Convention, Dr. Roy Sutton, would refer to his friend George Wilson as "Mr. Children's Home." Indeed, he deserved this title of distinction. It would not be an exaggeration to believe that Rev. Wilson had visited most of the Southern Baptist churches in Arizona and several in Texas. The burden of raising money for the children's home was on his shoulders, and he keenly felt

that burden, albeit a tender burden. It would not be uncommon for his voice to break when he pleaded for the needs of his children to be met, and he did consider them "his children."

He was a tireless writer making sure that Arizona Southern Baptists learned something from every issue about this ministry through the *Baptist Beacon*, BGCA's newsmagazine. He also started a newsletter for the children's home, which he titled *Love in Action*. It contained stories about the children and itemized the needs of the ministry. It contained inspirational articles and special emphasis like the "Mother's Day Offering." Articles like "Train Up a Child" or "Be Ye Kind" emphasized the importance of proper child rearing. Several issues have been lost, but it is believed that the newsletter began around 1961 and continued at least through 1971 when the new superintendent, Don Cain, changed the name to *Footprints,* creating an entirely new format.

Also the board would be looking soon at the prospect of Rev. Wilson's retirement. Fifty-four children had been served from the beginning of the children's home in 1961 until his retirement in 1970. Fifty-four does not seem like many children to be served in a nine-year period, but it was a solid start against many obstacles. Support was slow in coming, and these godly men and women had no previous experience in these matters.

They overcame many years of resistance of people who didn't feel such a program was the business of the convention. They had to compete for support with an aggressive new church mission program and the fledging Grand Canyon College, which the convention solidly supported. Like most pioneers, the Wilsons deserved more credit than they ever received, and for that reason, they are included in the dedication of this book.

References

Annual. 1950. Baptist General Convention of Arizona (BGCA), October 24, First Southern Baptist Church, Tucson, AZ.

_____. 1960. BGCA, First Baptist Church, November 16-18, Winslow, AZ.

_____. 1962. BGCA, Calvary Baptist Church, November 14-16, Tucson, AZ.

_____. 1963. BGCA, First Baptist Church, November 13-15, Kingman, AZ.

_____. 1964. BGCA, Central Baptist Church, November 11-13, Phoenix, AZ.

Baptist Beacon. 1961. Children's Home is Granted License. January 26, 1961.

Book of Reports. 1945. Central Baptist Association. October 8-9, Tolleson, AZ.

Cain, Don. 1979. Letter to Grady Gammage, Jr., dated February 21. Filed in ABCS Correspondence Archives.

Crotts, Glen E. 1960. Baptist Children's Home Employs First Superintendent. *Baptist Beacon*, March 10.

Dupree and Walmsley. 1961. Annual Audit. November 3, Phoenix, AZ.

Flint, Gerald David. 1986. The building blocks of the ABCS: the Arizona Baptist Children's Services. An independent research project conducted through the Department of History, Grand Canyon College, Phoenix, AZ, 36. Filed in the ABCS Archives.

Hacsi, Tim. 1995. From Indenture to Family Foster Care: A Brief History of Child Placing. *Child Welfare*, January-February: 162-180.

Jennings, Lester E., Jr. 1997. Early beginnings & growth of Arizona Baptist Children's Services. Unpublished paper presented at a regular meeting of the Arizona Baptist Historical Society, Phoenix, AZ, March 15. Located in the archives of Arizona Baptist Children's Services.

Johnson, Bill. 1965. Minutes of the executive board, Arizona Southern Baptist Convention, February 21, 1979.

Minutes. *1961*. Executive Committee of BCHA Board. 1961. Minutes. April 6

_____. 1961. Executive Committee, BCHA Board, July 18.

_____. 1966. Executive Committee, BCHA Board, February 28.

_____. 1970. Executive Committee, BCHA Board, September 24.

Minutes. 1961. BCHA Board, March.

_____. 1961, June 5.

_____. 1961, September.

_____. 1961, December 5.

_____. 1962, September 10.

_____. 1963, May 27.

_____. 1964, November 24.

Pair, C. L. 1989. *A History of the Arizona Southern Baptist Convention*. Phoenix: The Arizona Southern Baptist Convention.

Procedures While Child is in Residence. n.d. Minutes *of* BCHA Board. Exact date not available but between 1960-1970.

Richard, Glen H. 1962. Letter in board minutes 1960-1970 to Rev. George Wilson from Mr. Richard, licensing representative, Children's Agencies and Institutions, Department of Public Welfare, Phoenix, AZ. The letter is dated November 5 and filed in ABCS correspondence archives.

Wilson, George. 1963. Foster Home Care License Received by Children's Home. *Baptist Beacon*, February 7.

Part III: From Giving a Home to Providing Services

Chapter 5

A Change In Direction

The Period 1970-1983: "The Cain Years"

The Leadership Change

The only houseparents the children's home had up to this point, Mr. and Mrs. Otis Dickson, publicly announced their intention to retire. This was due to Mrs. Dickson's poor health. One can only marvel that houseparents who had already raised a family could continue for nine more years providing twenty-four-hour care for twelve dependent children. The emotional drain of caring for that many children, many of whom had been deprived of the love and care of two parents, would be stressful for body and spirit. Three other couples would try their hand at this houseparent business only to leave after a brief time.

In the fall of 1969, it was announced that Mr. and Mrs. Sidney Cox would begin houseparent duties in September. On the ninth of that month, an emergency meeting of the board was called because the Coxes had announced their resignation. "The children were not responding well to the authority of Mr. and Mrs. Cox, which was resulting in a discipline problem in the home" (Flint 1986, 43). Another board meeting followed on the sixteenth to develop a solution. At this point, the board extended Superintendent Wilson's employment, at his request, from December

31, 1969, to April 1, 1970. The date would be extended another time to July 1, 1970.

Mr. and Mrs. Vernon Mims would follow the Cox couple, together with some temporary substitutes. Mr. Mims was a senior at Grand Canyon College, and both were musically talented. The children enjoyed being entertained by the couple, and they appeared to work well with the children. They remained only a few months before Mr. Mims was inducted into the military. Mr. and Mrs. Watts came next (Flint 1986).

The board was beginning to feel the pressure of obtaining competent, permanent replacements for its superintendent and houseparents. At the

1971 ABCS Board

November 20, 1969, meeting of the board, board chairman Lester Jennings, Sr., was authorized to travel throughout the southwest to visit other Baptist child-care agencies (Minutes 1969, Executive Committee, BCHA Board). Mr. Jennings had volunteered to do this at his own expense. It was this kind of dedication and sacrifice by the "few interested people" that started the Baptist Children's Home of Arizona and would keep it alive in the early years of its history. On this tour, Board President Jennings, accompanied by his wife Marie, would observe the facilities and programs of other state Baptist child-care programs and hopefully interview prospective houseparents and superintendents.

Mr. Wilson's tenure of office was again extended, this time until June 30. The Jennings's son, Les Jennings, Jr., observed all that was taking place and later wrote,

> With a list of homes and superintendents in hand, in March, 1970, Les & Marie Jennings commenced their trip. A mandate was given: "To seek out a person who could analyze the needs of children in Arizona, and design programs to meet those needs." That mandate remained a guiding force in the life of ABCS to this day. (1997, 7)

The journey that began in early March would take them to Baptist children's homes at Portales, New Mexico; Oklahoma City, Oklahoma; Monticello, Arkansas; Monroe, Louisiana; Beeville, Texas; San Antonio, Texas; and the Texas Baptist Children's Home at Round Rock, Texas, near Austin. Mr. Jennings would discover who he was looking for at this last Texas Baptist agency.

Charles Wright was the executive director of the Texas Baptist Children's Home. He had seen the leadership potential in Mr. Don Cain and had offered him the job of assistant director of his agency with responsibility for all campus operations. Charles Wright then devoted his energies to working with the board on some serious financial matters he inherited from the former director. Everything was working smoothly. Charles Wright knew about the Baptist Children's Home

Don Cain

of Arizona through his association with the Child Care Executives of Southern Baptists, but he knew nothing about the couple from there that called upon him that day in March 1970.

After introductions, time was spent getting acquainted, and then Mr. Jennings shared with him the mission of their visit. A dread slowly came over Mr. Wright as he realized the person the board chairman was looking for was his assistant. Mr. Jennings visited with both Wright and Cain for several hours discussing the board's need to fill the vacancy left by George Wilson's retirement. This was a difficult moment for Mr. Wright who was torn between helping the career advancement of his assistant or attempt to keep him at Texas Baptist Children's Home. Those who know Charles Wright, as does the author, would know what his decision would be. Mr. Wright recommended his assistant with no reservations because he knew he had the qualities that the Baptist Children's Home of Arizona needed.

Personnel Committee chairman Gordon Green contacted Rev. Don Cain to set up a time for him and Mrs. Cain to visit the Phoenix agency (ibid. 1997). Mr. and Mrs. Jennings had done their work well. At the August 4, 1970, meeting of the BCHA Board at Sir George's Restaurant,

Don Cain was interviewed and offered the position of superintendent of the Baptist Children's Home of Arizona. He would move to Phoenix September 1, 1970, and begin work soon afterward.

The New Direction Defined

The young Rev. Cain appeared to be an ideal choice. He had served four years in the United States Air Force. He was an ordained Baptist minister and received his bachelor's degree from Baylor University, as well as a master's degree in religion and counseling. While a student at Baylor, Rev. Cain worked as a chaplain at the Waco State Home for children. During that period, he baptized approximately one hundred children into the First Baptist Church. His six years as chaplain ignited in him an interest in children who were in out-of-home care.

Don Cain spent the greater part of the first month getting acquainted with the program and mapping out his strategy to recommend to the board. At a special called meeting with the board's executive committee, Rev. Cain presented his findings regarding current program operations and proposed directions for the future. Following his report, the committee made the following recommendations:

(1) The Arizona State Welfare Department would be asked to pay the maximum allowance for its children in care. The payment would be based upon the actual cost of care and closer to amounts received by other agencies.
(2) A vehicle would be purchased for Rev. Cain's use.
(3) A recommendation would be made to change the name of the agency from Baptist Children's Home of Arizona to Arizona Baptist Children's Services.
(4) The agency would establish a satellite home (foster care) program and employ a social worker to supervise the program.
(5) Office space would be developed on the agency site. (Minutes 1970, Executive Committee, BCHA Board).

George Wilson retired July 1, 1970, and was honored at the annual meeting of the Arizona Southern Baptist Convention on November 12, Mr. Cain made his first report to the convention in which he shared the dream that he and the board had for the children's services. He commended the work of those before him and urged support from the convention for the work ahead. He shared with the convention a summary of the goals recommended by the board. Cain's heart for this work was seen in the following statements in his report.

> In any given month in the state of Arizona, there are approximately 2,500 children living in foster homes and institutions and another 2,500 children who are on trial-living arrangements with parents or relatives. This makes a total of 5,000 children. With our present cottage facilities, we can take care of, at the most, twelve of these children. Obviously, this is just a drop in the bucket to what we should be doing . . . I have found the Baptist Children's Home to be held in the highest regard, but I am continually faced with this statement, "I just wish you could take more children. (Cain, 1970, 90)

The first office space occupied by Rev. Cain was in the Arizona Southern Baptist Convention (ASBC) offices at 316 W McDowell, the site where George Wilson's office had also been. His part-time secretary was Mrs. Roy Sutton who also worked for the convention. The other part-time worker in the BCHA office was the social worker Phyllis McFarland. The only full-time staff were the houseparent and the new director, Rev. Cain. The Baptist Foundation of Arizona was also located there.

When Don Cain first arrived, he found the financial management of the children's services different than he expected. The convention handled all the finances. They received all gifts and payments and paid all the bills. At the end of the month, Rev. Cain would be given a financial statement from the convention. Apparently, this was the method used throughout the Wilson administration for financial management.

Mr. Wilson had started the idea of asking people to send "cents-off" coupons to be used in grocery and household purchasing. Cain talked about being inundated with coupons of ten and twenty cents off coupons, which didn't made a big difference in the grocery bill but did give people a sense of having a part in the program. The new executive director discovered that the Arizona Southern Baptist Convention (ASBC) had waived their right to join the Social Security program. Rev. Cain had that changed for the BCHA associates since he already participated in the program and believed it would enhance staff recruitment to have that benefit.

The Expansion of Services

The new superintendent, whose title was changed to executive director, brought with him valuable experience he had gained at Texas Baptist Children's Home. While there, he had served under their director, Charles Wright, one of the most respected and progressive child care and social work leaders among Southern Baptists. Mr. Cain recognized early on, as did the board, that times were changing in Arizona and the nation, and the needs of children were becoming more complex.

Cain's experiences at the Waco State Home and Texas Baptist Children's Home were not his only resources. He was no newcomer to the current technology and culture of working with dependent, neglected, and troubled children. His master's degree thesis on "The Role of Religion in the Placement and Care of Dependent and Neglected Children by the State" gave him a feel for the unmet spiritual needs of children in out-of-home care. Because the juvenile courts placed most of the children in those institutions and many were faith-based, Rev. Cain believed there could be church-state issues in this practice.

Don Cain also had read a report written by Dr. Edmund V. Mech, a professor in the School of Social Work at Arizona State University. The special study, requested by the Arizona legislature, was completed in April 1970. The report, "Public Welfare Services for Children and Youth in Arizona," described the sad state of affairs of children in Arizona and outlined possible solutions to the problems.

Cain met with directors of the various state agencies responsible for children and educated himself regarding the needs of children in the state. As a result of the ASU professor's report, laws were passed to create Child Protective Services in the state. Mr. Cain heard the question from state social workers, "We will need to pick up these abused and neglected children, but where will we put them?" With this information in hand, he wrote a paper for the board, outlining his future plan for Arizona Baptist Children's Home. This plan was approved by the children's home board and became the guiding beacon for future program development. Rev. Cain's plan quoted Dr Mech's report,

> According to practitioners on the firing line, receiving homes, especially for emergency cases, and group homes for teenagers, are the two resources most desperately needed throughout the state. (Cain, "A Brief History," 1970, 1).

These were the two programs that Cain and the board proceeded to develop in the early 1970s.

A New Name

Specialized services for children would need to be developed. Because of this, one of the earliest changes to be made was the name of the agency.

ARIZONA BAPTIST CHILDREN'S SERVICES
400 W. Camelback Rd. / Suite 101
P.O. Box 27128 / Phoenix, Arizona 85061

By action of the board on May 21, 1971, the name of the Baptist Children's Home of Arizona was changed to Arizona Baptist Children's Services. The initials of the name, ABCS, would better capture people's attention and be more easily understood and remembered. While not spelled out more clearly at this time, it would also reflect the broader scope of services to children beyond just custodial care.

A few years later, the children's home campus would be renamed to Little Canyon Center because of its adjacent location to Little Canyon City Park. It also made a more palatable term for the children to describe where they lived. It was easier for them to say, "I live at Little Canyon Center," rather than, "I live at the Baptist Children's Home."

Executive Director Don Cain was a step ahead of his time, particularly regarding Southern Baptist child-care programs. An anti-institutional fever had swept the country in the 1960s, and most of the state mental-health institutions had been closed in favor of community-based services. This move was economy-driven and left much to be desired as the public and mental health professionals would soon discover. The increase in the numbers of homeless people and mental-health problems would be a not-so-silent testimony to the shortcomings of deinstitutionalization. The same mentality carried over to children's homes but with better results.

The realization was settling in that children needed to be reared by families and not institutions. The fact that this approach was more cost-effective also encouraged the growth of this trend. In addition, fewer children were being placed in children's homes. In an article written for *Child Welfare* journal by Eve Smith, assistant professor in the School of Social Work at the University of Windsor in Ontario, she quotes from a study completed by Wolins and Piliavin, "The percentage of children in institutions dropped significantly, from approximately 43% in 1951 to 31% in 1962 . . . Most institutions either closed or were transformed into residential treatment centers for the emotionally disturbed" (1995, 135).

Rev. Cain understood this direction and focused his efforts to dismantle the children's home program format in favor of promoting specialized services. Campus group care would be utilized for providing specialized treatment care that could not be met in a homelike setting. The "best practice" approach would later be developed in providing those specialized services in family settings, but Rev. Cain and the ABCS Board were not quite to that point. It was to their credit that their thinking was as farsighted as it was in the 1970s.

Following his study of the existing programs at ABCS and the current needs of children and families in Arizona, Cain would design a program that would embrace the following directions:

1. The children's home would become a residential treatment facility to care for troubled children.
2. Dependent-neglected children, formerly served by the children's home, would be served in foster family care, or through satellite homes, as he called them.
3. A critical need existed in Arizona for emergency care for children, and that need would be met through group homes and foster family homes.
4. A program of counseling for the families of children in care would be started.

Family Counseling

Family counseling was the first specialized program put into place by Rev. Cain and the board in November 1971. Counseling was generally not a part of the earlier "orphanage" or "children's home" program. In fact, it was a common practice for children's

Modular Building in Front Used For Administration and Counseling on Little Canyon Campus

homes to require temporary custody of children so they could manage the young lives without "parental interference." This was never the case at BCHA/ABCS. There was little, if any, understanding of the importance of families to children. In time, "best practice" would include family counseling as a means for many children to return to their own home.

Another point of view was that children needed to be placed in institutions "to straighten them out." In other words, the child was "broken" and not the family, and the institution would "fix" their children so they could go back home. Family counseling was started at ABCS as part of the dramatic transition from "child serving" to treatment for children and families. In November 1970, preparation was started for this program, which went into operation in 1971. Space was provided for this in the first mobile building moved to the Little Canyon Center that same year (Jennings 1997). Early in his administration, Cain understood the importance of counseling to prevent placement of children outside of their home, or to facilitate the return of a child in placement to their home.

A full-time director of social services, Elaine Bennett, MSSW, was employed who would do the counseling as well as provide social services on campus. She received her master of science in social work from LSU and served the children's services several years until her husband Harold,

Elaine Bennett, MSSW,
Social Worker

director of the Arizona State Personnel Commission, accepted a similar position in another state. In Executive Director Cain's brief history of ABCS, he writes, "In a number of situations in 1971, family problems related to children were resolved through counseling and children did not have to be removed from their own homes, or in some cases, only had to be removed for a short time because such regular counseling was available through Arizona Baptist Children's Services" (Cain, "A Brief History," 1971, 4).

Rev. Cain later told the writer that Mrs. Bennett was very good at helping children return to their families, but it created a financial problem for him since he needed to keeps the beds full on the campus to meet budget. Of course Rev. Cain was glad when a child could return to his/her own home, but this paradox would be the bane of every campus administrator's existence in the future.

Emergency Shelter Care

In 1971, following enabling legislation, Maricopa County Juvenile Court judge William Holohan, in cooperation with the county supervisors, had the responsibility to develop a temporary shelter care program for dependent, neglected, and abused Maricopa County children. The outcome was that ABCS was awarded a one-year contract to provide services. The first site for the ABCS emergency shelter was leased at 1225 E. McDowell and opened March 5, 1971. It had no yard and was less than ideal, but it was a start and was used to provide emergency shelter care for dependent and neglected children. This was a home loaned to ABCS by a member of North Phoenix Baptist Church. This followed a change in plans for the church to purchase a house for the children's home use. There was no playground space, and it became overcrowded very quickly. The first residents were two black children who had been beaten with a battery cable by their parents.

The shelter was later moved to property at 1480 E. Bethany Home on March 5, 1971. This property was purchased for fifty-two thousand dollars (Cain 2005). North Phoenix Baptist Church contributed two hundred dollars per month toward the cost of its operation. (Minutes, Executive Committee ABCS Board, January 4, 1971, 1). The financing would be done through Western Savings Association at 8 percent interest.

The shelter was open twenty-four hours a day, seven days a week. In the beginning, children of all ages were brought there by the police at any hour of the day or night. They could stay up to fourteen days before they would need to be placed in a foster home or returned to their own home or that of relatives. The average stay would be two to three days. The facility was staffed by a live-in houseparent couple.

During the first year, the shelter cared for over five hundred children. The second year saw nine hundred children come through the doors. The third year, one thousand three hundred children received care. The executive director, Don Cain, talked about receiving calls in the middle of the night from the houseparents saying that the police had brought in a family of children, and every bed was already occupied. Cain would tell the houseparents to accept the children, and then he would get up and go to the shelter to help make arrangements for their care (ibid).

In the beginning of the shelter care program, there was disagreement between the welfare department and the juvenile court as to who would pay for the care. Child Protective Services (CPS) had just been started, and new legislation made provision for removal of abused and neglected children from their homes. The juvenile court finally agreed to pay; and all children in Maricopa County who were found to be abused, neglected, or dependent and in need of immediate care were brought to the ABCS shelter. Upon arrival at the shelter, the children would be bathed, fed, and provided clothing and medical treatment if necessary. They had access to recreation and group activities (Whiteaker 1978). ABCS was paid a rate of five dollars per diem for each child with a minimum guaranteed payment of five hundred dollars per month, which would mean a fifty-thousand-dollar annual savings to the county (Minutes, Executive Committee, ABCS Board, 1971).

The home had a capacity for twenty children, but the expectation was that no more than ten or twelve would be there at one time. Regarding this decision to utilize the services of ABCS, Judge Holohan commented,

> I'm very happy with the kind of services this group (ABCS) gives to children. The parents involved are sort of missionaries and they are very much concerned with the children. (*Arizona Republic* 1971).

Overcrowding was always a problem. In 1976, built-in beds were installed as well as new carpeting. Because of the overcrowding, maintaining the property and managing the children constantly challenged the staff. The same welfare department workers who licensed the facility for a limited number of children had no hesitation about placing more children than the license permitted.

On several occasions, the church people would drop in unexpectedly and discover the chaos created by the overcrowding. Rather than spending some time helping, they would go back to their pastors and complain about the "sad condition" of the ABCS facility. Then Rev. Cain would get the calls.

Director Cain promised the convention that plans were being made to resolve the problem (Annual 1977). In time, the infants would be cared for by Crisis Nursery. The girls were later cared for by Patterdell Catholic School at Nineteenth Avenue and Northern. The Patterdell School was originally the Good Samaritan Home for unmarried pregnant girls. After Patterdell closed, the girls were cared for by the Florence Crittenton Home, which also began as a maternity home. Because of these developments, there were no infants or girls in the ABCS shelter after 1977. In 1982 the Bethany Home shelter site was sold for $325,000.

One of the early efforts to deal with the overcrowding at the shelter was to obtain a house to handle the "overflow" from the shelter. In 1973, the residence at 5915 W. Laurie Lane in Glendale was secured for this purpose. It later became a group home for boys. The executive director and staff became concerned about older boys who would reach eighteen and be discharged from the ABCS program to live independently but with little or no skills. The Laurie Lane home became a specialized facility to train older boys in independent living skills. When the Bethany Home shelter was sold and the program moved to Myrtle Street in Glendale, the boys group home on Laurie Lane was closed and the independent living program moved to the new Glendale property. Bob Garrett took over the leadership of this program and named it "the Wrangler Program."

On February 1, 1982, property was purchased by ABCS at 5125 W. Myrtle Avenue in Glendale, Arizona. The four-thousand-six-hundred-square-foot Glendale Bunkhouse, as it was called, was located on an acre of land and was licensed for seventeen boys.  The program at the Bethany Home property was relocated to this site and made available to both the court and the DES. The Bunkhouse had been built by a couple who were foster parents, and they expanded their interest to include a larger group of children. They were active in the Arizona Association of Child Care Agencies where they met ABCS director Don Cain. In time, they asked Rev. Cain if ABCS would be interested in their facility, and the purchase was made soon afterwards.

A temporary sheltered-care home for children in Tucson was opened November 15, 1971, at 3801 N. Swan Road. It served approximately fifty children the first year. All children in Pima County who were found to be dependent, neglected, or abused and in need of immediate care were brought to the shelter. All minority ages were accepted and could be brought to the shelter at any hour of the day or night (Cain, "A Brief History," 1971).

Wrangler Program: Independent-Living Preparation

The Wrangler Program for independent living preparation for boys began at the 5915 W. Laurie Lane group home as noted earlier. When relocated to the Glendale Bunkhouse in February 1982, it became known as "the Wrangler Program." It would later be moved July 1, 1985, to a house on adjoining property at 5115 W. Myrtle. This would allow the shelter program in the Bunkhouse to be increased from ten to eighteen beds and the Wrangler Program increased from six to eight beds. The

Wrangler Program coordinator was Bob Garrett who, at the writing of this book, is the senior-tenured ABCS associate with twenty-one years of faithful service to ABCS. The Wrangler Program assisted older boys with life-skills training leading to independent living. Forty-five boys were served in this program from 1984 through 1988.

Robert Garrett

Satellite Homes

The following story will be familiar to many.

The princess and her royal entourage had no more than stepped into the edge of the water when a faint whimper broke the early morning stillness. The women followed the sound which led them to a mound of straw shaped into a floating basket, which was caught in the reeds of the Nile River in Egypt. A Hebrew baby had been discovered by Pharaoh's daughter. His name was Moses. (Exodus 2:5-9)

Pharaoh daughter took Moses to the royal palace and raised him as her son. Moses was not the last child to be saved through foster care, but he surely is one of the most famous! Satellite home was the name that Rev. Cain gave to what is generally referred to as "foster family care." Cain wanted to distinguish the ABCS foster family care program from that of state foster homes and thus used the new title.

Foster family care had been started earlier by Superintendent Wilson in 1963. The Arizona Department of Welfare had granted the Baptist Children's Home a license to care for six children, ages six to fourteen, in foster family care (*Wilson 1963*). While the number is uncertain, we know that at least six foster family homes provided this care from 1963 until 1969. No other records regarding foster family care are found until the satellite program started under the leadership of Rev. Cain in 1971.

During the first nine months, eleven preschool children were served. The satellite program would continue throughout Rev. Cain's administration. In the beginning, only active members of Southern Baptist churches would be enlisted in the program. That would change as accepting public funding would require implementation of a nondiscrimination policy in hiring. In addition there were not enough Baptist homes to meet the need.

Social worker June Patton headed up the satellite program under the supervision of Dr. Phyllis McFarland. Beginning in July 1979, the foster-home method would be employed to care for young, handicapped, abused, and neglected children in what would be called "therapeutic foster care." During the first year of this program, twenty children were served

L-R: June Patton, Phyllis McFarland

through twelve therapeutic care foster homes (Annual 1980). In 1980, fourteen families were in this special program caring for children between the ages of four to eighteen (Annual 1982).

The difficulty in enlisting families to provide this service for children was indicated in early records. This shortage not only characterized the

ABCS program, but it characterized almost all foster family care programs in all agencies throughout its history. It should be noted that there were no "regular" foster homes during the Cain administration. The satellite home consisted of therapeutic care for special needs children. The emergency receiving homes were specialized homes to provide temporary emergency care until a child was returned to his/her own home or to a more permanent type of foster care or adoption.

Emergency Receiving Homes (ERH)

On December 1, 1977, ABCS entered into a contract with District I of the Arizona Department of Economic Security (DES) to provide emergency care for the district's children ages birth to twelve. Teenagers would be accepted only when they were part of a family group. This would be done through use of private homes, much like the Satellite Home program. ERH parents could be licensed to have from two to five bed spaces. These homes would be available twenty-four hours a day, seven days a week, to receive children that were abused or neglected or for whatever reason required immediate removal from their family. ERH parents would have a respite time (no children placed) one week each quarter. Eventually, twenty-nine families were licensed to provide this service (Annual 1979).

Children could remain in the emergency care home for up to three weeks before being returned to their parents or another form of permanent care. Most of the periods of residence were one or two days. Very few remained more than twenty-one days. The rule of thumb was that the older the children, the longer would be their residence in the emergency home. The children could be any age of minority. The families were trained and supervised by ABCS staff and paid by DES. In 1979, there were 554 children served in this program (ibid.). ERH parents were required to have twelve hours of training each year to maintain their annual license.

The work of caring for troubled children in one's home was stressful and demanding. This resulted in a large turnover in receiving home parents, even though support services were available to make the job easier. The contract with DES called for a transportation worker who would do most of the transporting of children to and from the ERH, as well as transport the children for medical, social services, and parental visits. ABCS social workers assisted the parents by visiting in their homes two times weekly to discuss behavior management and to deal with the impact of the placements upon their family life. Each social worker served an average of fifteen children allowing sufficient time for adequate support. Other social work staff did the recruiting and licensing of new ERH parents. DES provided reimbursement for the cost of care to the families and paid ABCS an administrative fee for management of the program.

The following chart * provides information about the children who were served in the first seven months of the program.

1977-78	New Children Placed during Month	Total Number Children Served in the Month	Number of Child Care Days in the Month
December	6	6	17
January	14	14	89
February	12	15	96
March	28	37	501
April	33	52	568
May	53	91	834
June	54	88	848

*   Source: Undocumented report (no source or date) on the ERH Program in the ERH files, ABCS archives.

Another report indicated that from July 1, 1979, to June 1, 1980, ABCS had twenty-three different receiving homes licensed for fifty-seven to sixty bed spaces. From the period of July 1, 1979, to March 1, 1980, there were 287 children in placement and 7,184 child-care days. The average length of stay was 24.9 days. Fifty-one percent of the children were girls.

The following is a percentage of age breakdown: **

Birth through age five	50.2%
Six through twelve	45.4%
Thirteen through seventeen	4.4%

**   Source: 1980 Annual Report of the Arizona Baptist Children's Services, p. 6. In the ABCS archives.

In another report, the following reasons were listed for children being placed in the ABCS ERH program in September 1980:

Physical abuse by mother; disrupted adoption; abandoned in apartment; chronic runaway from other ERHs; mother severely retarded; placed by hospital; placed by police after abandonment; voluntary by mother from hospital; disrupted foster care placement; father arrested for kidnapping child; found at shopping center; mother arrested for drunkenness/disorderly conduct; Sexual abuse by mother's boyfriend; custody dispute; mother in jail on felony warrant; voluntary placement by parents; parents evicted; no resources; mother entering rehab. (Undocumented report in ERH files, ABCS archives)

One of the receiving home families was that of George and Doris Jones, active Southern Baptists. This licensed family's story was featured in the Arizona Republic newspaper. They had provided emergency care for forty children in their first eighteen months as receiving home parents. The story told of the fact that many had never attended church before nor experienced the warmth of a Christian home. Most of the children were abused or neglected. All needed protection. They were accepted regardless of race, color, or religion. Mrs. Jones was quoted as saying, "Our opportunities are unlimited for touching the lives of others" (1979, 6-10). George Jones would later become director of maintenance for ABCS and remained with the agency until his retirement, July 1993. Doris served many years as a volunteer after serving as a receiving home parent. The contract for the receiving home program was cancelled in 1981 (Arizona Department of Economic Security 1980). DES claimed that there was no longer the need for such care and that it was too costly. The closure was met by a large outcry and protests from the statewide Southern Baptist community. Executive Director Don Cain believes that the true reason for the program's closure was ABCS's questioning of certain Child Protective Service practices. Following numerous verbal and written protest to judges and legislators, the matter was heard by a joint Senate/House committee. As a result, several bills were passed improving the system, but the Receiving Home Program remained closed for ABCS (Annual 1981). Cain summarized the issue for the *Baptist Beacon*: "We're on the road to accomplishing reforms in DES, but it took sacrificing our own contract to do it . . . I don't see any way possible that we could have sat by and not said something when we saw what was going on." The Emergency Receiving Home program served about 11,000 children in its nine-year history (Young 1980, 1-2).

Group Homes

Two features characterize group homes for children. First, they are community based. Children live in a regular neighborhood and go to public schools and community churches. The house is usually a large house with four to six bedrooms. The size and many other features of the home are regulated by state standards for health, safety, and program matters. The group home may be supervised by live-in houseparents or staffed by associates who rotate by shifts based upon various staffing styles, much like those of hospital nursing shifts.

The second feature of the group home for children is the number of children who can be in residence. Facilities for out-of-home care for children get somewhat confusing at this point. A foster family care license, depending upon the particular state regulations, can provide care for up to six children, and in this case, the home may be called and licensed as a foster family home. A foster family home differs from the group foster homes earlier described, mainly in size. Group foster home parents may own or rent their own home, or the home may be owned by the agency by which it is licensed. A group home may care for up to sixteen children.

A group home that cares for more than sixteen children but less than twenty-five may be licensed as a "group residence." It may or may not be located in a residential community. The group homes developed by Arizona Baptist Children's Services generally served no more than twelve children and were located in residential communities. The various states have different standards for different types of out-of-home care for children, depending upon their classification of residential services.

One of the most popular methods of community-based services for children during the Cain administration was the group home. He was familiar with the unique joint sponsorship of group homes in Texas between local churches and Buckner Baptist Benevolences during his time on the staff of Texas Baptist Children's Home. In this arrangement, a local church would furnish a house and the cost of operation, and Buckners would provide the staff, child placement, licensing, and supervision of the children cared for in the home. It was a way in which churches could share in the direct responsibility in caring for dependent, neglected, and troubled children; and it would significantly help cash-strapped child-care programs.

Unknown to Rev. Cain at the time of the writing of this book, its author developed this model and established four such cooperative group homes in South Texas. Cain knew of Baker's employment with Buckners in San Antonio but did not know of his connection with the joint-sponsored group homes.

Rev. Cain believed this model of church-agency cooperation would work in Arizona and approached several churches about the plan. Cain explained to the author that he didn't realize at the time that the Arizona Southern Baptist Churches were smaller and just didn't have the resources that the Texas Baptist Churches had (Cain 2005). There were some attempts by churches to explore this plan, but those attempts never materialized. North Phoenix Baptist Church did provide two hundred dollars a month toward the operational cost of a group home and later extended that to five hundred dollars per month. First Southern Baptist Church in Yuma offered the use of a house they purchased February 25, 1977. The logistics of setting up a group home proved unworkable at that time in ABCS's history. It would be a different matter twenty years later when ABCS had established regional offices throughout the state.

Even without support from a local church, Rev. Cain, his staff, and the board began establishing a series of group homes to house the state's dependent, neglected, and troubled children. The following is a list of the group homes developed during the Cain administration. Some have already been described in detail but are listed again here to give readers a sense of the extent of the group home program.

** The first group home of ABCS was an emergency shelter opened at 1225 E. McDowell in Phoenix.

** A group home was opened for six adolescent girls February 22, 1971, at 309 W. Almira in Phoenix (Minutes Executive Committee, ABCS Board February 1, 1971).

** A group home for adolescent boys opened May 18, 1972, at 2018 N. Ninth Street, Phoenix. This program was short-lived because of better facilities, which later became available.

** In 1973, a boys shelter-overflow facility was leased and opened at 5915 W. Laurie, Glendale, Arizona. This residence would later become a group home for boys and the first independent living program site.

** The Glendale Bunkhouse at 5125 W. Myrtle, Glendale, opened February 1, 1982. It would contain both the boy's shelter and independent living (Wrangler) programs. The latter program would later have its own residence adjoining the Bunkhouse.

** The Camelback Girl's Home at 3324 E. Camelback Road opened December 15, 1972. This facility was in existence under another authority before being turned over to ABCS.

** A Group Home for Girls was leased at 3741 Hazelwood, Phoenix, and opened in 1973.

** Efforts were made to begin work in Tucson, and an emergency group home was established. The property was sold by the owner, and zoning restrictions prohibited further work in the area.

Residential Treatment

The original Baptist Children's Home site at 3101 W. Missouri, Phoenix, consisted of a single brick residence on five acres of land. That would soon change as other properties and programs were added to the work that had started under George Wilson.

In the early days of the Cain administration, the West Missouri campus would continue to serve as a children's home. The activities were consistent with the care of dependent-neglected children. Rev. Cain's legacy from the Wilson administration would include some horses as well as dependent children.

There were horses on the campus, which the children loved to ride. The horses attracted flies, and the hay cost about thirty dollars a month per horse, which was a big expense at that time. After several broken arms, Cain decided that the horses had to go. He was concerned about the repercussions since he was new, and the horses were donated for the children. He bravely took "the steer by the horns," so to speak, and summarily discharged his equine legacy. Surprisingly, there seemed to be little concern about the decision.

When the children's home was transitioned into a residential treatment center for emotionally troubled children, the name of the campus was changed to Little Canyon Center. The original facility could care for twelve children, ages twelve to eighteen. Following the campus transition from a children's home to a treatment center, two houses were purchased across the street at 3114 and 3118 W. Missouri, bringing the capacity of the campus up to thirty. A permanent residence and four portable buildings would be added during the Cain years. Two of the temporary units were modular buildings (trailers) measuring twelve by fifty-six feet and were moved onto the campus to provide office, counseling, and classroom space. The first was moved onto the campus in 1971 at a cost of eleven thousand five hundred dollars, and the second was moved in 1974 when the Papago Indian Children's Home was closed. One additional small building was brought in as a classroom.

The following story about one of the treatment-center residents illustrates the work of the program and the problems of the children who were served.

Robert (not his real name) came to the ABCS campus at the age of eight. This was at a time when the campus was still a children's home, and children of a wide range of ages were accepted. He was the type of child "that at first glance stole your heart away." He was bright, charming, and very cute. Nevertheless, he had a variety of problems that made management of his care very difficult. He was unable to read and possessed a learning disability. The boy would erupt easily and forcefully. He was a hyperactive child who talked constantly. He was your basic "whirlwind of activity."

His mother was ill and could not manage him at home. The teachers at his school had difficulty controlling his behavior. His parents were divorced, and his mother eventually died due to a heart attack. Robert received care, security, and developed a strong sense of values in the treatment program.

Years after he left ABCS, he corresponded with the campus associates and expressed appreciation for the love, care, and direction he received. He mentioned how special Christmas and birthdays were to him because of the thoughtfulness of his caretakers. He had found work as an aide in a nursing home and found he enjoyed giving of himself to others as other had given themselves to him. He pursued a nursing degree at Northern Arizona University in Flagstaff. Robert summed up his time at ABCS by saying, "I thank God for ABCS and the values and the knowledge I received from my stay. It was a warm and growing experience for me". Robert's experience has been repeated numerous times and gives the kind of encouragement needed by the associates to work harder to serve children and their families.

Don Cain related the following story that took place early in his administration. A secretary, whom Rev. Cain knew at Texas Baptist Children's Home, introduced him to a lady who was interested in children and would soon be moving to Phoenix, where Rev. Cain was also moving. She had previously worked for them on a part-time basis—possibly as a relief houseparent. The secretary thought that the lady might be of help to Rev. Cain after they both had moved to the new location in Phoenix. Don Cain told the writer, "At first, I thought little about it, but later remembering the introduction, and needing all the help I could get, I contacted Dorothy Law who was interested in helping." She did some relief houseparent work but really found her niche in buying groceries for the home. She was a high-energy lady with several talents and also located property sites needed for group homes. Dorothy found the property for the Bethany Home shelter.

In the course of her volunteer work, Mrs. Law, a widow, met Jim Hite, a widower who was in real estate. They became interested in one another and eventually asked Don Cain if he would perform their wedding ceremony, which he gladly did. They continued to purchase groceries and convinced stores to donate food and other goods. They eventually set up a commissary off campus. This continued for several years. Cain mentioned that later in life, Jim was pastor of one or two small churches. They are both deceased now but were among the many unsung heroes whom the children's services has had over the years (Cain 2005).

Other changes would take place in addition to the name change and upgrading of facilities. Cain early recognized that the physical facilities at 3101 W. Missouri were substandard and would prove to be a challenge in qualifying for accreditation by the Joint Commission on Accreditation of Health Organizations (JCAHO). The quality staff and strong programs carried the agency through its first accreditation, but it would be highly unlikely that continued accreditation and Child Welfare League membership would take place unless dramatic improvements were made. This belief was to be affirmed in the Whiteaker study, which stated "A complete rework of facilities on the Missouri Avenue Campus is necessary in order to maintain national and state accreditation and to improve the results of this program" (Whiteaker 1978, 17).

Wage and hour laws were making it difficult to maintain the "houseparent" model on the campus. This was not only true for Little Canyon Campus, but it was a ubiquitous problem in children's residential group care throughout the nation. Since houseparents spend twenty-four hours daily with the children, questions arose as to payment for sleeping time if in fact they were still "on duty." Also, it became a challenge to fit their work into a forty-hour week. It became a nightmare to calculate the work time and interpret the wage and hour law. In addition, it was increasingly difficult to find qualified houseparents.

Another challenge for live-in houseparents was the complexity and stress of caring for and living with the increasingly troubled children that were coming into care. The earlier orphans and dependent children were happy to have a place to stay and responded with respect and obedience to their caretakers. The troubled child, beginning in the 1970s, did not want to be away from his/her own parents in spite of abuse and neglect, and they resented redirection and counsel from those caring for them.

All of these factors made it necessary to move to a "counselor" or "shift" model. In this model, child-care counselors worked with and supervised the children for an eight to ten hour shift, and then went to their own homes away from the campus. Instead of a single set of houseparents who lived in the house with the children, there were now three shifts with two associates on each shift. No staff slept overnight, and the night staff did laundry and some cleaning while the children were sleeping. At ABCS, instead of three sets of houseparents and their relief workers, now there would be thirteen child-care counselors. In addition, with the increased staff, there would have to be shift supervisors to coordinate the staffing and ensure coverage was adequate at all times. Such a change would increase costs.

Convention Offices at
400 W. Camelback

When Mr. Cain first came to ABCS, his office was in the Baptist convention building at 316 W. McDowell. Feeling the need to be located closer to the Little Canyon Campus, he was able to relocate when the first modular building was moved to the campus. However, because of the space needs for the child-care operation, Rev. Cain's office would again be moved and this time from the modular unit on Little Canyon Campus to the 400 W. Camelback building where the Arizona Southern Baptist Convention offices had been relocated.

In addition to all the other changes, the residential treatment program at the Little Canyon Campus was first accredited by the Joint Commission on Accreditation of Health Organizations (JCAHO) February 10, 1975. This was a big step for the children's services that would qualify the program to accept Medicaid (Title XIX) money for eligible children. It would also qualify the residential treatment program to receive payment from private insurance. In 1979, another big step was taken as ABCS was accepted as an accredited member of the Child Welfare League of America (CWLA). At this time the campus had a capacity for thirty-two children.

In spite of the many problems, it is important to realize that membership in CWLA and accreditation by JCAHO are no small achievements. Agencies work for years to reach the stringent standards of both of these organizations, and ABCS had met the standards for both. The agency was frequently given positive recognition by the state departments that used its services. By this time, ABCS was accepting children from the Maricopa County Juvenile Court Center as well as from the welfare department. In an evaluation that was done by the court in the mid-1970s, the following assessment was given:

> Arizona Baptist Children's Services is one of the best and most valuable resources available to wards of the Juvenile Court Center. This agency's concern with programs to help children and their families has made this agency popular among probation officers. The fact that this agency has just received accreditation as a psychiatric treatment facility attests to this agency's strivings for excellence in child care (Institutional Review, Maricopa County, 1795, 3).

Plans were being made in 1972 for constructing additional cottages on the campus (Minutes, ABCS Board, May 17, 1972, 1). No more information about the building program is mentioned until 1978. This was a result of the difficulty experienced by the ABCS administration to obtain the necessary zoning approval from the City of Phoenix. This delay was further compounded by lack of funds and growing problems in the neighborhood because of the increasing complexity of the children's problems. The ABCS children became the scapegoat for any vandalism or theft experienced by the neighbors. Certainly, the ABCS children did act out in the community, but they received far more credit for the community problems than they deserved.

There were many good experiences and positive outcomes for children that far overshadow some of the difficulties. Executive Director Don Cain related the following true story in one of his many letters to pastors.

One year ago a seventeen year old girl came to live with us at ABCS. She came to us having been charged by the court as being incorrigible and incapable of being controlled by her parents. There was a history of drunkenness and drug abuse as well as stories of violent episodes in which people and property were damaged. There had been several unsuccessful suicidal attempts on her part and the most recent was the precipitating event which led to her placement with ABCS.

The sad part of the story is that the home she came from was also a home in which alcoholism was a big part of the problem of the father and mother. The girl recognized this fact and whenever she had contacts with her parents over the following months (after she was placed with ABCS) she became quite depressed as she recognized that there was no hope for her ever returning home.

Just a few months ago, this girl made a profession of faith in Christ which has resulted in a dramatic change in her life. Those who are closest to her say there is no comparison as to the difference in her outlook and behavior since she made this positive decision. Her teachers have commented that her school work has become noticeably better and she has recently started on a vocational training program that should make it possible for her to establish a good life for herself in a few months when she is eighteen years of age. (Cain 1976)

Rev. Cain's comments in the letter to pastors focused upon the purpose of the ABCS ministry.

As Jesus many times found it necessary to provide for the physical needs of people before he faced them with their spiritual needs, so we many times find it necessary to provide a stable home environment, food and clothing, and emotional security in order that the teenagers with whom we work can settle down and hear the truth of the Gospel. (ibid.)

Special Education—Coed School

ABCS' CO-ED SCHOOL

In December 1972, ABCS accepted the responsibility for operating the Camelback Girl's Residence (CGR) located at 3324 E. Camelback Road in Phoenix. This was a residential and academic program for troubled girls. The educational part would eventually serve all ABCS children who could not attend public school because of their behavior (*Love in Action* 1973). The CGR Board, affiliated with the Camelback Bible Church, requested that ABCS manage the program, and in return, they would hand the program over to ABCS in the future. The ownership of the property remained with the Camelback Girl's Home Board. Conflicts arose in the spring of 1974 between the ABCS and the Camelback

Camelback Girl's Residence and School

Girl's Residence (CGR) boards. The issues involved the change of ownership, financial assets of CGR, and control of the agency to which they had been transferred.

Rather that turning over the program and facilities to ABCS, they wanted to sell the program. The issues were not resolved, and in November 1974, GCR was closed, and the girls were moved to the ABCS Girls' Teen Cottage on Little Canyon Campus (Feick 1986). In addition to the conflict, the CGR facilities were in disrepair, and ABCS did not want to put money into a facility it did not

One of two mobile buildings used for class rooms on the Little Canyon Campus

own. A final resolution was reached with termination of all ties with the former CGR ownership (Minutes, ABCS Board, 1976, 1). This came after an agreement by the ABCS Board's Executive Committee to pay for one-half of the legal expenses that had been incurred (Minutes, Executive Committee, ABCS Board, March 1976, 1).

Bob Walker was employed as the director of the program after it came under ABCS management. The program had a capacity for fifteen troubled girls. It offered twenty-four-hour residential care for its residents and contained its own special education school with three teachers. As previously mentioned, a modular building was moved onto the Little Canyon Campus, which would contain the special education school. A smaller building would later be added to provide additional educational space. Several students in residential treatment could attend public school on a part-time or full-time basis depending upon their strengths and the severity of their emotional handicap. The school accepted a few day-school students from the community through contracts with the school districts. The special education program would continue to be a major part of the residential treatment program. The special education program was accredited by the State Department of Education in 1974. Later, in the new school facility, it was accredited also by the North Central Association.

Medical, Nursing, and Social Services

As early as the second year of the children's home operation, the program was commended by the state licensing division for its quality

Martha Decker, RN

health and social services. In the first licensing review, Glen H. Richard, DPW licensing representative, wrote to Superintendent Wilson, "In the short time of its existence, the Baptist Children Home has developed a program of medical and dental services, maintained a fully trained caseworker on its staff, and providing a family living experience with normal school and neighborhood participation" (Richard 1962, 2). The medical care during these early days consisted of regular medical and dental exams. Baptist Hospital provided emergency and in-patient care.

When the children's home was converted into a residential treatment center, both on-site nursing and psychiatric services were added. In the late 1970s, Martha Decker, RN, was employed as the full-time nurse and coordinator of Health Services. Dr. James Joy became the ABCS medical director and attending psychiatrist. As the program grew and the use of psychotropic medication became more widespread, additional nursing staff were added providing twenty-four-hours-a-day and seven-days-a-week coverage. In addition to giving the prescribed medications to residents, the nursing staff made medical and dental appointments and saw that the children had transportation to their appointments. Health care records, including immunizations, were kept for the children and became a part of the medical record that would follow them wherever they lived.

Pat Kaminsky, RN, made arrangements for medical and dental appointments for the Emergency Receiving Home program. Pat also arranged for the transportation with the ABCS transportation worker to get the children to their appointments.

Social services were also a part of the professional program from the beginning. It was doubtful if the first superintendent George Wilson even knew what a social worker was or what they did before he had to employ one. Mrs. Eddy of the Department of Public Welfare patiently educated him and the board

James Joy, M.D.
Psychiatrist and
Medical Director

regarding the need of the home to have a social worker to meet licensing requirements (Minutes 1960, BCHA Board, 1).

The social worker would make an assessment of a child's needs and family circumstances to determine if placement in the home was appropriate. The worker counseled both with the child and his/her family and developed a plan whereby the child would return home or to some other form of permanent care. This would be true for admissions to the children's home and to foster care. The previous chapter listed the first social worker who began on a part-time basis, Mrs. Mayola Miltenberger. Bill Johnson and Phyllis McFarland followed her as the home's social workers. It will always be to the credit of these early children's home associates that they were wise enough to get counsel regarding "best practices" in serving children in group out-of-home care.

At the time of Don Cain's employment as executive director, the home was without a social worker. The board authorized him to "find a qualified social worker from the ranks of Southern Baptists, if possible . . ." (Minutes, BCHA Board, September 27, 1970, 1). Elaine Bennett, MSSW, would fill this position in the home for several years. Following the opening of the residential treatment center and the addition of other programs, more social workers would be added to the staff.

Early Regional Program Efforts

The needs of children and families were not confined to Phoenix although it was much easier to develop programs there than other areas of the state. Interest was expressed that work with children and families begin in places outside of Phoenix. There were even promises of financial support for such expansion, but no money.

Tucson

The first effort to set up programs for children and families in other regions of the state was in Tucson, the state's second largest metropolitan area. On November 15, 1971, a temporary shelter for children was opened by ABCS at 3801 N. Swan Road (Cain 1971). This program operated similarly to the ABCS emergency receiving homes in Phoenix. All children in Pima County who were declared dependent, neglected, or abused would be brought there. This involved children of all ages who could be brought to the shelter any hour of the day or night. The children would be relocated when suitable long-term care could be found. The children were usually emotionally upset and sometimes would have cuts and bruises. They were usually dirty and in need of clothing and food. This program was also supervised by a live-in couple (ibid).

The shelter closed November 1, 1973, due to sale of the property. Several attempts to relocate the shelter failed due to unsolvable zoning problems with the City of Tucson (Krajnak 1973). Director Cain and others literally walked the streets in Tucson neighborhoods attempting to get signatures for approval to open a group home in the area (Cain 2005). Mr. Richard Huff, active in Baptist work in Southern Arizona and a realtor, tried on several occasions to secure property for use by ABCS. Zoning requirements and the cost in retrofitting houses to meet licensing standards were roadblocks that stymied these numerous efforts.

Tohono O'odhan[2] Children's Home in Sells, Arizona

The ABCS Board of Directors discussed the need for a children's residential program on the Tohona O'odhan Indian Reservation in Sells, Arizona, following a request by the tribal council. The need for such a program was great among the Tohono O'odhan people who were the poorest Indian people in the Southwest (Feick 1986). Boys and girls,

abandoned by their parents, were placed in the local jail because no other shelter was available (*Footprints* 1991).

A program for thirteen children on the reservation was approved by the ABCS Board on February 28, 1972 (*Love in Action* 1972). A building was offered by the Baptist Church in Sells, but it would need

Tohono O'odhan Children's Home at Sells, AZ

remodeling. When the need for help was made known, forty-five members from the First Southern Baptist Church of Chula Vista, California, and volunteers from Arizona Southern Baptist churches responded and completed the renovation project (ibid.). Mr. and Mrs. Vernon Furrow of Tucson offered a matching gift of one hundred thousand dollars for a children's home in Sells. (The offer was originally presented as an anonymous offer in a December 18, 1975, letter to Don Cain). The money was never matched, and the gift offer was forfeited.

---

[2]   Formerly known as the Papago Indian Reservation

On July 29, 1972, the children's home and emergency shelter were opened in Sells, and by October, forty children had received care. The program was operating at full capacity within two years of its opening. Several members of the tribal community worked full time at the facility. It was a challenge to keep the children there once they were placed in the home. The Indian people had such a strong belief in the sanctity of family life that the Indian women who worked in the home gave support to those children who wanted to return to their own homes without administrative approval.

It became increasing difficult to obtain payment for services from the Papago Community. The Bureau of Indian Affairs received so much criticism in the financial management of the program that they turned the payment process over to the tribe, who in turn mishandled the process. Eventually, this resulted in an eighteen-thousand-dollar revenue loss. This led to the closing of the home (Annual 1976). In addition, twenty thousand dollars had been embezzled from the program by a Phoenix ABCS staff member. It came about when the executive director had his signature put on a rubber stamp to be used for checkwriting when he was out of town or otherwise unavailable. On one occasion, he opened the bank statement usually opened by the staff member who paid the bills. He discovered that checks had been written to this staff member with his signature stamp. He took the matter to the agency's bonding company who called the authorities and pressed charges against the ABCS employee. The bond limit was ten thousand dollars, which ABCS was paid, and the employee was placed on probation and required to make total restitution (Cain 2005).

Earlier, ABCS staff had moved a trailer to the Sells's campus to provide needed office space. The tribal council claimed ownership of the trailer and wouldn't allow its removal after ABCS discontinued its services. ABCS employees simply moved it to the Little Canyon Campus where it was used for classrooms. Apparently nothing was done about it by the council.

Yuma

On April 10, 1972, property was offered to ABCS in Yuma, Arizona by First Southern Baptist Church through ABCS Board member, Mr. Bill

Jewett, and his wife, Barbara. The Jewetts and First Southern Baptist Church would each play important roles in the future development of ABCS work in southwestern Arizona. The termination of the effort was believed to result from lack of cooperation by the Department of Economic Security (DES) (ibid.). In any event, board minutes state, "There will be no child care work started there by us at the present" (Minutes, ABCS Board 1977, 1).

The Chaplaincy Program and Religious Training

From its beginning, the ASBC founders expected the children's home to be a ministry to children, which included meeting physical and spiritual needs. That ministry would later be expanded to include education, behavioral health care, and family counseling. However, two purposes seem to stand out throughout its history—protection and meeting spiritual needs.

In the early years of the children's home, children were required to attend church services on Sunday. Children attended at several Southern Baptist churches, but the children and staff primarily attended Love Baptist Church. One report indicated, "All of the children you have helped to support have been converted and baptized into the fellowship of Love Baptist Church, since coming to the home" (Annual 1962, 55). The intentions and hearts of the staff were in the right place, but one cannot help but wonder how much of a choice these young vulnerable children from broken homes really felt they had when it came to understanding spiritual matters. In 1975, a part-time chaplain Jim Preston was employed. At that time Sunday worship services were held on campus, and children and staff members were required to attend, unless by prearrangement they attended off-campus churches. The children's home at no point excluded children of other faiths or no faith.

With the growth of the ABCS foster-care programs and pressure from DES to conform to nondiscrimination hiring policy, foster parents of various religious traditions, or none, came into the program. It would be some time before the ABCS administration could develop methods of adhering to nondiscrimination hiring policy and still carry out its spiritual mission. Until that time came, there would be a great deal of conflict and heartache eventually resulting in the resignation of the executive director. Concerns were raised from time to time about the morals and spirituality of certain staff members.

Two things must be noted about this criticism. First, there are always weak and careless people in every organization, even in churches and Christian institutions. ABCS had its share of those individuals who were not strong examples of Christian character. On the other hand, bearing the name "Christian," or "Baptist," did not bring assurance of splendid Christian character. Two of the most glaring examples of misconduct were on the part of a Baptist minister on the ABCS staff (not a chaplain) and a houseparent who was a deacon in one of the local Baptist churches. Both incidents involved sexual misconduct. The administration throughout the ABCS history sought godly, professional people to care for children. Their experience, however, would be that wearing a "Christian" or even "Baptist" label did not guarantee spirituality or competence.

Susan Cain Teaching
Sunday School at the shelter

Oversight of the personal habits and morals of staff was much easier to monitor in the children's home or group homes because of the presence of several staff who encouraged accountability on a day-to-day basis. It was different in foster care where each home was an isolated living unit. Monitoring was difficult and loose, except for the occasional visit from the agency social worker.

Expectations for foster parents were practically nonexistent when it came to religious practices. It must be recognized that many of the foster parents were active Christians in their churches. It would always be a source of irritation to some of the constituency that they weren't all Southern

Baptist Christians. The agency had two problems with that viewpoint. The first was the difficulty in recruiting any kind of Christian foster parents, much less limit the qualifications to denominational preference. The board president at that time remembers telling some who objected to non-Baptist foster parents that if Baptist foster parents would step forward, they would be hired. He concluded, "That didn't happen." Secondly, because state funds were federally matched, federal nondiscriminatory rules applied to private state vendors, of which ABCS was one.

In Mr. Cain's 1976 annual report to the ASBC, he stated that Jim Preston, pastor of Longview Baptist Church in Phoenix, had been appointed as a part-time chaplain for ABCS (Annual 1976, 105). At the same annual meeting that year, an ABCS part-time foster parent made a recommendation on the floor of the convention "that a full investigation be made of ABCS by a committee of five to be appointed by the president. This committee would include one woman and a report would be made and published in the *Baptist Beacon* within ninety days" (ibid., 25). To justify his recommendation, the foster parent contended in the report that "his experience as a foster parent convinced him there should be more emphasis on teaching Christian precepts to the children coming to ABCS through the shelter care program, and that more spiritual instruction should be given." He further explained that if the children's spiritual needs were better met, "they wouldn't need medication" (ibid.). A committee was appointed by the president of the convention. (In looking back, this writer wonders why the matter was not referred to the ABCS Board.) When the written report was published, it suggested the appointment of a full-time chaplain.

This foster parent mentioned above owned a ranch outside of Phoenix and would take ABCS teenage boys there on weekends. The boys enjoyed the opportunity to get away from campus life and ride horses. The foster parent was a member of a paramilitary group, and sometime later, a Phoenix newspaper article indicated that he had been arrested in relation to that activity. That ended the weekend trips to his ranch, as well as criticism about the "lack of spirituality" in the ABCS program.

The committee asked that ABCS be very specific in writing responses to the goals requested by the convention. In response to the earlier request by the convention for a study to be done, the ABCS Board developed a written statement of its "philosophy" and "objectives," which were preceded by a "preamble," which summarized the entire document.

> Arizona Baptist Children's Services is an agency of the Arizona Southern Baptist Convention, chartered to minister to the very immediate urgent needs of children committed to its care, in compliance with its charter, the constitution, and the by-laws of the convention. It operates with the conviction that a part of the Christian ministry which Christ left for us involves the recognition and addressing of physical and social needs, as well as spiritual needs. It is the conviction of all—the Agency, its Board and Administration and the parent convention—that all ministry to physical and social needs must be administered manifestly in the name and for the glory of our Lord and Savior, Jesus Christ. (Policy Manual, ABCS, 1978).

The first full-time chaplain, Jim Rawls, was employed as director of religious activities in July 1977 (Annual 1977). This position became one of continuing importance throughout the remaining history of ABCS. Rawls would remain until 1980, at which time Jerry Bailey was employed in this position.

Paul Kinnison, a recent graduate of Southern Baptist Seminary in Louisville, KY, would become ABCS's third full-time chaplain in 1983. Kennison was a skilled communicator with the children and would later fill an expanded role in the agency's administration. He was a caring man who helped many children discover a personal faith in their lives. Kinnison laced much of his repartee with the children with humor, endearing himself to them and opening the doors for real spiritual searching and discovery.

This concern for more spiritual emphasis never completely went away during Don Cain's administration and continued into the next administration. A board member suggested to Cain's successor, President Baker, that "soul winning" classes should be taught to the staff. This was not an uncommon point of view and reflected a lack of understanding of the distinction between the goals of a church and those of a church-sponsored social service agency.

Finances

CEO's of nonprofit agencies dream of working for programs that were started by large endowments such as the Hopewell Children's Home and the Duke Endowment, both in South Carolina, or the nationwide Casey Family Care program. The reality for most administrators is one of hard work in securing the funds that their agencies need to meet budget and capital needs. This was George Wilson's challenge, and it would also be that of succeeding administrators of ABCS. The budget approved by the board of directors on August 4, 1970, was $112,000 for the 1971 year. Four years later, it jumped to $723,000 following the dramatic program expansion. In addition to donations from individuals, churches, and the Arizona Southern Baptist Convention, fees for service were received from the Arizona Department of Economic Security (DES). The fees for children placed through the courts were also paid by DES (Feick 1986). Later in the Cain administration, ABCS would receive payment for children served by contracts with the following government agencies:

** Department of Health Services and their statewide regional authorities
** Arizona Department of Corrections, Juvenile Division (later known as the Department of Youth Treatment and Rehabilitation)
** Arizona Health Care Cost Containment System (AHCCS)
** State Supreme Court (Administrative Office of the Juvenile Courts—AOC)
** Arizona Department of Education

** Various school districts
** Various tribal communities and the U.S. Bureau of Indian Affairs

When Don Cain came to ABCS, the state was paying one hundred dollars per month for each of its children in care. This was well below what the state was paying to several other providers. One of the first actions of the board was to increase the fee to two hundred dollars per month. This new rate would begin January 1, 1971 (Minutes, Executive Committee 1970). Each of these state agencies had different program and licensing requirements, quality assurance procedures, utilization reviews, and case management systems. Complying with these regulations, together with national safety standards and national accreditation requirements, was a monumental challenge.

From time to time, ABCS was questioned about its acceptance of fees for service from the state. To clarify this in relation to concerns about church-state separation, the executive committee of the ABCS Board reported the following statement in its minutes. Such action "does not violate the Baptist principle of separation of church and state so long as the payment does not exceed the actual cost of this care . . ." (Minutes, ABCS Executive Committee 1970; later affirmed in the ABCS Board meeting minutes of May 30, 1974).

One of the issues which Baptists did not understand at first was that payment by DES for its children was not the same as government grants or "support." The government was not *giving* anything to ABCS. It was paying for the care of its children in the same way that any parent would be expected to pay for the care of their children. Sadly, there were few parents financially able to pay for the cost of this type of specialized care. It was true that expensive behavioral health treatment often required that parents give up custody of their children to receive state help.

While no one was completely comfortable depending so heavily upon contract income, this was the only way to provide for the care of large numbers of children. The ABCS administration would make continuous efforts to encourage support from individuals and churches, as well as increasing the program income from state agencies.

Don Cain had knowledge of fund-raising from his experience at Texas Baptist Children's Home. Moreover, he understood the mechanics of working with state agencies, and both gifts and program income dramatically increased under his leadership. From 1971 through 1983, gifts increased from $42,650 to $112,375 and totaled $1,427,634 for that period, averaging $109,817 per year. The fund balance for that period increased to $756,821. (Taken from annual ABCS reports in the ASBC Annuals for those years. Those annuals are located in the Arizona Southern Baptist Convention Historical Commission Archives.)

Special offerings such as the "Mother's Day offering" would provide occasion for yearly information about ABCS to be provided to the churches. It would also challenge individuals and churches to support this ministry. The prayers and financial support of the Women's Missionary Union (WMU) in Arizona was a consistent resource throughout ABCS history. Not enough can be said about their interest, encouragement, and personal involvement.

Large gifts of money and land occasionally added much needed resources to the finances of ABCS. In 1974, the agency received a bequest of forty acres in Chandler, which was sold the following year, and the proceeds added to ABCS. In 1983, a gift of eighteen thousand dollars was received following the sale of property bequeathed by Mary Lizenbee. Two hundred acres of land in Texas were donated and subsequently sold for five thousand dollars. Royalties from the sale of western author Slim Ellison's books would come to ABCS and an additional five hundred dollars cash from his estate (Minutes ABCS Board, 1983). Several churches in Phoenix sold property and gave ABCS portions of the proceeds from those sales (Minutes, Executive Committee, ABCS Board 1976).

As Mr. Cain began urging increased support from the churches throughout the state, people in various areas began expressing their desire for ABCS to begin work with children in their area. They indicated a more favorable penchant for giving to local work. This local interest is understandable, but two factors were explained in response to these desires. First, children from over the state would be accepted in the Phoenix facility. Second, because of the high cost of care, it was necessary

birthday offerings and Mother's Day offerings made the difference that kept the children's home alive during some of its darkest times.

The simultaneous campaigns were not the extent of ABCS' fund-raising problems. The ABCS fund-raising organization's director, Byron Welch, and the ABCS Board were becoming disenchanted with each other. Welch did not believe the convention and the board were sufficiently "supporting" the campaign, and the board believed that Welch's expectations of them were excessive. Mr. Jennings describes this confusion.

> One of the issues which later developed with Welch Associates was their interpretation of that support. They never could grasp the fact of the make-up of our unpaid board of directors, and that few, if any, of us could contribute one to five thousand dollars to the campaign. Throughout the following seven months, there was a constant harping back to this issue with the claim that 'Until the Board is in support of the campaign, we can't do anything about getting funds from others,' or words to that effect. (Minutes, ABCS Board 1974).

There is more. Teachers of the Cordova Elementary School, where most of the children from the children's home attended, circulated a letter to all of the Southern Baptist pastors in the Phoenix area. The letter was harsh and critical of many perceived bad practices regarding the children's home. These allegations were unfounded, but the damage had been done.

In February, 1975, Mr. Cain informed the board that the Little Canyon Residential Treatment Center had just received Joint Commission Accreditation as a Psychiatric Facility. Rather than being perceived as a positive step for the program, many Baptists looked with disfavor on psychiatry and social work in general and were not pleased that the children's services achieved this accreditation (Jennings 1975).

"When it rains, it pours," is an often used expression that certainly applied to the factors behind the unhappy fund-raising experience in 1975. In addition to the above matters, the First Baptist Church of Chandler expected ABCS to use a vacant house adjacent to the church and forty acres of property south of town for the care of children. This property was a bequest that came to ABCS through the "Rucker Will," which the church had been instrumental in establishing. The house was too small for use as a children's facility; and it, along with the land south of town, was put on the market, much to the disappointment of several members in the church.

There was one more item that helped create the poor ABCS image at that time. The ABCS administration had made numerous unsuccessful attempts over the years to begin work in Tucson. Zoning problems and reluctance of city officials to open doors for a "Phoenix-based" program resulted in defeat at every turn for ABCS to begin work in that city. This led Pima County Southern Baptists to believe that ABCS was strictly a Phoenix-centered operation, and they "had no desire to support it" (ibid., 5).

Much criticism was leveled by those who were unhappy with ABCS contracting with public agencies. ABCS' board president wrote a letter to the president of the ASBC reaffirming their strong alignment with the convention. The president wrote, "At no time has there been any intention or desire, expressed or otherwise, for the Arizona Baptist Children's Services to be or become anything other than . . . ministering agency of the Arizona Southern Baptist Convention . . ." (Pair 1989, 330). This did not diminish the growing concern about ABCS' loyalty to the convention or concern about its ministry focus. The executive board of the ASBC instructed its Committee on Plans, Policies, and Programs to make an in depth study of ABCS (Hunt 1994).

On August 28, 1975, the ABCS Board discontinued the financial campaign. From the beginning on January 1, 1975, to October 31, 1975, the proceeds from the campaign were $8, 332.12. The expenses were $71,013.97 (Minutes, ABCS Board 1975). To say that the reason for its failure was because it was "ineptly managed" (Pair 1989) was hardly fair or accurate.

One of the public-relations problems created for the Cain administration among his Baptist constituency was the Baptist people's failure to understand the subtle changes that had taken place in residential child care. Cain, himself, was unable to adequately communicate those changes to the people of the Arizona Baptist churches.

When Don Cain came, he realized, as did the board, that the need was diminishing for care of the dependent, neglected child. The Arizona Department of Welfare would care for those children in foster homes, which was better for the children and more cost-effective for the state. What was needed were resources for the teenagers and troubled children of all ages. The additional services that were required for this new breed of older troubled children would be very expensive. In addition to three shifts of houseparents (now called behavioral health techs), there would be the costs of various therapies, high property maintenance, and personnel supervision.

The income from churches, interested individuals, and groups could no longer support this higher cost of service. The choice that had to be made was either to get out of the business of providing services for children or accept the fees paid by the state to care for their troubled children. Obviously, the choice Cain and his board made was to continue serving troubled children and their families in the name of Christ and accepting the higher fees from the state for their care. By doing this, the Arizona Baptist Children's Services not only remained alive but grew dramatically.

Raising money, which was still needed in addition to purchase of care (POC) for troubled teenagers, was a different story. The needs of troubled adolescents just didn't have the appeal which little children had. To make matters worse, these rebellious, mouthy, angry teenagers "turned off" the adults and simply weren't as appealing as objects of charity! But they were the children who needed help, and Cain and the board chose to help them even without the understanding and limited support of its constituency.

In spite of the adversity and negative publicity the children's services had received, the convention began giving ten thousand dollars annually to ABCS. This was the first, but not the last, expression of consistent support to be given by the parent body.

The Advisory Council and Publicity

A feasibility study about ABCS was conducted by Robert R. Whiteaker in 1978. Mr. Whiteaker was a member of North Phoenix Baptist Church.

The study was done as a requisite for the next financial campaign they would soon begin. His report sums up very clearly the needs of children in this country in the 1970s, and it affirmed the direction the agency had taken eight years earlier.

During the past decade, the children's home "business" in this country has changed drastically. Whereas children's homes were once orphanages where homeless (children) were kept when their parents died or were incapacitated, the improvement of insurance coverage and State/Federal Welfare programs have progressed today to the place that most children in these circumstances are placed in permanent foster home situations rather than institutions. Many Baptist children's services in other states who have programs of long-standing are running out of

COMING SOON

Photo by Rick Bell

THIS IS ALICE. She has just been battered by her mother. The latest in a never-ending series of beatings that only get worse. There are many Alices in Arizona. Abused, neglected and homeless. They all need someone who cares. But few are the people who put feet to their prayers and actually do something. Arizona Southern Baptists are an exception. They are doing something through **Arizona Baptist Children's Services.** The **ABCS** story is touching. It is educational. It is dramatic. And now that story is on its way to your church in the film...

SOMEONE WHO CARES

Time _____ Date _____

Place _____

ARIZONA BAPTIST CHILDREN'S SERVICES **ABCS**

children; therefore, there is a change in programs taking place throughout the country into those (programs) which are similar in concept to the programs offered now by ABCS. Today, there is a need to help children who need temporary care until a permanent home can be found or their own family situation can be rectified. (Whiteaker 1978, 17).

In the Whiteaker study, one recommendation was to do "a first class public relations campaign" to educate people about ABCS and "build support." This would be followed by a capital-funds drive to secure the funds needed to complete the campus plan (ibid., 21). To do this, a thirty-minute film was produced, titled *Someone Who Cares*. It was professionally produced and later nominated for a national award. High praise from several sources was received for the film. Several copies were made and offered to churches for viewing. The film featured simulated situations about children caught up in family conflicts, or found homeless, which resulted in their placement in various ABCS programs. It was viewed in several of the churches and was well received. Doug Geeting was director of development at this time and worked with the group who made the film.

Another recommendation to come from the Whiteaker study was that ABCS create an advisory council composed of people in the community

who would assist with public relations and fund-raising. The committee consisted of twenty citizens in the Phoenix area. The chairman was Dr. Dwane Averill, a local minister. The vice-chairperson was Mrs. Paula Smith, and Mrs. D. Swan was the secretary (*Footprints* 1982). Dr. Averill was a highly educated man with many interest and involvement with the community. The committee was made up of men and women who were interested in children and committed to helping the agency raise resources to complete the Little Canyon Campus.

Dr. Dwain Averil, Advisory Council Chair, and Don Cain

"Building for Tomorrow"

A second attempt to raise funds through a major campaign came in 1981. By this time, the previously troubling zoning issues had been resolved, and serious preparations began for the first phase of a five-year capital campaign titled "Building for Tomorrow." This included the construction of a brick and wrought-iron fence at a cost of fourteen thousand dollars that would separate the campus from Little Canyon Park.

It was an ambitious plan involving the construction of five buildings, the perimeter fence, a sports court, remodeling of the school, and landscaping. Because of their disappointing earlier experience with a fund-raising organization, the decision was to implement the goals of the campaign without outside help. The project would be carried out in six phases with a total cost of $1,250,000 with campaign costs totaling $30,000.

Phase	Project	Costs
1.	Boys Cottage	$316,000
2.	Wall and Landscaping	$ 54,000
3.	Administration Building & Chapel	$280,000
4.	Girls Cottage	$350,000
5.	Dining Hall and Storage	$200,000
6.	Remodel School	$ 50,000
	Total	$1,250,000
	Campaign Costs	$ 30,000

Very attractive materials were designed and mailed out. This campaign was more successful, raising thirty-two thousand dollars in 1982 (Minutes 1982). Several events were planned as part of the campaign, including a benefit concert, a 10K or half-marathon, and a benefit Phoenix Suns Basketball game. Another benefit basketball game between ABCS staff and KPNX-TV personalities raised over $370.

As a result of the publicity generated by the campaign, support and donations came from many sources. Phoenix Baptist Hospital offered to treat ABCS children if there were no other resources for medical care. Sixty Bibles were donated from Robin's Stained Glass Studio in 1981. A Colorado company provided twenty-five boxes of clothing, which ABCS shared with another agency (Minutes 1981, 2). No doubt the film *Someone Who Cares* also inspired and encouraged support from the public at large as well as the members of Arizona Southern Baptist churches.

Boys Cottage Built in 1982

Phase 1, the perimeter fence, and phase 2, the boys' cottage, were constructed as a result of the campaign. Groundbreaking took place on the West Missouri Campus March 31, 1982, and the dedication took place September 24, 1982 (*Footprints* 1982). The new cottage for sixteen youth, designed by Dean Glasco, was a state-of-the-art model cottage for residential care. It was a duplex building composed of two eight-bed units separated by a common wall. A connecting passageway gave the building extra flexibility for various types of utilization.

Each unit contained two double rooms (for two children), four single rooms, a kitchenette, storage room, laundry room, two student bathrooms, a large office for the counselors, and a very large living-room area.

Changes in Facilities and Support Services

At the time of Mr. Cain's arrival at the Baptist Children's Home, the administrative offices were located in the same building occupied by the Arizona Southern Baptist Convention at 316 W. McDowell. In the latter part of 1970, a modular unit was purchased and moved to the West Missouri Campus for offices (Minutes, ABCS Board 1970). In July 1975, ABCS leased approximately one thousand eight hundred square feet for administrative and financial offices from the Arizona Southern Baptist Convention, by then located at 400 W. Camelback in Phoenix. As space became available to the children's services, they would increase the size of their office area to meet the increased demands. By the time this building was sold in 1991, ABCS would occupy one-half of the first floor.

Storage was always in short supply. A small warehouse was leased at 6819 N. Twenty-first Avenue in Phoenix, which was used as a commissary for food and other supplies. A small used cold storage building was acquired from an old barracks at Luke Air Force Base. The building was being salvaged by First Southern Baptist Church in Payson in 1973, and arrangements were made through the board president Les Jennings, Jr., to give the cold storage unit to ABCS. It was moved to the main campus and used as a storage building until it was torn down to make way for new buildings.

Summary

It would be difficult to imagine the 1983 Arizona Baptist Children's Services to be the same organization as the 1960 Baptist Children's Home of Arizona. The only thing recognizable would be the little brick house on the five-acre campus at 3101 W. Missouri in Phoenix, and even it had been modified. The year 1983 was a new day with new facilities and new programs to meet the changing demands of troubled and neglected children and their families. Perhaps one of the most significant changes was the fact that the transformed organization included the children's parents in its outreach of care and services and offered community-based services both in and outside of Phoenix.

Teacher Peggy Lancaster Checks a Students Paper

In the beginning of his administration, Executive Director Cain worked closely with both the Arizona Southern Baptist Convention and the public agencies. During his thirteen years as executive director, Rev. Cain attended every annual associational meeting, except when two or more were scheduled at the same time. The convention even put ABCS into its mission program budget, which was something his predecessor, George Wilson, was never able to achieve. But Cain never felt that the convention was totally behind the agency or him. In time, this began to trouble him to the point that he gradually withdrew (emotionally) from the parent body and slowly began to draw more support from his colleagues in the community and the state agencies. This was a subtle shift that even Cain was unaware of, but his growing distance began to be felt by convention leadership. Looking for something to explain this drift of interest and loyalty, some pastors would accuse him of not being "spiritual" enough. Those closest to Cain knew better. He was a deeply spiritual man whose own children grew up to be capable Christian citizens reflecting the strengths of their parents in many ways.

Rev. Cain was at the helm of a private Christian agency at the time when federal nondiscrimination policy became a rigid qualification for contract eligibility. With as much as 90 percent of revenue coming from government agencies in the form of purchase of care, the director had to make a hard choice. ABCS would either obey the law and maintain a high level of service to children and families or cancel the contracts and return to the 1960s level of service—providing care to fifty or sixty children a year! He and his board chose the former option and continued to maintain religious training to the limits of allowable discretion. That would not be sufficient for some of his critics. They complained to their pastors, and the pastors complained to Don Cain and the ASBC. On one occasion, a report was made by Rev. Cain to the ASBC Executive Board in defense of some of the charges made against him:

> I remind you that we are not an orphanage caring for children without parents. We are seeking to minister to troubled kids who in most cases, cannot function at home or school. Many times to reach them spiritually, we have to care for their physical and mental needs first. We are endeavoring to do this and we urge your prayers and understanding of this most difficult work. (Minutes, Executive Board, ASBC 1977, 1)

It cannot be overlooked that Don Cain was the catalyst in this alchemy of growth and expansion. Gerald Flint said it best in his 1986 brief history of ABCS:

> The founders of the agency had moved cautiously to establish an organization which was solvent and efficient, but their perception of child care and the agency had mired into a continual struggle to survive. Their struggle prevented them from embracing an attitude of growth and change with the zeal necessary to accomplish such goals. Mr. Cain was a breath of fresh air who revived ambition and inspired Baptists to venture forward rather than stand in place. The future had become a landscape of potential service. (Flint 1986, 50-51)

Arizona Southern Baptists owe a debt of gratitude to this Christian leader whose vision and courage moved the agency out of the dark ages of orphanage and children's home mentality into the bright sunlight of inclusive, knowledgeable family ministry and specialized treatment for children. Progress can be a costly matter. It was in Cain's situation. It cost him his job and a career in the ministry to which he had given his life and commitment. He resigned, effective May 1, 1983, because he refused to compromise his values and to break the law regarding nondiscrimination in hiring practices. He was highly respected in the community and among his peers in the Child Care Executives of Southern Baptists. He gave the Arizona Baptist Children's Services a reputation for integrity and skill like it had never before experienced. It is a discredit to the Arizona Southern Baptist Convention that they did not give him the support and affirmation at that time that they gave him years earlier when the agency lost its Emergency Receiving Home contract. Cain and his family would go on to establish and operate a very successful awning business in Phoenix until his retirement.

Don Cain led the agency into a relationship that illustrates that church agencies and government can work together without either dominating the other. He embraced the concept of licensing and state oversight of health and safety issues. He used the advice that was available from state social services to improve the program.

(Note to readers: It must be noted that while Don Cain served on the Edit/ Writing Committee for this book at the request of its author, the summary paragraph of this chapter was in no way a part of his contribution.)

References

Annual. 1962. Arizona Southern Baptist Convention (ASBC) held at Calvary Baptist Church in Tucson, AZ. November 14-16.

_____. 1976. ASBC held at Twenty-Second Street Baptist Church in Tucson, AZ. November 16-18.

_____. 1977. Arizona Baptist Children's Services. ASBC held at Trinity Baptist Church, Casa Grande, AZ. November 15-17.

_____. 1979. ASBC held at First Southern Baptist Church, Yuma, AZ. November 13-15.

_____. 1980. ASBC held at First Southern Baptist Church, Tucson, AZ. November 11-13.

_____. 1981. ASBC, held at First Baptist Church, Chandler, AZ. November 10-12.

_____. 1982. Arizona Baptist Children's Services. ASBC held at Casas Adobes Baptist Church, Tucson, AZ. November 9-11.

Arizona Department of Economic Security. 1980. Letter to ABCS dated November 7. In ABCS archives.

Arizona Republic. 1971. County Shifts Care of Abused Children. March 30.

Cain, Don. 1971. ABCS Opens Services in Southern Arizona. *Love in Action* 10 (November): 5.

_____. 1970. Children's Home. ASBC report in a meeting at First Southern Baptist Church, Tucson, AZ. November 10-12.

Cain, Don. 1971. A Brief History of Arizona Baptist Children's Services. An unpublished report submitted to the ABCS Board of Trustees.

_____. 1976. Letter to Arizona Southern Baptist pastors dated February 2. Filed in ABCS correspondence archives.

_____. 2005. Interview by C. Truett Baker. Taped telephone conversation. February 12, 2005.

Fleick, Tam Marie. 1986. The Arizona Baptist Children's Services 1970-1983: Expansion of the Dream. An independent research project conducted through the Department of History, Grand Canyon College, Phoenix, AZ.

Flint, Gerald David. 1986. The Building Blocks of the ABCS: The Arizona Baptist Children's Services. An independent research project conducted through the Department of History, Grand Canyon College.

Footprints. 1982. ABCS Advisory Committee. (Summer.)

Footprints. 1982. (Fall): 4.

_____. 1991. A Look Back. Spring.

Hunt, Theresa. 1994. Organizational Dynamics—Arizona Baptist Children's Services. Unpublished research paper prepared as an academic requirement in the Graduate School of Social Work, Arizona State University.

Institutional Review for ABCS. Maricopa County Administrative Office of the Court, Phoenix, AZ, February 20, 1975. Filed in ABCS Archives.

Jennings, Les, Jr. 1977. Early Beginnings and Growth of Arizona Baptist Children's Services. Presented by the author to the monthly meeting of the Arizona Baptist Historical Society in March, Phoenix, AZ. Filed in ABCS Archives.

_____. 1975. An Explanation of the Traumatic Years of 1974 and 1975. 1975. Filed in ABCS Archives.

Jones, Doris. 1979. Children Put On Hold. *The Arizona Republic*, November 4.

Krajnak, Debby. 1973. Children's Home Being Opposed. *The Arizona Daily Star*, July 22.

Love in Action. 1973. Camelback Girl's Residence Becomes a Program of ABCS. 12 (March): 1.

Minutes. 1960. Baptist Children's Home of Arizona (BCHA) Board, December 1.

_____. Baptist Children's Home of Arizona, Board, September 27, 1970.

_____. 1970. BCHA Board, September 27.

Minutes. *1972*. Arizona Baptist Children's Services (ABCS) Board, May 17.

_____. 1974. ABCS Board, May 30.

_____. 1974. ABCS Board, July 16.

_____. 1974. ABCS Board, December 16.

_____. 1975. ABCS Board, October 31.

_____. 1976. ABCS Board, August 20.

_____. 1977. ABCS Board, August 26.

_____. 1982. ABCS Board, December 3.

_____. 1983. ABCS Board, December 2.

_____. ABCS Board, 1981.

Minutes. 1977. Executive Board, ASBC, June 9.

Minutes. 1969. Executive Committee, BCHA Board, September 23.

_____. 1970. Executive Committee, BCHA Board, September 24.

_____. Executive Committee, Arizona Baptist Children's Services, January 4.

_____. 1971. Executive Committee, ABCS Board, February 1.

_____. 1976. Executive Committee, ABCS Board, March 26.

_____. 1976. Executive Committee, ABCS Board, June 25.

Pair, C. L. 1989. *A History of the Arizona Southern Baptist Convention.* Executive Board of the Arizona Southern Baptist Convention, Phoenix, AZ.

Love in Action. 1972. Papago Indian Children's Home: A Progress Report. 11 (March): 1.

Policy Manual. 1978. ABCS, General Operating Procedures, A-1.

Richard, Glen H. 1962. Letter to George Wilson dated November 5. ABCS Correspondence Archives.

Smith, Eve P. 1995. Bring Back the Orphanages? What Policymakers of Today Can Learn From the Past. *Child Welfare*, January-February:115-142.

Whiteaker, Robert R. 1978. Feasibility Study, ABCS Missouri Avenue Expansion. October 27, Phoenix, AZ. Report filed in ABCS Archives.

Wilson, George. 1963. Foster Home Care License Received by Children's Home. *Baptist Beacon*, February 7.

Young, Elizabeth. 1980. Children's Services Battles State Over Foster Care. *Baptist Beacon* 41 (December): 35.

Chapter 6

Establishing a Foundation for Growth—
1984-1993

The Period 1984-1988: "The Baker Years," Part 1

The Change Begins

After the resignation of Don Cain, the board asked their president, Mr. Jack Willis, to serve as interim executive director. He accepted, resigned his position on the board, and immediately began his duties. His background as an administrator and his experience on the board served him well in these days between permanent executive directors. The board authorized the Personnel Committee to begin the search process. The new board president, Sam Williams, and the chairman of the Personnel Committee, Dr. Simon Tsoi, would work together in announcing the vacancy and in receiving and screening applications.

The board received several applicants that met the qualifications for which they were looking. One was from the director of Regional Programs for Virginia Baptist Children's Home and Family Services (VBCH&FS), who lived in Richmond, Virginia. God's timing is always right, and this was no exception. C. Truett Baker had been employed by VBCH&FS in 1978 to establish regional centers in the populous Virginia Urban Corridor, which ran from Washington, D.C., along the eastern coast of the state to the Tidewater area. As Baker described it, "The three offices I had been hired to establish were set up, furnished, and staffed. Advisory councils and policies were in place as well as a strong foster care and adoption program. My job was done. What do I do now?" In reality, he had the option of remaining in Richmond and supervising the three offices, but that didn't seem very challenging.

Then one evening in October 1983, a call came from a man in Phoenix, Arizona, who introduced himself as Sam Williams, president of the Board of Trustees of Arizona Baptist Children's Services (ABCS). He wanted to know if Baker was interested in being considered for the executive director position at ABCS in Phoenix. The rest is history, as they say.

The Arrival

The antecedents of his arrival are described in an article he was asked to write for *Footprints,* the agency's newsletter.

I could not imagine what lay ahead for the Baker Family when I greeted Mr. Sam Williams and Dr. Simon Tsoi as they stepped off the plane in Richmond, Virginia, October 22, 1983. Nor could I imagine the impact these two godly men would have on my life from that day forward. Dr. Tsoi was pastor of the First Chinese Baptist Church in Phoenix and chairperson of the Board Personnel Committee of ABCS. Mr. Sam Williams was a Phoenix realtor and builder and Chairperson of the ABCS Board of Trustees. We had agreed upon that week as a time

Dr. Tsoi and Mr. Williams at Lottie Moon's grave in Crew, VA

for interviews and just getting acquainted. And did they ever interview!

I think they talked to everyone I knew in Richmond from my secretary to my banker. They ate dinner at our house and went with me to speaking and preaching appointments. Never had I been so thoroughly scrutinized! Two visits to Phoenix followed and on December 2, 1983, the board extended a call for me to become the third leader of ABCS. I prayed and Carolyn packed and our house sold in December and we were on the field January 1, 1984. We had sensed Divine leadership from the first contact and the fact that everything fell into place came as no surprise, but we were very grateful.

The board was clear with me about their desire that two directions be followed. The first would be to strengthen the relationship of ABCS with the Arizona Southern Baptist Convention and its churches. This was done through participating in as many convention and associational activities as possible. I visited churches, met pastors, and frequently supplied in the pulpits of the churches, always telling the story of ABCS as well as presenting the Gospel. In addition, area dinner conferences were held around the state during the first four years. This enabled me to get acquainted with Arizona Southern Baptists and to share the new vision for ABCS. As a result, support from the convention and the churches began to grow. During the first year, the convention put ABCS in its budget on a percentage basis discontinuing the earlier practice of an established annual amount.

The second mandate from the board had to do with ensuring that the agency focused upon meeting the spiritual needs of children as well as their other needs. I didn't find that those needs had been neglected, but their expression had not been very visible to those outside of the agency. The ABCS leaders had been following the direction set forth in the 1978 study done by Robert Whiteaker which read, " . . . ABCS employs the services of a full-time director of religious training and chaplain who provided individual counseling to both employees and children. The basic belief underlying all the child care services of ABCS is that each individual is a creation of God and made in his image. This conviction places upon each staff member the responsibility for providing an environment which will promote maximum growth and development for the children as individuals, and which will lead them to a personal commitment to God through Jesus Christ our Savior." (Whiteaker 1978, 5)

Rev. Paul Kinnison had joined the ABCS staff as chaplain prior to my arrival. He was a godly man who feared not the devil nor the authority of the new agency executive director, and I'm sure he thought at times they were one and the same! Over the next five years, 139 children would make commitments to Christ. In my annual report to the Arizona Southern Baptist Convention (ASBC) that year, I made it clear as to the spiritual direction of the agency. "We affirm that Arizona Baptist Children's Services is a Christ-centered ministry to troubled children and their families. We are the benevolent arm of the ASBC and our goal is to serve Christ by caring for his children" (Baker, "Getting Ready," 1999).

The board had given Baker until January 15, 1984, to officially begin work. His resignation in Virginia was effective December 31, 1983; and he and his wife, Carolyn, were in Phoenix the first week in January. The following weeks after January 15 were spent in getting acquainted with staff, board members, convention staff, community leaders, and state department personnel with whom ABCS was contracting for services. Preaching appointments were scheduled in an effort to get better acquainted with the new ABCS executive director. There were organizations to visit such as the Arizona Chapter of the National Association of Social Workers and the Arizona Council of Centers for Children and Adolescents. Baker would later hold office in both of those organizations. He would attend the Arizona Southern Baptist Convention's Monday morning devotional period at 9:00 AM and eventually have a part in leading the devotions. There were weekly pastor's conferences to attend and monthly associational meetings. There were lunch meetings with staff and pastors, and contract meetings with Department of Economic Security (DES) personnel. It seemed to Baker that there was a staff meeting of some kind every day; and in addition, there were occasional trips to Tucson, Yuma, and the White Mountains and other Arizona communities.

Baker believed early on that relationships were the key to achievement, and success was never a solo journey. This was not a "business" in the traditional sense of the word but a fellowship of pilgrims helping one another on a common journey. All of us, at times, would stumble and fall, which gave us opportunity to pick each other up and move on. Grace is not only for the children and families served by ABCS but for the associates who provide those services. With this philosophy, Baker would launch a ministry of fifteen years that would be inclusive and embrace both the religious and the public communities.

The New Management Team

Baker believed that the programs a social service agency offered would never rise above the level of its leadership. He also early recognized his own limitations and lack of experience in financial management. His expertise had been in program administration, and the nuts and bolts of financial management and fund-raising had been shifted to others. Therefore, this awareness led him to gather around him competent people who would complement his own skills in addressing the total demands of agency administration.

(L-R) Phyllis McFarland, Jack Willis, Truett Baker, Diana Browning

A new management structure was recommended and approved by the board during the first year. In addition to the new executive director, other staff roles would be modified in the new management team.

Dr. Phyllis McFarland's role was changed from that of director of residential treatment to director of Program. *Services for the agency.* Mr. Jack Willis, the interim executive director was asked to remain on the staff as director of Administrative Services. Rev. Paul Kinnison was director of Chaplain Services. Mrs. Diana Browning, who had joined the staff in 1983, was appointed administrative assistant to the executive director.

This team was the core leadership that would work with the board in developing the values and direction the agency would take throughout the Baker administration. However, this was the start—not the completed picture. Gradually this core leadership would pull in other managers and staff of the programs to spread the leadership opportunity and marshal the collective creative thinking from every level of agency life. The terms "strategic planning" and "focus groups" would become familiar and frequently used terms used to describe the implementation of the shared leadership and planning process.

With some modifications over the years, the agency would operate through three divisions in addition to the board of trustees. These were the Operations Division, Program Division, and Executive Office and Development.

The Operations Division

This division was led by director of Finance and Administration, Jack Willis. Mr. Willis was associated with the radio and television industry for thirty-four years prior to his work with ABCS. He was general manager of KHEP AM-FM, Phoenix, for the last twenty years of that period. He received a number of awards including election as president and honorary life member of the Arizona Broadcasters Association and received the National Radio Broadcaster's 1979 Award of Merit for distinguished leadership in the  field of religious broadcasting and for excellence in Christian station ownership and operation. Mr. Willis received his bachelor's degree from Northern Arizona State University. He was president of the ABCS Board and, following the resignation of Executive Director Don Cain, was asked to serve as the ABCS interim executive director. When Mr. Baker filled the executive director's position in 1984, Mr. Willis was asked to remain on the staff as director of Finance and Administration and later was appointed vice president of Operations.

The Operations Division was first located at the 400 Building on West Camelback Road and later moved to the new ABCS corporate offices at 8920 N. Twenty-third Avenue in Phoenix. The division included budget and accounting, billing, facilities management, computer services, and human resources. Later the thrift industry and Sunglow Ranch would become the responsibility of this division. Jack and Sarah Willis have four grown daughters, and Jack is a deacon at Phoenix First Southern Baptist Church.

The Program Division

The Program Division was under the leadership of Phyllis McFarland, Ph.D. She grew up in Oklahoma, New Jersey, and Texas. Dr. McFarland's employment history included experience as a medical secretary, interior designer, administrative officer in an alcoholism rehab center, director of Christian education, social-group worker, social caseworker, and chaplain. She received her bachelor of arts degree from Grand Canyon College in 1968.

Dr. Phyllis McFarland

Dr. McFarland attended Texas Christian University in Fort Worth, Antioch College and Presbyterian School of Christian Education in Richmond, Virginia. Graduate degrees included both a master of arts in education and master of counseling earned in 1971, both from Arizona State University. She was awarded a Ph.D. from Arizona State University in Philosophical Foundations of Education and Counseling Psychology in 1975. Dr. McFarland came to ABCS in 1966 as a social worker and remained there throughout her career with the exception of two educational leaves of absence and a short tenure in private practice. She was a member of several professional organizations and was recognized in Arizona as a leading expert in special education and residential treatment. Dr. McFarland was awarded Lifetime Honorary Membership in the Arizona Council of Centers for Children and Adults. Her career with ABCS spanned the three administrations of Wilson, Cain, and Baker. She was a deacon and Bible teacher in the Heritage Presbyterian Church in Glendale.

Dr. McFarland was honored at ABCS for her twenty-seven years of service, the longest tenure of any associate at that time.

The Program Division included supervision of residential treatment, counseling, Bunkhouse Emergency Shelter, foster care, group homes, and health services. In addition to supervision of individual programs,

Dr. McFarland directed admissions, contract management, licensing, and quality assurance.

Executive Office and Development

The third and final division was the Executive Office and Development. The division included executive director (later president), C. Truett Baker; administrative assistant, Diana Browning; development associate, Shirley Cravens; director of Development, Ray Shelton; church and public relations coordinator, Karen Merrick; volunteer coordinator, Debi Siwek; and secretary, Lori Boettcher. At a later time, another division, Church and Community Resources, was added; and Dr. Paul Kinnison was appointed director and later vice president of that division. In later years the directors were called the executive officers, and this management structure would be there for the

Shirley Cravens

duration of the Baker administration. There would be some changes in the composition of the council, but the model of shared management would be the driving force behind Baker's administration.

Strategic Planning

Strategic Planning would become one of the hallmarks of the Baker administration. The planning process would evolve in its design. It would eventually result in a detailed document containing the mission statement, overall objectives, specific goals, and implementation strategies. Retreats were held to give the staff opportunity to brainstorm ideas and focus their attention upon very specific goals. At the end of each year, the agency would review its progress on the goals as a part of the planning process for the following year.

Reference was made in chapter 4 to the Convention Executive Board's frustration because they had difficulty in understanding the direction the children's home was to take in helping children (Annual 1962). The technology of long-range planning in nonprofit organizations was not well developed at that time, contributing to the confusion. Lack of planning may have contributed to the poor outcome of the fund-raising campaign sponsored by the children's home in 1964.

Little thought was given to planning as a management strategy. It was the Arizona Southern Baptist Convention that would force the children's home administration and board to do some long-range planning following a meeting of their executive committee on February 28, 1966. The executive committee asked that goals for seven years be developed and presented to their committee (Flint 1997).

This was done. (The goals are listed in chapter 4.) Serious efforts were made to attain these goals, and progress was made. It was the first experience in planning which was done by the children's home, but it would not be the last. In 1970, the same year Don Cain began his service as the executive director, he led the board to establish five goals. These were described in the preceding chapter.

All of these goals were met, but planning was sporadic and largely facility-focused. In some ways, it was a frenzied, crisis-oriented approach in an attempt to meet an urgent need brought about by statutory changes in child protection. Rev. Cain's vision was not confined to Phoenix. He envisioned a counseling office in Tucson that would also provide supervision for local programs. His vision would also include "group homes in strategic sites throughout the state . . . satellite homes over the entire state" (Cain 1971, 8).

In 1984, "strategic planning" was not a part of the agency vocabulary, but serious planning had been done and would continue that first year of Baker's administration. The board approved six goals outlined in his first annual report. The goals were as follows:

(1) To complete, debt-free, our building program on the West Missouri Campus within the next two years;
(2) To completely redecorate and refurnish the Glendale Bunkhouse;
(3) To develop home-based and preventive programs to strengthen family life and prevent placement;
(4) To establish regional counseling and ministry centers;

(5) To develop various avenues of additional funding;

(6) To continue to spiritually develop and strengthen our program.
  (Baker 1984, 3)

All the goals were achieved but not in the short time span of two years as envisioned by Baker. A process was set in motion to plan goals and evaluate progress that caught fire among the staff, and in time, this method of planning would guide the agency like a lamp in the darkness. This process was called "strategic planning" and will be described in more detail in chapter 7. The conviction that ABCS services must be offered statewide began with Don Cain.

Baker's vision was to see that home-based family services were established throughout the state. This dream was embedded in the earliest planning and would carry over into each year's planning after that until the dream would be fully realized in the Jakes' administration.

Program Development

Counseling

Counseling the families of children at the Little Canyon Center was started in the Cain administration. In 1984, counseling was expanded to include a broad range of needs. This resulted from the realization that it was not enough to work with children if families were not helped. This program would be enlarged into a new Division for Family Ministry (counseling) under clinical psychologist

Dr. Ron Willcoxon

Dr. Ronald Willcoxon, who began work with ABCS March 18, 1985.

Initially the program was located on the second floor of the 400 Building. By 1987, additional space was needed and became available on the first floor of the building previously occupied by Hanson Realty. In addition, family ministry centers would soon be started in Tucson, Show Low, Casa Grande, and the East Valley. All of these offices were in rooms made available by Baptist churches, and the offices were staffed on a part-time basis by Dr. Willcoxon and others from the Phoenix counseling program. The church secretaries in these various churches would make appointments for the day that the ABCS counselor would be in their office. The amount of driving would eventually be too much for the staff, and these out-of-Phoenix programs were temporarily discontinued. Counseling services outside of Phoenix would not be stable and permanent until the opening of regional offices in or near those same areas. From 1984 through 1988, 756 individuals and families received counseling services.

The Bunkhouse Emergency Shelter

The Bunkhouse started in 1982 and was licensed for sixteen boys. Only ten beds were used as shelter beds, while the remaining six beds were reserved for the Wrangler Independent Living Program. When the Wrangler Program was moved into an adjoining residence, the emergency shelter could again accommodate sixteen boys. During the 1984 through 1988 period, 755 youth were served in the Shelter program.

One of the gratifying benefits for tenured associates was to see the positive outcome of their efforts with the boys who later made a success of their lives. No true story better exemplifies the ministry of the emergency shelter than the life of one of its residents, Darryl Williford, who later earned his master's degree and became vice-principal of the ABCS special education school.

Darryl was brought to the Bunkhouse when he was a teenager. His foster parents left him there when the family left for a vacation at Disneyland. Darryl's story began in a home he believed was his biological family. He would later learn they were foster parents. Darryl's comment, "It was a big shock when they told me they were not my real parents." They informed him he would have to leave home when he was eighteen because they would no longer receive payment for his care. He would sometimes be locked out of the house and many times went to bed without dinner. He did give his foster parents credit for taking him to church and instilling high moral standards in him.

Darryl was an exceptionally good athlete and was awarded scholarships both at Glendale Community College and Grand Canyon University in Phoenix. He earned several awards for his basketball skill as he studied for his bachelor's degree in criminal justice. While in college, he found work as a behavioral health tech at the ABCS Glendale Bunkhouse, where the troubled children related well to this associate who himself had been a resident in the program.

When the Bunkhouse was closed, Darryl went to work in the Little Canyon School as an educational tech. He married another ABCS associate and in 2004, ABCS filmed his dramatic story, which was seen at the annual meeting of the Arizona Southern Baptist Convention. Darryl's statement, "I always wanted to help someone with some of the things I went through."

The story gets better. Darryl wondered about his biological parents and spoke to the shelter coordinator, Mike Ransbottom, about his interest. Mike began a search, and in time, both of Darryl's parents were located, and Mike accompanied Darryl to this joyful reunion. They continue to keep in touch.

Wrangler Program—Independent Living Preparation

The Wrangler Program, the first of its kind in the state, grew out of a need to prepare foster children who would soon be "aging-out" of the foster-care system. The program, which began at 5915 W. Laurie Lane, the shelter overflow house, later moved to the Bunkhouse in Glendale when it was purchased. On July 1, 1985, a house adjoining the Bunkhouse at 5115 W. Myrtle was purchased for the Wrangler Program from George Duff. It had four large bedrooms with three thousand square feet. It was licensed for ten boys.

Bob Garrett, the founder and longtime coordinator for the program, described his earlier sadness in watching eighteen-year-olds pack up their things and leave, upon reaching the end of their minority, with nowhere to go but the streets. Prior to this program, little or no independent-living preparation was given to these older teens when they reached their eighteenth birthday. Some of the higher functioning youth could join the military, but more often than not, they headed for the streets to support themselves any way they could.

It is helpful to note that foster children are even more ill-equipped to live on their own than children with families. They do not have parents to help them with this transition and support their new independence. Furthermore, growing up in foster care often encourages dependency from well-intentioned people who did everything for them.

Children who have been in multiple placements are exposed to a variety of lifestyles and often conflicting values, and their sense of who they are (identity) may be diffuse and confused. They were ill-equipped to live on their own. In addition to the skills they would learn and money they would earn, the Wrangler House was the only stable home that some of the boys had ever known. It was there for them to come back to for support and direction even after living on their own.

Laws were changed to allow for eighteen-year-olds to remain in foster care as long as they were in high school or trade school. This would help many, but even then, most had no idea of how to create and live on a budget, buy food and plan meals, open a checking account, purchase a car, lease an apartment, etc. The Wrangler Program would teach all of these skills to the fifteen- to eighteen-year-old boys who qualified for the program. In addition, they would have part-time employment to learn work skills and develop a savings for the time when they would be on their own.

Training could include completing high school or earning their GED and learning a trade. The most popular trade that students adopted was cooking, and they could be certified in fast-food preparation and work up to being chefs. Additional trades available were cable-television installation, welding, construction, auto-body repair, and painting. One young man became a beautician, obtaining his license and a job in an exclusive salon. Another talented musician would have a career in the performing arts.

An important feature of the training was saving money. The boys were required to save a good portion of their income from employment so they would have start-up funds for living on their own. They would save anywhere from hundreds to thousands of dollars that would give them resources for an apartment and utility deposits and perhaps a down payment on a car. They would have money to live on until their earnings began from their new job.

Wrangler Program

Steve (not his real name) was placed in the Wrangler Program by the Maricopa County Juvenile Court Center. He came from a family where violence was the norm. An older brother was in prison, and the violent gang life that Steve had been leading promised a similar fate if he wasn't killed on the street first. He was part of an auto-theft gang that exported cars and other stolen goods into Mexico. His diagnosis upon admission was "conduct disorder and intermittent explosive disorder." During his early residence in the program, he continued to have violent outbursts, threaten staff, and destroy property. He did have many strengths, and the staff knew they could build upon those strengths if given the chance. He began to form relationships with counselors, the psychiatrist, and others who worked with him, as well as the other boys in the program. Because of his gang associations, he could not go to public school, but he did complete his GED.

Mississippi Volunteers Replace Bunkhouse Roof

Steve used the program well but left when he was eighteen years old. The staff did not hear from him again for some time, and one day he just appeared. He wanted to say that he had accepted Christ, and his life was changed, and he wanted to find the friends that planted the Gospel seed and share that decision with them. He explained to the staff that he had a full-time job and was studying biology and education in college. He owned a house and car and had rebuilt relationships with his family. He further shared that one result of his new life was his work with the Christian Car Ministry, an outreach to gang members who cruise their cars on weekends.

Steve now uses cars, which he once stole, as a tool in reaching gang members for Christ. This writer saw a light in the young man's eyes that expressed the happy face so different from the angry face of earlier years. Sections of the information describing the Wrangler Program were written by Robert Garrett, the ABCS associate who developed the program and supervised it for many years (Baker, "Love Keeps," n.d.).

The new Wrangler house at 5115 W. Myrtle and the adjoining Bunkhouse at 1525 W. Myrtle were in serious need of repairs and redecorating. Through the Southern Baptist Convention Home Mission Board (name later changed to North American Mission Board), ABCS was able to obtain the help of thirteen volunteers from the North Delta Baptist Association Brotherhood in Mississippi in the summer of 1986. First Southern Baptist Church (FSBC) of Phoenix allowed ABCS to set up cots in their fellowship hall, and the volunteers were given breakfast at the nearby Grand Canyon University dining room.

Both Grand Canyon University and Phoenix FSBC would befriend ABCS on many occasions. In the four-day period that they were there, the volunteers replaced tile, painted the exterior of the new Wrangler house, replaced the Bunkhouse roof, and completed many other smaller tasks. Jack Willis, Director of Administrative Services, planned and coordinated the projects with the able help of George Jones, maintenance supervisor; Larry Gallaugher, Bunkhouse coordinator; and Bob Garrett, Wrangler House coordinator.

The coordination and planning involved obtaining the needed materials, transportation for the volunteers, project assignments, and feeding the volunteers. It was a beautiful thing to see and was a morale booster for ABCS in addition to being a tremendous financial help. One of the added benefits was to see the positive interaction between the volunteers and the children.

Therapeutic Foster Care

Pat Jenson

The foster care program at ABCS would eventually include three types of foster family care: (1) Regular Foster Care, (2) Therapeutic Foster Care, and (3) Professional Parenting. Because of the need for therapeutic foster care, ABCS focused upon recruiting, training, and supervising these specialized foster homes at this period of its history. Pat Jenson, coordinator, reported on the special problems that children had who were referred to this program:

> There are children who have severe medical problems as well as emotional problems. A three year old has severe seizures approximately every five days. A seven year old boy has been in eleven different homes in two years before an ABCS foster parent took him in. A nine-year boy couldn't tie his shoes and had been out of school most of his life. Many children have been abused from a very early age. (*Footprints*, "Introducing the ABCS," 1986, 3)

Foster-care capacity at ABCS doubled from ten to twenty beds during this time. Pat Jensen and her staff organized the first Annual Foster Care Awards Banquet in 1986.

The foster-care program was a cooperative effort between the Arizona Department of Economic Security (DES) and private agencies such as ABCS. The private foster-care agencies organized into the KIDS Consortium and did recruiting and training for new foster parents as a collective effort. The consortium was supported by DES, which provided funds for recruiting, training, and other expenses. Other state agencies,

Patty Gordon (center, back) receives congratulations from ABCS foster care employees after being named Foster Parent of the Year during the agency's Appreciation Luncheon June 9

such as the Maricopa County Juvenile Probation Office, would also use the therapeutic foster-care program.

Pat Jenson had given strong professional leadership to the foster-care program but resigned in 1987 to accept a social work leadership position with DES. Carolyn Harvie was employed to take her place (Baker 1987, 2). Alice Hardy Thornton began work in 1986 as a behavioral health tech on Little Canyon Campus. She completed her bachelor's degree from Grand Canyon College and began work on her master's degree in social work from Arizona State University. While working on her master's degree, she transferred to the foster-care department. Alice took a three-month leave of absence from the social work department to complete her graduate degree.

In the fall of 1988, Carolyn Harvie resigned, and Alice returned from her leave of absence with a master's degree in social work and was appointed the new foster-care coordinator. The department continued to grow under Alice's leadership, and she, like her predecessor Pat Jenson, took an active role in the KIDS's Consortium.

Therapeutic activities are a valuable component in the arsenal of resources for helping troubled children. Medical care, counseling, education, and religious training are all vital to a comprehensive program, but special activities often act as a catalyst that can enhance the other treatment modalities. One such program used by foster children at ABCS was "Blazing Saddles Equestrian Academy" run by foster parents Bob and Debbie Gladding. The program was described in *Footprints*.

After purchasing Ironwood Ranch near Cave Creek, Arizona, the Gladdings saw the effectiveness of working with horses with their own children. They were already foster parents, but after the move, they took in additional children. The program was open to all foster children who would benefit. In the program, children learned riding skills and the responsibility of taking care of the horses. "Standing face to face with an animal as large as a horse can be intimidating. But if you can stand face to face with a horse and control its behavior, it becomes inspiring. The majority of the kids have lives that are out of control. When they get on a horse and see that they have control, they see that they can take control in other parts of their lives."

There is more to Blazing Saddles than riding horses. Weekday classes involve recreation, life skills training and community service activities in addition to riding. Saturday classes, which are longer, include a session on agriculture as well.

Debbie summed it up. "In the end, Blazing Saddles is effective because it helps kids become good at something, and shows them they can take control of things that seem bigger than they are. Self esteem is really the most measurable of the results" (1998, 6-7).

Little Canyon Center—Residential Treatment

Following the study done by Rev. Cain in 1971, the decision was made to convert the children's home into a residential treatment center. An unpublished paper dated December 7, 1970, described the services offered by Arizona Baptist Children's Services. It read, "The program is designed for boys and girls six to seventeen years of age whose family is unable or unwilling to provide care . . ." (Cain 1971, 3).

3114 W. Missouri

Sometime after 1972, the original cottage at 3101 W. Missouri, the mobile office at 3115 W. Missouri, and two houses across the street at 3114 and 3118 W. Missouri were considered part of the "West Missouri Campus." Later it was named Little Canyon Campus for the city park that adjoins the ABCS property. As the program grew, the girls and boys would live in various units on the campus, which included the two houses across the street from the original cottage. The boys would later move to 3118 W. Missouri, and then to 3114 W. Missouri. When the new Jennings cottage for boys was constructed in 1982 on campus, the girls would remain in the original cottage at 3101 until their new residence was constructed in 1985.

During this period, the coed school at the Camelback Girl's Residence was moved to the Little Canyon Campus. The school would provide special educational classes for the children at Little Canyon Center who could not attend regular classes in the public schools.

The residential treatment center at Little Canyon Campus was a specialized program designed and licensed for thirty (later thirty-six) children ages twelve to eighteen years. These were youth who had serious emotional or behavioral problems requiring more intensive care than could be provided in a foster home or group home. Their caretakers are referred to as "mental-health techs," and they supervised the children over the course of three shifts each day, such as is characteristic of the nursing-coverage model in hospitals. The day shift of staff was primarily the teachers since the children were in school during this time. The children attended special education classes on campus and received the services of social workers, psychologists, psychiatrists, nurses, teachers, recreation leaders, and a chaplain. Other support staff, such as administration, housekeeping, dietary, maintenance, and clerical staff, completed the human resource network at the center. From time to time, as people with special skills were available, other activities and therapies were used.

Stephanie Sowter, who had extensive background in music, began teaching art and music classes at Little Canyon Center in 1990. She designed and implemented a therapy program for the center's children that served over four hundred children/youth in a four-year period. "Many of these kids see the world as a grey, dark, dreary place . . . we give them a chance to explore colors and to see art as an outlet" (*Footprints* 1995, 8-9). Ms. Souter worked with the caseworkers to tailor the therapy

Joint Commission
on Accreditation of Healthcare Organizations

needed by each child. Some learned to play musical instruments, and some took voice lessons. Musical performance and art shows for parents, teachers, caseworkers, parole officers, and friends gave a venue for showcasing the results of their work. In addition to classes, field trips were taken to cultural events such as museums, galleries, and symphony concerts. Materials and supplies were donated by individuals, churches, Grand Canyon University, and other groups.

The residential-treatment program was initially accredited by the Joint Commission on Accreditation for Healthcare Organizations (JCAHO) in 1974. The accreditation was lost when standards were increased, and the Little Canyon Center could not measure up to the new standards due the poor physical conditions on the campus. When additional buildings were constructed and the program upgraded, it would again be accredited in 1992 and has maintained that accreditation until the campus was sold. From 1984 through 1988, the residential-treatment center served 179 children.

Jennings' Building for Boys

A new cottage for sixteen boys was built in 1982. The girls continued to live in the original children's home building, which also contained the campus kitchen and dining room. Part of the first plan developed in the Baker administration contained the goal to complete Little Canyon Campus. It is important to understand that children in residential treatment have a disposition to act out in proportion to the quality of the facility. In the parlance of the profession, this is called "the loose thread syndrome." The analogy is to a garment or some type of material that has a loose thread, and the tendency of all of us is to pull on the thread, which of course further damages the garment. It is just too tempting not to pull on a loose thread.

The maintenance was costly and frequent. It was difficult to teach ego-impaired children to take pride in themselves and the property when their surroundings were shabby. The board made a decision that a cottage for the girls should be constructed, which was "child proof," as was the boy's new cottage. The money was borrowed, and groundbreaking for the new girls' cottage was held September 21, 1984 (*Footprints* 1984).

At the same time, a memorial made by the family of Timothy Westmoreland was recognized. This young man had died earlier, and the family wanted to make a gift to ABCS in his memory. This was recognized in the form of a plaque that was placed in the original building. The family were members of Glendale's First Southern Baptist Church; and Rev. Paul Kinnison, friend of the family, presented the recognition at the dedication of the building.

The cottage, designed by Dean Glasco, was identical to the boy's cottage. The construction was done by J. R. Porter Construction Company and the financing by Valley National Bank. Mr. Ron Riemer was president of the board at the time of this decision. It was a great day for the children of ABCS when the entire group of thirty-two children could live in quality facilities on the campus. Dedication of the girls' cottage took place June 22, 1985 (*Footprints* 1985, 5).

In addition to the cottage dedication, two families were honored by having buildings named in their honor. The original children's home  cottage was named in honor of Mr. and Mrs. J. B. Carnes who provided the money for construction. It would be referred to as the "Carnes Building" from

Girl's Cottage

that day. The boy's cottage was named in honor of Mr. and Mrs. Lester Jennings, Sr., who gave the money for the property at Little Canyon. The boy's cottage would be referred to as the "Jennings Building."

In addition to the new girls' cottage, a sports court was constructed in front and between the boy's and girls' cottages. This would be used for basketball, volleyball, skating, and other activities. The money for this was given by the Kiwanis Club of Phoenix. Their president, Mr. Doug Dunipace, was invited to the dedication to accept recognition for the gift. A breakfast had proceeded this happy occasion on that morning at the Camelback Sahara Hotel, which gave the board and the associates an opportunity to meet those involved in the construction, as well as meet the benefactors. Mr. Jack Willis, active in the Phoenix Kiwanis Club, was instrumental in encouraging this gift.

Sunglow Mission Ranch

Chiricahua Mountains

Mr. and Mrs. Richard Huff of Tucson were longtime supporters of ABCS and had worked hard to help ABCS start a group home program in Tucson. They owned an eighty-acre guest ranch in the Chiricahua Mountains east of Tucson, which had been used extensively by their church, the Casas Adobes Baptist Church. Eventually, the Huffs placed the ranch in a trust with the Baptist Foundation of Arizona (BFA). The trustees were the Huffs, Casas Adobes Baptist Church, and BFA. In 1988 the decision was made to donate Sunglow Mission Ranch to ABCS. This was a wonderful gift and was used by ABCS as a retreat center for its own staff and a fee-based guest ranch opportunity for churches and other groups to use. The several efficiency apartments could accommodate up to twenty-eight people and were completely furnished, including kitchenware and linens. There was an attractive chapel that was used for worship, conferences, or a gathering room for family reunions. Meal preparation was available for groups in "Roxanne," a converted post office from the days when Sunglow was a community. It is still listed as a community on older state maps. A fishing pond located a few hundred feet from the casitas was a popular spot for fisher people.

Mark & Nancy Pitts

This would become a favorite site for ABCS Board retreats and group gatherings. It was used one summer as a training site for a group from the University of Arizona. The first full-time resident managers of the ranch for ABCS were Mark and Nancy Pitts of Tucson, and they enabled the ABCS operation of the ranch to make a good start (Baker 1987). Mark served as manager and frequently filled the pulpits at local churches. Nancy was a gracious hostess and accepted the reservations, cooked when requested, and did the housekeeping.

Later managers included Marvin and Ginny Humble of Tucson. Marvin was a former trustee and served as the first regional coordinator for the Southern Regional Area of ABCS. Ron and Edna Gilliland also

managed the ranch until it was closed (Baker 1995, 8). A nearby neighbor to the ranch, Mrs. Louise Smith, helped with cooking and cleaning. Her familiarity with the area and the history of the ranch made her a valuable source of information

Sunglo Mission Ranch

as the staff gathered background information about the ranch. Of course, Mr. and Mrs. Huff were also sources of information about their former guest ranch and its surroundings and culture.

Spiritual Life

The spiritual welfare of the children was of the utmost concern and had been from the beginning. To capture the full extent of this program, it must be explored in two parts. The first part will be called the "informal" part. It was always the intent of the board and executive officers that Christian values and attitudes should permeate everything that was done at Arizona Baptist Children's Services. This would mean that the children would be treated

with unconditional love. They would be valued as objects of God's creation and love in spite of how the children themselves might behave. Every associate, as one local juvenile judge would describe, "was a kind of missionary." ABCS would be a place that lived and breathed spiritual affirmation. It would be a natural and not a scripted matter. Children are experts at sensing phoniness and the artificial.

The Christian Gospel is about hope and healing, and the thousands of children who came to ABCS could experience both. God gave and used the sciences of medicine; psychology; social work; education; and

155

above all else, relationships to heal the brokenness in the lives of the children he sent to ABCS.

The second part of the religious program would be called the "formal" structure. This would consist of structured activities, such as the Sunday worship services held on each campus and weekly Bible study. Each child, who so desired, would receive a Bible. Children were encouraged to attend religious services, but attendance was voluntary. This was never a problem, and from time to time, a child would stay in his or her room during the services. This was not a punishment for not going to church. Children were not allowed to roam the campus anytime without supervision. On occasion, family members or friends would take individual children to the church of their faith or denomination. This was worked out in advance through the social workers as a part of the visitation schedule.

Other capable chaplains joined Rev. Kinnison when the task became too much for one person. Rev. Ed Kines was enlisted to work with the boys on the Glendale campus and would later serve in the outpatient counseling department. Both Kinnison and Kines made quite an effective team and eventually earned their doctor of ministry degree. Dan Fosnight joined the chaplain team in 1988, and Bill Helm joined in 1989 to work with the boys on the Glendale Campus. Paul Kinnison and Dan Fosnight both left ABCS in 1992 to work in similar roles at the Baptist Retirement Home (Minutes, Executive Committee, ABCS Board 1992).

President Baker became concerned about the turnover in chaplains. This was such an important position because effectiveness with the

youth depended upon consistency and stability. Relationships take time to build, and frequent changes in chaplains were distracting to a stable program. The men who served in this position were capable and godly men and well received by the children, but Baker saw the value in long-term

Mike Ramsbottom leads a Bible study for a group of boys at Little Canyon Center.

service in this ministry with children whose families were often fragmented and undependable. The spiritual needs of these children were very basic, and relationship was more important than advanced education. Up to this time, only seminary-trained ministers were considered, but it didn't seem necessary to be able to parse Greek verbs or explain theological concepts to children who so badly needed someone who could speak their language and love them unconditionally as a part of the ministry.

Baker believed there was a godly man on the staff already who had been with ABCS for many years and more than likely would stay until retirement. He was a large "bear of a man" who could handle aggressiveness as skillfully as he could teach the Bible. Baker asked Mike Ransbottom, the shelter coordinator, if he would be interested in serving as chaplain. After recovering from the surprise, Mike agreed and became the stable, down-to-earth mentor and spiritual leader whom the children and program needed. To this day, the ABCS president believes this was one of the best personnel decisions he made.

Numbers of children would make professions of faith each year and be baptized. This was always with the consent of the parents or legal guardian. Beginning in 1996, one or two spiritual emphasis weeks would be conducted each year with special services and other activities planned. Youth groups from area churches would come to the campuses to entertain and interact with the ABCS children. They nearly always brought goodies, which were much appreciated. President Baker told the following personal experience on several occasions.

> The printed bulletin indicated that the worship service would begin with an "invocation." Chaplain Paul Kinnison, who was leading the worship service for the youth, asked if any of them knew what an "invocation" was. Teaching the children about worship was part of the total religious program at ABCS. One of the younger boys immediately answered, "It's the beginning prayer." The same boy then volunteered to lead the opening prayer.

I sometimes attended the worship at our campuses on Sundays when my schedule allowed. I also wanted to be at our emergency shelter that day to examine improvements that were being made in our electrical service. Those improvements required that the electricity be shut off during a few hours which included the worship time. However, it would be turned on again before nightfall, but apparently this was not clear to the boy who said the opening prayer. He prayed, "Dear God, don't let any of us get hurt while the lights are off tonight . . ." I wondered what this little boy's experience had been in the dark before he came to our shelter.

His prayer touched me and I wanted to go up and down the streets turning on the lights in every house where children lived. A few hours later that same day, I sat in my own church, but I didn't hear much of the marvelous sermon our pastor preached. My mind and heart were flooded with the words of the boy's prayer. Tears finally warmed my cheeks as phrases of the Christmas sermon penetrated my melancholy, and I realized that Jesus came into the world to dispel the darkness for all of us.

The lights came on again in the shelter a few hours after the earlier worship service. I have prayed many times since, that the light could be turned on so easily in the young, trouble lives God sends our way. (Baker n.d.)

Health Care

The standards of the Joint Commission on Accreditation of Health Organizations (JCAHO) required very specific and extensive health care and nursing services. Nursing coverage was now twenty-four hours, seven days a week. As new programs were added, nursing and medical services had to be extended to the youth in those programs. Martha Decker had done an excellent job in setting up the nursing service during the Don Cain administration and into the Baker administration.

Ms. Decker stated in one of her quarterly reports in 1986 that 297 medical, dental, and psychiatric appointments had been made during that period (Baker October-December 1986).

In addition to meeting the medical needs of the children, the nurses scheduled outside medical, dental, and other appointments. They conducted in-service training classes in first aid, CPR, blood-bourne pathogens, psychotropic medications, and numerous other health-related areas. They worked with a dietician in meal planning. They treated student illnesses and administered the patch test as part of annual staff medical exams.

Ms. Decker left ABCS and was replaced by Valerie Porter in 1989. Because of the comprehensive nature of nursing, health care, and dietician services, the director's title for this program was changed to "coordinator of health services." Janie Pudoka followed Ms. Porter and became the coordinator of health services in the same year. One of the strengths of this department was staff's ability to garner other needed health resources. Dr. Jerry Sparks, DDS, provided free dental service to the ABCS children. Dr. Galen, a retried physician, provided physical exams. Alice Goodrich, an employee in the Bell Group Home, was a licensed dietician and assisted in planning the menus. Lisa Kandall followed Alice as the registered dietician for ABCS.

David Goot, pharmacist and owner of Goot Pharmacy, provided many services to ABCS staff and children beyond filling prescriptions. He often prepared and delivered "unit doses" (each dose measured out individually to the children based upon physician's orders on script) to the home, making it possible for mental-health techs to give the medications to the children. Otherwise, only nursing staff could give out the medications. This took place evenings and weekends when nurses were not present, although available on call.

In addition to Dr. James Joy, the ABCS psychiatrist and medical director, other psychiatrists would provide services. In the East Valley location of the Bell Group Home, Dr. Rick Manganero provided those services. Special diagnostic procedures, such as electroencephalograms

(EEG) and neurological exams, were available. As state wards, most of the children were covered by Medicaid. Others were covered by private insurance with parents responsible for medication charges.

Sharon Whipple Burkhart, RN, became coordinator of health services in 1993 and remained throughout the Baker administration and part of the Jakes administration. At the time of this book's writing, she continued her relationship with ABCS as an on-call nurse. The work of this department and its talented corps of nurses were best described in one of Sharon's annual reports to the president:

> This year has come and gone quickly and the Health Services staff has been very busy. From July 1995 to July 1996 at the residential treatment center alone, we have transported children to the following appointments: 212 sick visits (including E.R. visits); 71 vision appointments; 63 history and physicals; 67 T.B. tests; 82 dental appointments; and 44 hearing appointments. This totals 539 medical appointments. We also have had two children hospitalized after surgeries. One child had surgery on her knees and one child had an appendectomy.

> Our sick visits and E.R. visits have consisted of ear infections, sore throats, strep infections, fractures, upper respiratory infections, ringworm, cysts, urinary tract infections, sutures and appendicitis. In addition to the above, staff have given approximately 87 nursing physical assessments. All the above were done in compliance with standards that have been set by JCAHO and Arizona Department of Health Services. (Whipple 1996, 23)

Maintenance

When ABCS was a small group home with live-in houseparents, the husband did what little maintenance was done. This included yard maintenance as well as repairs. As the program grew and additional facilities were acquired during the Cain administration, maintenance became a full-time job. One of the earliest of these maintenance supervisors was Dawayne Slagel who was employed by Rev. Cain on January 2,

1973. Mr. Slagel's work would be limited to grounds maintenance after the employment of Mr. George Jones in 1984. Mr. Jones and his wife, Doris, had been receiving home parents for ABCS and were no strangers to the program. Doris was forced to retire from foster-care work in 1979 because of illness (Merrick 1993). Jones was an electrician but proved to be proficient in every aspect of property maintenance. A popular expression became, "Let George do it." At this time, in the words of ABCS media coordinator Karen Merrick, it "was a one-man job" (ibid., 3).

In a short time, four more associates would be added to the maintenance crew. They did repairs of every nature, including electrical, plumbing, carpentry, heating/cooling, and automotive. They moved furniture, built shelves and cabinets, repaired roofs, painted thousands of square feet, remodeled building interiors, poured concrete, and did all of the lawn and landscape services. Very little repair work was outsourced, and then usually, it was because the ABCS maintenance crew was backlogged with work orders. Jack Willis, vice president for Finance and Operations, supervised the maintenance coordinator and helped the department organize and prioritize its work.

With the addition of new facilities, Selwyn Harris was employed as facilities coordinator in September 1990. This would free up Vice President Willis from the day-to-day facilities management and give him more time for agency operations and business administration. George Jones would now work with Selwyn Harris in the maintenance and repair of the buildings and utilization of space (Baker 1990).

Selwyn's background in hospital administration gave him the skills he needed in exploring possible property acquisitions for various programs and supervision of the completion of the Little Canyon Campus. Selwyn also accepted the responsibility for disposing the mobile buildings (trailers) on the campus. He retired in early 1993 but remained long enough to head up the construction of the new kitchen/dining room on Little Canyon Campus. Selwyn's move to the White Mountains was a loss to the Operations Division.

George Jones retired June 15, 1993, after nearly ten years as ABCS' maintenance supervisor. He was appreciated, and he in turn described his experience with ABCS as the most positive work experience of his career (Merrick 1993).

Les Jennings, Jr., was employed as the new facilities coordinator, a combined and expanded position of the former maintenance coordinator's position and the facilities coordinator position held by Selwyn Harris. Les's parents, Mr. and Mrs. Lester Jennings, Sr., were among the founders of ABCS, and Les himself had served on the ABCS Board of Trustees in a leadership capacity. For some years, he had managed the facilities of the Arizona Department of Corrections and was both a capable administrator and craftsman. He began his work as an ABCS associate in November 1993 (Willis 1993, 7). Les Jennings, Jr., reorganized the work-order system and developed many policies and procedures that would streamline the maintenance and facilities management program. Additional maintenance technicians would be employed, and agency purchasing was enhanced for economy and efficiency.

Recording ABCS history has been a hobby of Les Jennings for many years. His data has been a valuable contribution to the writing of this book.

Maintenance was never just about repairing broken things. It was about helping children who were troubled and often had weak ties to their families. It took a great deal of patience and understanding to repeatedly repair holes in walls made by angry children, and repair furniture and equipment resulting from aggressive outbursts. The hero in the following story is not a psychiatrist, social worker, or nurse. Charles Reynolds is an ABCS maintenance tech.

> Tommy (not his real name) never knew his father, and his mother was addicted to drugs. He was removed from his home at an early age and bounced from foster home to foster home. One of his recent placements was in an emergency shelter at which time he got in trouble with the law. He was then sent to an ABCS group home and required to complete community service hours. To meet that obligation, he was assigned to work with ABCS maintenance tech, Charles Reynolds.

Charles had always had a special place in his heart for the boys at ABCS. As they worked together Charles would on occasion remind him of God's love and a relationship began to build. Charles and his wife prayed daily for Tommy. After living in the group home for several weeks, Tommy attended a Bible study and worship service for the group home residents. Chaplain Mike Ransbottom concluded the service by telling the boys he would be available if any of them had anything they wanted to discuss. Without hesitation, Tommy spoke up and told the chaplain that he wanted God's love in his life. After asking God into his life, Tommy's attitude became more positive and he became anxious to learn all he could about the Bible and his new faith. He has maintained the highest level that can be achieved in his behavior program and began telling other boys about his new friend, Jesus (*Footprints* 2001, 3).

Much of the credit for the growth and strength of ABCS must go to the maintenance and facilities department personnel and to the Operations Division's vice president Jack Willis.

Human Resources (HR)

Human resources associates are included with the other "unsung heroes," along with maintenance, dietary services, accounting, administration, and development. They are the support people who enable the frontline associates to do their work with children and families. Without these services and the people who perform them, there would be no therapy, education, child care, and health services.

Human Resources did recruitment, hiring, employee orientation, and training for the agency personnel. They attended career fairs, assisted with accreditation, and frequently had to call on temporary professional agencies to fill last-minute staff vacancies. The HR staff at ABCS held monthly president's luncheons to assist new employees in getting acquainted with the administrative staff. HR personnel kept records of each associate's training activities, and these became "grist" for the accreditation "mill."

Longtime staffer Larry Gallaugher set up the first HR Department; and Laura Miller, his assistant, became the second HR coordinator following his resignation. Larry was an outstanding member of the ABCS team, serving over twenty years in various leadership capacities. Laura felt very inadequate in taking his place; and yet her accomplishments have equaled, if not exceeded, her predecessor. While working for ABCS, Laura obtained her bachelor's degree and has taken advantage of workshops to strengthen her skills.

Finances and Fund-Raising

The finances were strong during the period of 1984 through 1988. Income went from $1,397,097 in 1984 to $2,595,326 in 1988. Donations went from $146,461 in 1984 to $346,308 in 1988. God used several factors to bring about this blessing:

1. Strong fiscal management was provided by director of administration, Jack Willis. Mr. Willis's business experience was a complement to the lack of business experience of the new executive director.
2. The new executive director,[3] Mr. Baker, and some of the ABCS associates toured the state in a series of "dinner conferences," which were informational, inspirational, and entertaining. The message about the Arizona Baptist Children's Services would be shared during a delicious meal and musical entertainment. These were wonderful times of fellowship and getting acquainted with Arizona Southern Baptists. They were well received and appreciated. The dinner conferences were held from 1985 through 1989. Attempts were made to have them in different cities and different churches from year to year to encourage a broader participation.

---

[3]   The executive director's title was later changed to president.

In 1985, the conferences were held in eight different locations throughout the state and had a total attendance of 503. In 1989, the dinner conferences were held in six different locations with a total attendance of 306. In addition to the entertainment, a media presentation would be made, and one of the ABCS service programs would be featured. This became a successful occasion for enlisting people as members in the Circle of Champions. These early dinner-conferences were instrumental in informing the Baptist constituency about ABCS and later facilitated the opening of the regional centers.

3. A support group called "the Circle of Champions" was started in1985 with twenty-one members. It grew to 110 by 1989. The club was made up of people interested enough in ABCS to support it by their prayers and gifts. Friends had the option of making a one-time gift each year or making their gifts on a monthly basis. Their gifts went from $5,107 in 1985 to $21,418 in 1988 for a total of $64,043 for the four year period. By March 1999, there were 337 members of the Circle of Champions; and at the year's midpoint, a record $132,564 was given by this faithful group (Craven 1988). Shirley Cravens, development associate, worked with this program from its beginning.

4. One of the areas in which Baker had little experience was fund-raising. He did know of a consulting firm, which had helped other agencies where he had previously been employed. Lloyd Wagnon of National Children's Services Association in Florida had assisted Connie Maxwell Children's Home in South Caroline where Baker had served on the staff. Wagnon made several consulting visits to ABCS and eventually produced an annual development plan. It was very specific and detailed. From this assistance, the Circle of Champions was born as well as the area dinner conferences. He gave direction to strengthen the Mother's Day offering. Good advice was given on better use of *Footprints* to tell the ABCS story. Mr. Wagnon encouraged ABCS to begin direct-mail appeals that resulted in the

"back to school" campaign and appeals sent out at Thanksgiving and Christmas. His service was discontinued in 1987. The learning curve of the staff, due to the effective consultation, was very noticeable, and the board and administration believed that the consultation had served its purpose.

Behavioral Health Revenue Is a Mixed Blessing

In 1992, Arizona's Health Care Cost Containment System (AHCCCS) joined many other states in accepting Title XIX (Medicaid) for its behavioral-health programs. For the first time, behavioral health would embrace the managed care model that had already adversely affected other health and human-service programs in the state and nation. It created chaos and confusion within the state's Department of Health and the provider community of which ABCS was a part. The infrastructure of the state's system was not sufficiently strong enough, and the Medicaid system overload caused reduction in quality and quantity of services. While attempts were made to correct the flaws in the system, the results were providers were not paid in a timely fashion, and many, including ABCS, ended the fiscal year with an unusually high aging receivables account. Even when the system was corrected and properly functioning, it appeared that the new billing-payment model would require agencies to operate sixty to ninety days or more before receiving payment of claims.

It would be years before some semblance of unity and cohesiveness would characterize the Arizona Behavioral Health System. In the meantime, some agencies would go out of business, and all agencies would suffer. Agencies that had multiple sources of income, such as ABCS, fared better than those that depended entirely upon behavioral-health contracts. Donated dollars would mean the difference between life and death for ABCS. In 1992, ABCS received $437,436, the largest annual amount of gifts that it had received in its thirty-two year history.

Deferred Giving

The board and administration of ABCS did not make a strong effort to obtain deferred gifts through wills and estate planning. The

Baptist Foundation of Arizona (BFA) performed that function for all of the Arizona Southern Baptist Convention agencies. In working with families on their wills and estate plans, BFA would always give people the opportunity to include one or more Arizona Baptist agencies or other agencies within the Southern Baptist Convention in their estate plan. This was not a pressured appeal but was an occasion for providing information about opportunities that would permit people to continue helping Baptist causes even after their death.

BFA would give periodic reports to the agencies regarding the value of the deferred amounts people had pledged in their wills. In the case of ABCS, that potential amount had reached over four million dollars. In addition, ABCS had an endowment account with BFA, which served as the repository of funds that actually came when wills and estate plans were processed. ABCS would be notified periodically when such action took place. The agency was notified in 1996 that the estate of Mary Cheatham had been settled. Mrs. Cheatham had lived at Thunderbird Baptist Retirement Center and died in January of that year. The first president of BFA, Glen Crotts, had helped her with her will in the 1960s. ABCS received $598,629 from her estate.

Peggy Evans and Lois Smith of BFA notified ABCS in 1996 that the ABCS endowment had received a gift of eighteen thousand dollars from the estate of Lillian Nugent (Baker, "Board Memo", 1996). ABCS received the proceeds from the Mae Naylor estate valued at thirty-one thousand dollars and from the Biffle Jones estate in the amount of twenty-five thousand dollars (Baker 1988). Similar instances of deferred gifts sent to the endowment, following the settlement of estates, would happen many times during the ABCS history.

The First Computer

In 1985, ABCS purchased its first computer for accounting. Prior to that time, all accounting was done on large paper spreadsheets. This new computer was a 2250 Prime minimainframe computer purchased from Titus, a local computer consulting firm. The consultant provided the equipment and trained the ABCS staff in using it. It would be several years before computers would be used for any function other than accounting.

The Thrift Industry

ABCS had high hopes for its thrift industry, which began November 28, 1988. The first store was opened in Plaza 19 located at 9020-40 North Nineteenth Avenue in Phoenix, Arizona. The goal was to make money for ABCS as part of developing multiple funding sources for the agency.

Grand Opening of 19th Ave. Thrift Store

Executive Director Baker had learned from colleagues in the National Association of Homes and Services for Children that money could be made for children's services in the thrift store business. One example was Idaho Youth Ranch, which had two such stores with plans to begin others. They had been making less than 10 percent on their endowment and used their endowment capital to establish their industry. From the later profits, the administration estimated that they earned about 30 percent, rather than 10 percent by investing their money in the thrift industry. Baker was inspired by this example and, after consulting with the Idaho Youth Ranch staff, decided that ABCS could do the same thing. The board approved the idea, and a fifty-thousand-dollar line of credit was established with the Sunglow Ranch property used for collateral. Final approval was given by the board on March 18, 1988.

The first managers were Duard and Elladee Bell. The early years of operation did not result in profits for ABCS, but

Thrift World

it did give the ministry a considerable amount of attention and interest. The store was never short on merchandise. Some of the donations were clothing, furniture, books, household items, tools, appliances, costume jewelry, and other items too numerous to list.

Used merchandise poured in after the word was spread to the churches that the industry needed used goods. The store became a supply source for the other ABCS programs which was one of the positive benefits. Later managers included Bill Abdoo, Jim Tripote, A. E. and Charlotte Minard, Alvin and Betty Francis.

The Nineteenth Avenue store lost money, and the belief was that several stores were needed to really earn a profit. A second store was added at 8933 North Seventh Street in Phoenix on September 18, 1995. This large eight-thousand-seven-hundred-square-foot store was brighter and more attractive, and the staff were encouraged by this addition. The stores did not make money although sales were high. ABCS associates were never able to contain the overhead since most of the labor was hired staff, and the building was rented. A number of people volunteered for special projects, but the day-to-day management cost was too much for the industry to make a profit.

Communication Was a Strength from the Beginning

The importance of telling the ABCS story was a goal developed early in the Baker administration. So many things were done to accomplish that, including the area dinner conferences, *Footprints,* and the Circle of Champions. Visits were made by the executive director to churches and pastor's conferences, and an audiovisual presentation called "A Place Called Hope" was viewed over forty times throughout the state.

Five of the eight area dinner conferences had been conducted by March 20, 1985. Paul Kinnison was in charge of arrangements and planning the agenda. Diana Browning and Betty Jean Suttill worked very hard to implement the planning. Board President Ron Riemar gave support by attending several of the meetings and offering his van for transportation for the ABCS associates. They were well attended by several hundred people from Baptist churches and the communities. Associates provided information about the children's services and provided musical entertainment.

Sydney Browning

One of these associates was mental-health tech Sydney Browning, daughter of Baker's administrative assistant Diana Browning and her husband, Don. She was gifted in music and handling troubled kids, and her quick humor made the hours go fast driving around the state. Sydney was tragically killed in her church in Fort Worth, Texas, by a lone gunman who then killed himself. The author wrote the following statement in honor of Sydney, a friend and colleague:

Her wit was excelled only by her musical talent. My fondest personal memories of Sydney go back to the mid 1980's when she worked for ABCS. In addition to her required responsibilities as a behavioral health tech, she and other members of our staff, traveled with me as part of a team that met at various sites across our state at what we called "Area Dinner Conferences." This was a part of my early effort as president of ABCS, to tell our state about this ministry, beginning with our churches. Sydney would charm the audiences with her self-accompanied singing as part of our evening program of information, inspiration, and entertainment. I don't remember much of what was said at those events, but I do remember the fellowship that took place in the car to and from those meetings! Sydney kept us in stitches. On several trips, our friend John Feree, would be a part of the team. If the witty bantering between John and Sydney could be recovered and recorded, it would be a best seller! Neither one would allow the other to have the last word. The only thing that would distract them was my driving. Sydney would later affectionately refer to these trips as "the death rides" (Baker, "In Memorium," 1999).

The area dinner conferences were a blessing to ABCS and instrumental in getting the word about this ministry out to Arizona Baptists. Sydney was an important part of that effort, and she will always be a burning ember in the fire of precious memories of ABCS.

The agency was blessed by the services of very talented people to design its communication material. The first consultant was Charlotte White who helped prepare the ABCS display

Paul Kinnison and Karen Merick

board for the Arizona Southern Baptist Convention annual meeting in November 1985. She also designed and published the Executive Director's Annual Report for that year.

The next consultant, Lloyd Wagnon, has already been mentioned. He assisted the agency in putting together an annual development plan and designed direct-mail appeal letters and special fund-raising events. Later,

Karen Merrick, formerly with the *Baptist Beacon* and winner of national awards for her work, designed eye-catching and heart-catching materials for many years. Her work is seen here and elsewhere in this chapter. Communication was not neglected internally. Baker visited the campuses regularly and urged other administrative staff to do so. He attended monthly

foster-parents' meetings and campus-staff meetings. Staff morale and effectiveness depended upon communication within the agency. At least two things contributed to the ongoing success of internal communication. The first was the Staff Advisory Council composed of the ABCS administrative staff and program coordinators. The council met monthly to address any concerns from the associates, do strategic planning, and develop a program of incentives for associates.

One of the most effective and entertaining tools was the in-house newsletter called "As the Agency Turns." Baker didn't select this title  but opened himself up for an unsavory outcome by holding an agencywide contest to name the new newsletter. Tom Graham, the ABCS accountant at the time, won the contest. As a reward, one of the "famous" ABCS T-shirts was presented to him. The title stuck, at least for a few years, and Baker reluctantly did his part in this hoot by titling his column "Rotcerid," which is "director" spelled backwards.

In addition to Baker's monthly column, each of the programs had a reporter who submitted news about his/her program. The exchange of wit became so fierce that associates were as interested in getting their copy of *ATAT* on the twentieth of each month as their paychecks, which were handed out at the same time. It would be unforgivable not to mention some of the down-home, earthy rhetoric that these program reporters penned.

SEPTEMBER 20, 1986   VOL. III NO. 9

The first contribution is from the reporter for the Bell Group Home. It was signed by "the Ringer" who chose to remain anonymous, but we strongly suspect it was the creative Group Home Coordinator, Sally Mason.

JINGLES FROM THE BELL

Well ALL is WELL
At the GROUP home BELL
CENsus at FOUR
But we're GETin' two MORE

RIGHT after SCHOOL
we're DOin' somethin' COOL
gonna MAKE it GOOD
In the PREScott wood

Here's a SHOCK
for the REST of the FLOCK
the STAFF right HERE
has BEEN the same all YEAR!

The PARents CLASS
is REALly a BLAST
we could STAND to GROW
 so we lET some churches KNOW

A visit we HAD from D-H-S
overall their COMment was Y-E-S
so JANie relax—you do good WORK
there's NOTHin' to FEAR where Margie LURKS

it's tIME to GO
i HOPE you really KNOW
your PRAYERS we NEED
and aPPREciate InDEED!

We WISH for YOU
lots of SUMmer fun TOO
but you BETter listen WELL
for a JINGLe from the BELL
(*ATAT* 1990, 4).   THE RINGER

    Fred Godejohn, Little Canyon Center reporter for their newsletter, had a sharp wit that brought heaves of laughter. Here is just one paragraph from his articles:

Wayne Ver Hoeve had been settling in his new position here at Little
Canyon Center. He and Larry Gallaugher had fun one afternoon stuffing
Margie Woodruff's purse with snacks stored in the office and then
asking her when she returned if she had any change in her purse. You'd

have to know Margie to imagine the expression on her face when she opened her purse and saw all the goodies. They then assured her that no one would find out about her kleptomania if she promptly sought professional help. (*ATAT* 1988, 5:11)

Sydney Browning, mentioned earlier, could banter with the best of them without ever letting anyone get the best of her. She was reporter for the Bunkhouse before transferring to Little Canyon Center. This is pure Sydney:

I've heard too much complaints of "no ink, no ink!" I think that's why Jim McGinlay works here . . . just to see his name in print! Oh Jeem, you must be quicker. Press-stopping news is at a low here at the mighty Bunko. So I'll see what I can drag up. Mike Ransbottom provided pizza for our last in-service . . . thanks Big Kahuna! My wonderful partner, Dana Plank, is in the process of growing a beard. You wouldn't believe the amount of restraint it takes NOT to call him "Teen Wolf." Due to the menus lately . . . Dawn Goods new middle name is "Egg." This chick hides eggs or egg-type products in everything! Speaking of good, how 'bout those BH (Bunkhouse) overnight staff. I just can't say enough about the fabulous job they do . . . Yes Fred . . . looks like the Sooners are in the top 5 of yet *another* sport. Almost forgot and he'll kill me if I Don't say it . . . Jim Waggoner is the best! Sidney Browning, Reporter. (ibid., 4).

The Associates: People Who Made the Difference

The writer wishes it were possible to list everyone who ever worked for the Baptist Children's Home of Arizona or Arizona Baptist Children's Services. The task would be almost impossible due to the large number of people and the absence of personnel records during the first ten years of its history. Each associate was a valued member of the team; and their work, whether short or long-term employment, was a contribution to the well-being of the children. Sadly, people who work with children on a day-to-day basis are underpaid. Therefore, it is understood that motivation for this type of work is not just for money. There is nothing wrong with wanting the best pay one can get for work, but there must be a higher motive for those who work in family and children's services. In spite of the low salary, the benefits were above average, and this was a motive for some associates. It was always important to the administration and the board that all associates have health insurance, life insurance, and retirement benefits to somewhat offset the modest pay; and associates were not required to pay taxes on the benefits. In recent years, salaries have been brought more in

line with standard wages.

The counselors or behavioral-health techs, as they were more often called, and the schoolteachers frequently endured verbal and sometimes physical abuse. They were the primary caretakers of the children and were often the objects

Annual ABCS Staff Picnic

of misplaced anger and aggression. When the troubled children were out of control, it would be these associates and their supervisors who restrained the children until they could control themselves. At those times, the associates were calm and attempted to "talk down" the violent behavior,

modeling for the children that anger can be managed. The core of the therapeutic model was the belief that healthy relationships were a vital part of "best practice."

The children came to ABCS because of broken relationships—with family, community, and with God. The goal of treatment was to aid in restoring those broken relationships. The relationship with God is the most important of all, and when that relationship is restored, the restoration of other relationships can follow. Always, the positive relationship of the associates with the children was the beginning step in the treatment process.

It is difficult for abused and abandoned children to conceive of a God who loves them. What they can understand is the love and care of people around them every day who demonstrate expressions of that love and care by their unconditional acceptance. The associates also provide living necessities, verbal affirmations, and faith in the youth even when they have no faith in themselves.

The associates were people who made a difference in the lives of troubled children. When these children realize that the people at ABCS cared about them, it opened the door to tell them of God's love and care for all of us. God bless the ABCS associates!

Summary

The first five years of the Baker administration, 1984-1988, were marked by leadership transition, strengthening the program and financial foundations, strong communication with the Baptist churches and community at large, strategic planning, and expansion of the counseling program. It was recognized that fund-raising had to be a major focus, and this was implemented by using help from a well-known development consultant. As a result, a strong emphasis was made upon developing a plan that called for direct-mail appeals, expanding the Mother's Day emphasis, use of quality publicity materials, statewide area-dinner conferences, and production of a video to tell the ABCS story. A volunteer program was started, and foster parenting was expanded.

Through all the planning and implementation, there was the conviction that the spiritual life of the children and their families was uppermost in importance. A full-time chaplain gave direction and support to a program of which all staff were expected to be a part. One hundred and thirty-four children, and several adults made professions of faith during this period. This priority would grow over the years beginning with four professions of faith in 1984 to fifty-six in 1988. Faith and spiritual life were not separate programs but a spirit that permeated all programs. "Let the children come to me," were the words of Jesus, and ABCS could do no better than flesh out his invitation.

References

ATAT 1990, ABCS Monthly Newsletter, May 20

_____. 1988. ABCS Monthly Newsletter, March 20.

_____. 1988, 5:11, November 20.

Annual. 1962. Arizona Southern Baptist Convention held at Calvary Baptist Church in Tucson, AZ. November 14-16.

Baker, C. Truett. 1984. Twenty-five years of service. Annual report. Filed in the Archives of Arizona Baptist Children's Services.

_____. 1986.President's quarterly report to the ABCS Board. July-September.

_____. 1986. President's quarterly report to the ABCS Board. October-December.

_____. 1987. President's quarterly report to the ABCS Board. October-December.

_____.1988. Executive director's quarterly report to the board. September- December.

_____. 1990. President's quarterly report to the ABCS Board. October-December.

_____. 1995. President's quarterly report to the board. October-December.

_____. 1996. Board Memo # 96-9. April 28.

_____. 1999. Getting Ready For 40. *Footprints*, Summer.

_____. 1999. In Memoriam: Sidney Browning. *Footprints*.

_____. n.d. Dear God, don't let anyone be hurt in the dark. Unpublished monograph in the personal papers of the writer.

_____. n.d. Love keeps reaching out. In the Church Bulletin Service series 3500, Southern Baptist Convention Sunday School Board.1996.

_____. 1990. Finance and Administration. A six-month report. President's quarterly report to the ABCS Board. October-December.

_____. 1993. Finance and Administration. President's quarterly report to the Board. July-September.

Cain, Don. n.d. A brief history of Arizona Baptist Children's Services, 1971. Unpublished material from the private papers of Don Cain given to C. T. Baker and filed in the ABCS archives.

Cravens, Shirley. 1988. Development and Public Relations Report. *ABCS Board of Trustees Reports*, March 19.

Flint, Gerald D. 1997. The building blocks of ABCS: Arizona Baptist Children's Services. Unpublished research paper completed toward degree requirement for Grand Canyon University, Phoenix, AZ.

Footprints. 1984. Construction Begins For Girls' Cottage. 4 (Fall): 4.

_____. 1985. Summer, 2.

_____. 1986. Introducing the ABCS Therapeutic Foster Parents. 6 (Fall): 3.

_____. 1986. Ron Willcoxon Joins Children's Services. 6 (Fall): 3.

_____. 1991. Back to the Bunkhouse. Fall:5.

_____. 1995. Power of Arts, The. Fall.

_____. 1998. Saddle-Up. Fall.

_____. 2001. It Takes Us All. October

Merrick, Karen. 1993. Kids Were First For ABCS Maintenance Supervisor. Baptist Beacon, July 8.

Minutes. 1992. Executive Committee, ABCS Board.

Willis, Jack. 1993. Quarterly Report to ABCS Board, July-September

Whipple, Sharon. 1996. Health Services annual report. President's annual report to the board. June 30.

Whiteaker, Robert R. 1978. Feasibility Study, ABCS Missouri Avenue Expansion. October 27, Phoenix, AZ. Report filed in ABCS Archives.

Part IV: From Services To Children—
To Statewide Family-Based Services

Chapter 7

The Building Takes Shape

The Period 1989-1993: "The Baker Years," Part 2

If the first five years was the period of "walking," then the next five would be the period of "running." In fact, the staff would question, at times, if ABCS was running too fast. Finances were strong, gifts increased, programs were expanded, buildings were built, and property acquired, and children's lives were changed. The word was getting out that ABCS was a credible, effective organization bringing honor to Arizona Southern Baptists and to our Lord.

Building Fiscal Strength

Agency income increased from $2,007,754 in 1989 to $4,365,003 in 1993. Donations remained fairly constant during this period, annually averaging $384,643, which was a disappointment. This led to a major capital campaign in 1993. Still, many good things were happening to offset this discouragement. The Arizona Southern Baptist Convention included ABCS in its annual mission's budget, on a percentage basis, which had been their desire for many years. Not only was the money important, but this affirmed to the agency that it was truly a part of the convention. In every year of this period, the income exceeded expenses for which the agency was very grateful.

"For the Children"

In the wake of the 1992 managed-care beginning in behavioral health and the growing need to complete the Little Canyon Campus, the board approved a financial campaign to be led by Cargill and Associates of Fort Worth, Texas. This successful

zona Baptist Children's Services Staff Campaign leaders look over ipaign materials.

campaign will be discussed in more detail in chapter 8.

Circle of Champions

The ABCS Circle of Champions support group grew from 21 members in 1985 to 252 in 1992. The development consultant, Lloyd Wagnon, suggested the organization of a support group. These support groups were effective in other states in which Wagnon worked. In the beginning, various levels of giving were recognized by bronze, silver, and gold seals on the certificates of membership.

Volunteers

The volunteer program was started and grew under the leadership of Jenean Grosskopf. Julie Blackshire continued the program after Jenean moved out of state. In 1991, fifty-nine volunteers gave 6,447 hours of service to ABCS. The first annual luncheon for volunteers was held in 1990, and each volunteer was recognized for the time he/she gave. Over fifty volunteers, spouses, and ABCS associates attended the event held at the First Southern Baptist Church of Phoenix. Mort Swickle and Debbie Hansen, who volunteered at Little Canyon Campus, were named the

Outstanding Volunteers of the Year during the luncheon. The following are but a few of the many activities and results of volunteer work:

- The National Junior Honor Society of Scottsdale Christian Academy raised three hundred dollars to buy camping equipment and to cover the pool table for the Bunkhouse.
- The youth group of Love Baptist Church of Glendale helped package Mother's Day materials to be mailed out to the churches.
- Two brothers, John and Kevin Forsythe, gathered hygiene supplies and remodeled a bathroom in the Wrangler House. These were projects leading to the achievement of their Eagle Scout rank in Boy Scouts.
- Toys and clothing were collected for Christmas gifts to children.
- Volunteers wrapped gifts at Christmas for the children.
- Youth groups collected a "mile of pennies" for the Children's Services.
- Individuals and groups gathered soup labels and cereal box coupons.
- Parties were planned; volunteers worked in the thrift stores; volunteers did construction, repairs, tutoring. Others collected school supplies, entertainment tickets, and the list could go on.

- Doug Cooper made a name for himself at ABCS as "the cereal man." Doug and Barbara saved grocery coupons and bought cereal and

Annual Luncheon Honoring ABCS Volunteers

household supplies for pennies on the dollar. One year they gave one thousand boxes of cereal to ABCS.

Only in heaven will we know the dramatic impact, which volunteers have made upon the children and associates of ABCS. One aspect of volunteering that must not be overlooked is that of board service. These men and women gave an enormous amount of time and resources to ABCS. They are a special group of volunteers who have provided guidance and support to the tender ministry of child care since 1960 (a list of all the board members will be found in the appendix).

Building a New Management Structure

Doug Cooper,
"the cereal man"

The Business Model

Because of the difficulty in understanding the scope of responsibility by titles such as director, executive director, superintendent, etc., the decision was made by the board in 1990 to move to the business model for titles

of administrative staff. The title of executive director was changed to president; the title of director became vice president; and the title of program director became coordinator. In this change process, a third division was established, Church and Community Resources. Paul Kinnison became the first vice president of this division, which included fund-raising, publicity, volunteers, and spiritual life. Kinnison was a 1978 graduate of Grand Canyon College and graduated from Southern Seminary in 1982. He would later earn a doctor of ministry degree from Golden Gate Seminary. In 1982, he was employed by Don Cain as chaplain and became director of Church and Community Relations in 1985. He worked part-time in counseling, and he and his wife, Norma, led marriage enrichment workshops. Rev. Kinnison was popular among the children and the associates because of his relaxed personality and strong sense of humor. He is a deeply spiritual man who had no hesitancy to question the agency president or any other associate when he believed that any activity or direction was not God-honoring. This was not only the right thing to do, but it gave confidence to the ABCS constituency that the spiritual mandates laid out earlier were being followed.

A New Corporate Structure

Growing concerns about liability and the need to preserve capital led to a decision by the board to restructure the ABCS Corporation. The new structure was organized into four subcorporations under the parent company, Arizona Baptist Children's Services Inc. The subcorporations were as follows:

* ABCS Little Canyon Center Corporation. This included the five-acre campus at Thirty-first Avenue and W. Missouri, which housed the residential treatment center and coed school.
* ABCS Behavioral Health Services Corporation. This would include all other services programs, such as comprehensive foster care, therapeutic group homes, counseling, and all family-based services to be later added.
* ABCS Endowment Corporation. This would be the holding corporation for the endowment.
* ABCS Thrift World Corporation. Current and future thrift stores would fall under the umbrella of this corporation. The board for the Arizona Baptist Children's Services Inc. would be the boards for all the subcorporations.

HELP CHANGE THE WORLD
OF A TROUBLED CHILD.
SUPPORT
ARIZONA BAPTIST CHILDREN'S SERVICES.

Mother's Day Offering • May 10

Building a Media and Communication Network

The structures to inform Baptists and others in the community about ABCS and the needs were slow in forming. These two activities must go hand in hand. People do not give to projects or ministries about which they do not know. Education must come first, and with that, people are inspired to commit themselves and their resources to support a program or ministry. In 1984, misinformation abounded in the state about ABCS. The administration and the board knew that before support could be expected, information had to be provided.

Don Cain had developed some attractive materials with the aid of his first director of development, Tom Newsom. He was skilled at creating good printed materials and began the ABCS news journal, *Footprints*.

Direct Mail Appeals

The production crew for "Making a Difference" was honored during a reception at the ABCS administration building. Pictured are (left to right) Marlene Klotz, Randy Meador and Dave Simpson.

Lloyd Wagnon helped the agency develop a series of direct mail-appeal letters that would inform people about ABCS and invite them to support the ministry. The Thanksgiving and Christmas appeal letter were combined into one holiday letter that would arrive in mailboxes the day after Thanksgiving. Mr. Wagnon's experience was helpful in designing these letters that would always feature the challenge of being a part of ministry to children in need.

The next letter was the Mother's Day appeal in the spring. This letter would be a part of the ABCS "Mother's Day offering" approved by the convention and annually taken in the ASBC churches. People had the option of giving an offering through their church or sending it directly to ABCS.

Mother's Day Promotion Materials

In the fall, just before the beginning of school, a "back to school" letter was sent. This emphasized the expenses that ABCS had in buying clothing and school supplies in preparing children for the beginning of school.

Publicity and fund-raising in the Baker administration were piecemeal in the beginning. Ray Shelton worked in fund-raising; Julie Blackshire headed up the volunteer program, and Karen Merrick joined the team in 1990 following her employment at the *Baptist Beacon*. Shirley Cravens, an administrative assistant, coordinated these functions in the president's office. When the Division of Church and Community Resources was organized in 1991 under Kinnison's leadership, these functions would continue to grow as part of the new division. This synergy would not see immediate results because it takes years to build a program culture that inspires confidence, but a good start was made. Marlene Klotz, as her gift to ABCS, directed and produced an audiovisual slide presentation with music and narration in 1992 that was both informative and inspiring. It was viewed numerous times across the state at area dinner conferences and various churches.

Enough cannot be said about the creativity and professionalism that Karen Merrick's award-winning design and writing brought to the overall ABCS media efforts. From Mother's Day material to annual reports, the materials were eye-catching, informative, and credible.

The Church Representative Network

A Church Representative Network was started in 1990 with twelve churches participating. This program involved enlisting a volunteer in each participating church who would be the ABCS spokesperson and advocate in that church. He or she would promote the Mother's Day offering, back-to-school offering, and Christmas appeal. They would also encourage people to participate in the Circle of Champions. This group would double in 1991.

Building Programs and Buildings

Barnicle Administration and Family Services Building, Little Canyon Campus

The Little Canyon Center had a reputation for quality care, but that reputation was not reflected in its unsightly appearance. Efforts were made to obtain funding for the administration building, which would accomplish several things. First, it would allow ABCS to remove the unsightly mobile buildings, which had seen better days. It would also provide for an attractive parking area, which would abolish the gravel and grass yard that people had to use to park their cars. Included in this

Barnicle Family Services Center Dedication

Dean and Betty Barnicle of Yuma see the completion of their dream at the dedication of the Barnicle Family Services

project would be an attractive fence across the front with a gate that would completely change the appearance of the campus. As Baker described this need to Dean and Betty Barnicle of Yuma, they looked at one another with one of those looks that says, "Can we do this?" Baker's heart nearly jumped out of his chest when they pledged the three hundred thousand dollars it would take to do all the things mentioned. Dean "Barney"

Barnicle, along with his wife Betty, owned the Barnicle Oil Company in Yuma, Arizona. Barney had served on the ABCS Board and knew of the challenges that the children's services faced daily. They had three daughters and several grandchildren, and Barney could hardly talk about this project without tears welling up in his eyes.

The facility would be a state-of-the-art administration building and family service center. It would contain a reception area for the public and one for the children. It had space for medical records and the people who worked with

those records. There would be a large conference room and a smaller one. In addition, there would be offices for the campus administrative staff and the social workers, as well as a two-room suite for the nurse and a locked medicine cabinet. A lower level contained a large storage area that would always be full, and a thirty-two-by-eight-foot vault for permanent record storage. The new lighted parking area, landscaping, and decorative fence in the front gave the campus a beauty it had never known.

When all the bids were in from seven contractors, the range of estimated costs was $402,391 to $491,900. The amount given for the project was three hundred thousand dollars, so this presented a dilemma for the board. The decision was made for ABCS to do the contracting itself and hire each of the subcontractors. To do this, Wayne Ussery of Glendale was retained as the project manager to supervise the project that Design Three Associates had estimated to cost $285,000. This estimate included the building, lighted parking area, and decorative wall in front. ABCS began to search for various subcontractors for foundation work, framing, electrical, plumbing, painting, mechanical, etc. An ABCS trustee, Wes Baker, owner of Brutinel Plumbing and Electrical in Casa Grande, provided plumbing services at cost. Others would discount their bids. The final cost was estimated at $390,000, which included the lighted and paved parking area. The earlier bids had included only the building.

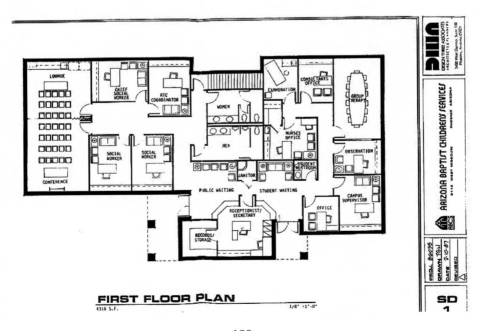

FIRST FLOOR PLAN

4316 S.F.　　　　　　　　　　　　　　1/8" =1'-0"

The dedication and open house were held June 2, 1989. Program personalities included Marvin Humble, chairman of the board; Dr. Jack Johnson, executive director of the Arizona Southern Baptist Convention; Wayne VerHoeve, campus administrator; Jack Willis, director of ABCS administrative services; Rev. Truett Baker, executive director of ABCS; Rev. Charles Tyson, pastor of Morningside Baptist Church in Yuma; Rev. David Gunn, pastor of First Baptist Church, Peoria, AZ; and Rev. Tom Wiles, pastor of First Southern Baptist Church in Buckeye, Arizona. Barney and Betty Barnicle were present together with their three daughters who assisted in the ribbon-cutting ceremony.

Upon its completion, the office contents in the mobile buildings were moved into the new administration building, and the mobile buildings were moved out! What a time of rejoicing this was!

The Bell Group Home

In this same period, 1989-1993, a Baptist couple in Mesa who were longtime friends of ABCS, decided to give a house they owned and all the furnishings to ABCS for a group home. The house had been a home-care facility for the elderly,

Duard and Elladee Bell of Mesa stand in front of the Bell Group Home.

and the Bells chose to close it and give it to ABCS. It would provide an East Valley residence for six boys ages six to twelve. The house and program would be called "the Bell Group Home" in honor of the couple who donated it (Board Resolution 88-PRO-3, 1988). The Bells would later play another important role in the life of ABCS by becoming managers of the Nineteenth Avenue Thrift World store during the early days of its history. The Bells were also among the most active volunteers in the program, and Mrs. Bell had been an ABCS trustee in earlier years.

Counseling

The growth of the family ministry program made it necessary to move to larger quarters. In addition, the ABCS strategy was to have counseling available in multiple locations to be more accessible to families. The first counseling location in the Baker administration was at the administrative offices in the 400 Building in 1984. Another office was started in 1990 at 2412 W. Greenway in Phoenix. The same year, both the counseling and foster-care offices moved from the 400

Family Ministry Staff (L-R) Betty Suttill, Ron Willcoxon, Paul Kinnison, and Ed Kines.

Building to 6122 N. Seventh Street in Phoenix. It was pointed out earlier that a counseling ministry began in Tucson in 1985, in Show Low in 1987, and in the East Valley in 1988. Casa Grande was another counseling site established during this time. New locations would be later added both in and out of Phoenix with the establishment of regional centers.

Journey Group Home

The two houses, 3114 and 3118 W. Missouri, across the street from Little Canyon Campus were sold. This took place after the boys' cottage was built in 1982, and the boys who had lived in those two sites were moved to their new home on the campus. By 1991, the owner of the two houses was unable to make his payments, and ABCS received back the property. The house at 3114 was in such a state of deterioration that it would not be restored but was then used for storage and much later maintenance. The adjoining house at 3118 was renovated, furnished, and made into a group home for five boys ages six to twelve.

It would be licensed as a therapeutic group home for troubled children. This home was too small to be cost-effective, but this was a temporary move. Since ABCS owned the house and there were no payments to factor into the cost of care, it was more cost-ffective than the Bell Home in Mesa, and the close proximity to Little Canyon Campus made supervision and needed resources more accessible.

Growth of Comprehensive Foster Care

The period of 1989 to 1994 saw the most dramatic growth years for foster care in its history. There were thirteen foster homes in 1989 and sixty-eight in 1994. Twenty-six children received care in 1989, and 164 received care in 1994. There was one level of foster care in 1989 and three levels of care in 1994. One of the reasons for this was the strong emphasis upon recruiting families to be foster parents. In the past, most of the families referred to ABCS came through the Kid's Consortium—the group recruiting and training effort of several agencies assisted by DES. In 1989, Executive Director Truett Baker and foster care coordinator, Alice Thornton, implemented a campaign to recruit families through the ASBC churches. From April through December 1989, the two ABCS associates scheduled fifty-six appointments with pastors to make a personal plea for new foster parents in their churches on Sunday mornings (Baker 1989).

Following each service, Baker and Alice Thornton would be available to talk to people interested in pursuing this ministry to children. This was another way to increase the visibility of ABCS, as well as make known the need for foster families. Baker also used this occasion to thank the pastors and their congregations for past support.

Training was a hallmark from the beginning at ABCS. It was never more evident than in foster care. In addition to first aid and CPR training, licensed foster parents would take in-service training classes in

Foster parent trainer, Dottie Bass. She and husband, Steve, are foster parents.

psychotropic medication, working with the ADHD child, helping children grow spiritually, and a host of other subjects. In addition to outside trainers, the coordinator would make use of other ABCS associates, such as the nurse, chaplain, dietician, and psychologist. Monthly meetings were held for all the foster parents, and much of this time would be used for training. Before an initial license was granted, parents were required to complete twelve clock hours of preservice training (ARS 8-509(B)). ABCS and most of the other Kid's Consortium agencies would require twenty-three to twenty-six hours. Each year prior to relicensing, foster parents were required to complete at least six clock hours of continuing education (DES 1997).

A cover story appeared in *Footprints*, the ABCS newsletter, written by an ABCS foster mother, Debby Littler, describing their first experience in caring for foster children. DES placed the shy, frightened five-year-old with Debby and her husband, Bob, from Crisis Nursery. As the new foster parents tried to make polite conversation to get acquainted, they were met with nothing but silence until the word "kitty" was mentioned. That opened the conversation door. The child was later presented with his very own blue-colored stuffed-toy kitty that he clung to like a lifeline to safety. The name "Kitty-blue" stuck. After three years of loving parenting, the little "scared rabbit" metamorphosed into a bright, healthy child that "exceeded our greatest hopes . . . the boy who was classified 'borderline mentally retarded' became a vibrant, intelligent child who no longer needed special education classes of any kind" (Littler 1992, 1-2).

This story of healing growth and grace is repeated numerous times in ABCS foster homes each year. The Littlers were never alone in their ministry of care. In addition to their spiritual resources, the foster-care coordinator Alice Thornton and other social workers were never more than a phone call away and were always available to give support and advice. It was truly a team effort, but the foster parents were the ones on the "front lines" making the difference, day by day, in lives that were damaged by neglect, abuse, and inadequate parenting.

ABCS Corporate Offices

ABCS' parent organization, the Arizona Southern Baptist Convention, experienced some financial challenges in the late 1980s

and early 1990s. As part of the financial restructuring plan of the convention, several properties were sold. One of those properties sold was the 400 Building, its headquarters for many years. It was sold in 1991. Since the ABCS Corporate Offices and some

ABCS Corporate Office at 8920 N. 23rd Ave
Phoenix, AZ

service programs were located there, it required that ABCS relocate. Several options were open, including a move with the Arizona Southern Baptist Convention to a new site in downtown Phoenix. The opportunity was presented to ABCS to purchase an eight-thousand-two-hundred-square-foot office building at 8920 North Twenty-third Avenue. The building was previously occupied by Blue Cross/Blue Shield of Arizona. At this time in 1991, the commercial real estate market in Phoenix was depressed, and several fine properties were available. The owner of this property was Great Northern Insured Annuity Corporation, which was willing to carry a note on the building with a reasonable down payment. ABCS was able to purchase this excellent building for $375,000. After minor repairs and decorating, the associates moved into the building on June 27, 1991, three days before its lease expired at the 400 Building. This was only one of many providential acts of God that protected and advanced this ministry over the years.

ABCS Children's Center:
Day Care at Phoenix First Southern Baptist Church

In 1980, Don Cain had received a feasibility study regarding day care in Arizona from Doug Miller, manager of administrative services for the Administration for Children, Youth and Families of DES. It included the cities of Phoenix and Tucson. The very detailed report had no recommendations, and apparently nothing more was done to implement this program idea. Baker believed that the concept of "family support" involved assisting families with child care when both parents worked outside of the home or where respite was needed for stay-at-home mothers.

The idea evolved into a belief that a quality day care center could become a model that other churches and businesses could use to establish their own day care centers. Dr. Virginia Furrow, a longtime friend of ABCS and of President Baker, believed the idea made good sense and, as a result, made a gift of one hundred thousand dollars to start the project. Plans for a day care ministry were drawn up and approved by the ABCS Board. A consultant was employed to assist in getting the program started with a feasibility study. The results of the study showed that only a few

194

families from staff members at ABCS, Grand Canyon University, the other state Baptist agencies, and Phoenix First Southern Baptist Church would use the service. That didn't diminish the enthusiasm to begin the center, so the decision was made that the day care center would be opened to any families in the area who wanted to use the program for their children. There were already several day care centers in the area, which should have been a red flag to the ABCS administration. "Red flags" are easy to ignore when one feels so strongly about a matter.

Readiness for the new children's center involved extensive remodeling of the preschool area at Phoenix First Southern Baptist Church. The church members, except for the pastor and maybe a few others, were not enthusiastic about the program; but their long association with ABCS and the fact that the president, a vice president, and many other ABCS  associates belonged to the church made them reluctant not to support the plan. The remodeling process began and resulted in a state-of-the-art child care center that would also benefit the children's ministry of First Southern Baptist Church, which would share the newly remodeled area. The best equipment was purchased, and an experienced director was employed, who in turn would employ her associates. They were trained, and programs were developed and put into place. On May 17, 1992, the ABCS Children's Center was dedicated and opened for inspection by the public. There was a good attendance, and Dr Furrow was honored for her generous contribution. Others were recognized, including Dean Glasco, the architect; and Kieborz Construction Inc., the remodeling contractor. The ABCS advisory council for the project was recognized consisting of Pam Hill, First Southern Baptist Church; Jane Castillo, Grand Canyon University; Paul Kinnison, ABCS; Ruth Wood, ASBC; and Perry Bramlett, BFA. The new program coordinator, Debbie Combs, was introduced; and in turn, she introduced her new teachers.

Advertising was sent out announcing that the center was "open to all families" (*Baptist Beacon* 1992, 3). The program received its license, and the children's center was open for business. The response was disappointing. Very few of the Baptist constituency responded due primarily to the fact that they already had satisfactory provision for their children. Some complained that the rates were too high for them, but the rates were based solely upon a budget with no provision made for earning a profit. One local day care consulting firm told ABCS that day care had to be subsidized when quality was important. Since the children's center paid only for utilities and not rent, it was believed that this in-kind support would be a sufficient subsidy to allow reasonable rates. It wasn't, and sadly the decision was made to close the center in 1995.

The ABCS president wrote an analysis of the "rise and fall" of the center and made that report available to churches who were interested in developing their own day care programs. The report, which helped several churches, was not so much a manual on "how to do it," as much as "what not to do." It was a costly lesson. The following were some of the lessons ABCS learned from this experience. It was believed that these would be helpful to churches who were considering a day care ministry:

1. There must be a need that can be documented by a valid survey.
2. A budget must be carefully designed that takes into account accurate costs, including living wages for the teachers. Teacher benefits, insurance, and transportation are often initially overlooked.
3. Insurance costs, including insurance for vehicles that pick up children, must be accurately determined.
4. After the budget is completed, the cost of care can be determined. Is the cost consistent with other day care centers in the area? Can the church members afford the costs? Will provision be made for accepting DES reimbursement from families?
5. Before any remodeling or other physical preparation, a church should consult with whoever will be doing the licensing to determine if standards can be met. If these standards cannot be met, then the church needs to know the cost of bringing the building into compliance with the local licensing standards.

6. Beginning a day care center should have the full support of the pastor, church leaders, and the congregation.

7. It is wise to employ people who do not belong to the church. Imagine what discord it would cause to have to fire one of the church members!

8. Provision needs to be made to keep the toys and supplies of the day care center in separate storage cabinets from those of the church's Sunday school. Friday cleanup, after all the children have left, involves not only sweeping, emptying trash, and wiping the tables but storing the toys and supplies that belong to the day care center after they have been sterilized.

There are other lessons, but these will lead a church a long way toward starting a successful day care program for children.

Building a Record of Memories—Thirtieth Anniversary

"His Word is Light"

The thirtieth anniversary celebration was held at the Mesa Hilton Pavilion Friday, February 15, 1991—almost thirty years to the day of the first child's admission to the home. It was a gala event attended by over two-hundred fifty donors, associates, trustees, and other friends of ABCS. The featured speaker was Mrs. Brenda Nordlinger, executive director of the National Association of Homes and Services for Children (NAHSC). Rev. David Gunn was chairman of the board and recognized President Baker for seven years of service (Merrick 1991, 1).

One of the highlights of the celebration was the presentation of a painting, which was commissioned for the occasion. The artist was

Carolyn Baker (not the wife of President Baker). The title of the painting was *His Word Is Light*. Greeting cards were produced from the painting. All rights to the painting were given by the Sedona artist to ABCS.

Building an Arizona Behavioral Health System [4]

When the children's services were started in 1960, the motivation was clear, and the system was simple. The early Baptist leaders just wanted to take care of needy children. It was as simple as that. When the home opened, Superintendent Wilson was approached by the state agency responsible for the care of dependent and neglected children—the State Welfare Department. This agency would later to be called the Division of Adults, Children, Youth, and Families (ACYF) within the Department of Economic Security (DES). The state offered to pay for the care of those children, and at first, their offer was turned down. As it became more and more difficult to raise funds to support the home, Wilson and the board decided to accept payment for state wards. Thus began a policy that would be followed to the present day in accepting purchase of care (POC) dollars for children in the care of the state. This initially took place within the state's child-welfare system.

In 1971, the Little Canyon Campus changed its focus from caring for dependent-neglected children to caring for troubled children, and began receiving state wards from the behavioral health and juvenile justice systems, as well as from the child-welfare system. Later, school districts and tribal communities would join the other state systems that needed behavioral-health services for their children.

Gradually, the behavioral-health system would dominate the referral base as more and more children needed behavioral-health services, and funding was increased for this need. It was not altogether a positive

---

[4]   In this book, "behavioral health" and "mental health" are terms used interchangeably.

move at that time as will be seen in the following description of ABCS's experience with this huge system.

The Beginning of the Behavioral-Health System

In Arizona, mental-health services date back at least to the establishment of the Arizona State Hospital by the legislature during territorial days. There were two significant events leading up to the establishment of a behavioral health system in Arizona. Congress passed the National Community Mental Health Centers Act in 1964, which provided federal matching grants to the states that would develop a state plan for a comprehensive, community-based program. The plan called for mapping out geographical areas into "catchment areas" with a full continuum of care required in each area. The Community Organization for Drug-Abuse Control (CODAC) was one of the early such programs developed in Southern Arizona. It was funded by the National Institute for Drug Abuse (NIDA) in the early 1970s and would become a part of the state's behavioral health system in future years (Hedgcock 2005).

The Division Is Born

Ten years later in 1974, the legislature gave birth to the Arizona Department of Health Services (ADHS) with a Division for Behavioral Health Services (DBHS), which encompassed the Arizona State Hospital, Southern Arizona Mental Health Center, and the Bureau of Community Programs. They began immediately to implement a plan to deinstitutionalize the Arizona State Hospital and used the savings from the hospital closure to fund community programs. During this period, the legislature passed Arizona Revised Statutes (ARS) 36-104, which stipulated that the ADHS was designated as the single state agency to develop and administer the State Plans for Alcohol and Drug Abuse.

ARS 36-189.B authorized the department to contract for mental-health services and established the 25 percent local matching funds mandate. ARS 36-141 authorized the department to contract with public and private nonprofit agencies for residential and other treatment services. One of those agencies was Arizona Baptist Children's Services.

Even a summary of Arizona's behavioral health system would not be complete without mention of the names of Fletcher McCusker and Boyd Dover. Mr. McCusker was the first executive director of the Arizona Council of Centers for Children and Adolescents (ACCCA) and in this role was an early voice for children's behavioral-health needs in the legislature.

Boyd Dover served as director of the division and wrote the first state plan for children's behavioral health in Arizona. Both men continue to be active in the Arizona behavioral-health system today. Other later standouts in advocating for children were Maria Hoffman, David Miller, David Hedgcock, Carol Kamin, Joe Abate, Morris Miller, Phyllis McFarland, Tim Dunst, and Joe Mann. There were others too numerous to mention who advocated for children's needs, including agency staff members, members of the legislature, parents of affected children, and other private citizens. This large group of advocates would be a deciding factor in obtaining resources for these troubled children on more than one occasion.

The Division of Behavioral Health Services Is Closed, and the Bureau Is Born

In December 1983, the division was abolished, and a system of bureaus was set up within the department. The Bureau of Community Services was established to develop a statewide network of services for which the department would contract. Prior to and during this time, the department contracted with approximately 125 nonprofit agencies through 20 umbrella agencies that coordinated the programs in each "catchment" area. Many believed that this system was duplicative and fragmented as well as costly.

And Behavioral Health Is Here to Stay . . . Sort Of

In 1984, following a study by department officials, legislators, and consumers, Arizona's Behavioral Health System was again reorganized. It would include a funding mechanism for mental health, alcohol, and drug abuse through nine statewide administrative entities called

RBHAs—Regional Behavioral Health Authorities. Acronyms would abound in names for these organizations such as:

CCN, ComCare, PGBHA, EVBH, ACCM, NARBHA, and CODAMA.

In 1986, the Division of Behavioral Health Services (DBHS) was reestablished by statute within the Department of Health Services (DHS) to oversee all mental health, drug, and alcohol programs, including programs for both children and adult.

While well conceived on paper, the program never received adequate funding, and even as early as 1985, Arizona was being ranked as last among the fifty states in per capita spending for mental health. Arizona was spending $12.06 for each of its residents, while the national median was $27.82. New York spent $90.12 per capita for its residents. Responsibility for providing behavioral-health services was fragmented and shuffled from one state agency to another. All too often, parents were forced to give up custody of their children to the state in order for them to obtain mental/behavioral health services.

Reform Follows McClure Report in 1988

In 1986, the Governor's Mental Health Task Force was formed to study the mental-health needs of the state's children and suggest a system in which to meet those needs. The task force was cochaired by Dr. Jesse McClure, dean of the School of Social Work at ASU, and Susan McBroom. Their report was presented to the legislature in January 1988. As a result of the committee's report and a strong grassroots citizen-advocacy effort, two major bills were passed in the legislature.

The first was House Bill (HB) 2338, which became Arizona Revised Statutes (ARS) 36-3431-35 authorizing the creation of a statewide, comprehensive Division of Behavioral Health System (DBHS) for all children in the state over a five-year period. ARS 36-3421-22 (HB 2335) authorized the establishment of a Children's Behavioral Health Council that would work with the DBHS to design and implement the plan. The cost of fifty-five million dollars was to be expended over five years. The first year began with an appropriation of $12.5 million. It was understood that the McClure Report would serve as a philosophical underpinning for the plan. This report was subtitled, "Beat'um Up, Lock'um Up, Give'um Up" (McClure 1988). The reference was to parents who had to give up custody of their children to Child Protective Service or Juvenile Probation as a means for getting help

The key issues were still not implemented after six years! In addition to the two landmark bills, the legislature passed ARS. 36-2907.01 (House Bill 2554), which was an emergency measure requiring the director of the Arizona Health Care Cost Containment System (AHCCCS)—the state's Medicaid Program—to develop a plan to phase in the implementation of mental-health services for eligible children beginning October 1, 1990. It was to be fully implemented by April 1, 1991. The bill also allowed AHCCCS to contract for services if an entity was unable or unwilling to contract with an AHCCCS plan or program contractor. The bill also opened the door to AHCCCS to implement a capitated system of reimbursement for services to be prepared by October 1, 1991.

The Advent of Title XIX . . . a Mixed Blessing or a "Mixed Up" Blessing

While the new plan was underfunded, it seemed to be working, and progress was being made; however, congress passed the Omnibus Budget Reconciliation Act of 1989, which included an amendment to Title XIX of the Social Security Act. This amendment (Section 6403, OBRA '89) included mental-health services as required coverage. These services had not previously been included in AHCCCS, Arizona's Title XIX managed care system. The services were required to be in place April 1, 1990. Through HB 2554, Arizona authorized a service-delivery system built upon the existing capacities of AHCCCS and the DBHS, ADHS.

Because of the stringent time lines, Arizona requested and was given a "waiver" from the April 1, 1990, deadline and received approval to implement mental health services for children in two phases, which would extend the mandatory coverage for all Title XIX eligible children's services to April 1, 1991. The total system for delivery of Early Periodic

Study, Diagnosis and Treatment (EPSDT) Title XIX services to all eligible children must be accomplished by October 1, 1991.

Prior to 1989, Arizona, as a Medicaid waiver state, provided almost no behavioral health services for children. In 1990 the legislature authorized ARS 36-2907.01, which would bring Title XIX funds for children's behavioral health into the state. This would be done by matching 40 percent of state money with 60 percent federal funding. The result was a near disaster for the state agencies, as well as the provider community and last but not least, the children. The new federal dollars were a mixed blessing.

Two major problems developed. First, Title XIX guidelines required that the state match those federal funds with state dollars. Rather than appropriating new state dollars to meet this requirement, the match was largely taken from the state dollars (subvention funds) originally intended to be used for *all* Arizona children with behavioral health needs. By siphoning off state dollars for indigent (Title XIX) children, all other children in the state ended up with inadequate funds for their care. Thus, Arizona had what was called a "Title XIX driven" system. This system left a "notch group" of children whose care was underfunded just as they were prior to 1988. For a time, outpatient children's behavioral health services were only offered to Title XIX eligible children. Even Title XIX funds were limited by the "medical necessity" requirement that would make some otherwise eligible Title XIX children ineligible for services.

The second problem created by the arrival of Title XIX had to do with the state's lack of preparedness for the new system, resulting in chaos. Overload, confusion, complexity only began to describe the abysmal condition of the system, which affected the provider community. Agencies went unpaid, building up enormous receivables and draining reserves.

Providers still shudder when they hear the term "BHMIS" (pronounced B-MIS), which was the acronym for the state's first experience with computerized billing and claims processing. It paled in significance to the frustration of learning to deal with "capitation" and "managed care," which providers realized was the wave of the future.

The system that resulted from the Title XIX advent was a complete distortion of the original intent of the 1988 legislation. The policy shift resulted from the funding change, rather than through publicly debated and formally established policy change. Letters poured into the newspapers complaining about the impact of the dysfunctional behavioral-health system upon the private agencies that provided services to children. Joel Nilsson, one of the popular editorial writers in Phoenix, titled his column "Mental Health Services for Poor Kids: No Way to Run a Business." He quoted from a letter and phone conversation he had with J. Dennis Wilkins, vice president and general manager of Del Webb Communities Inc., who was also chairman of the Arizona Baptist Children's Services Board of Trustees. Wilkins wrote, "If a company with 10,000 jobs was thinking of relocating, the governor would be moving mountains; yet an existing industry (of greater magnitude) whose presence is threatened is being ignored . . . what type of message does that send to the residents of Arizona?" Nilsson commented, "It's a question deserving of an answer." At that time, ABCS was owed five hundred thousand dollars by the state.

Another newspaper article revealed that ten million dollars would be needed to pay for services already received by the state. The same article described how the new behavioral-health director, Dr. Aletha Caldwell, planned to "begin a managed care system on November 1st to replace the existing fee for service plan to control costs" (Kull 1992, B1).

The escalating problems resulted in staff changes at the state department and division levels. DHS director Caldwell attempted to resolve the serious unpaid claims problems and eventually brought in the Electronic Data System (EDS) to handle the cumbersome payment process. This proved to be a generally effective system.

In addition, she reduced the number of Regional Behavioral Health Authorities (RBHAs) in Maricopa County from three to one and reduced the total statewide number of RBHAs to six.

Providers who were encouraged by the early changes were now protesting that the new system was not working much more effectively than the old system. Director Caldwell was asking for the providers to be patient, assuring them that the new programs needed more time to effectively come together. Providers were saying that they had been patient, and there was no more time. Agencies were financially strapped due to aging receivables going back two years in some cases.

Prior to July 1, 1992, many agencies would go ninety days or more without money for Title XIX services. The crisis was compounded by the fact that virtually no payments for Title XIX services were made during FY 91-92. Advances were made without those monies being reconciled to individual claims. The reconciliations for FY 91-92 billings were being made in the early months of FY 92-93.

And the Search for Solutions Begins!

A paragraph from the January 24, 1994, issue of the "COMCARE Communicator," a Maricopa County RBHA, best described the transition of the attitude "ain't it awful" to "what can be done" approach.

> As the system shuddered with the dynamics of massive change, the focus shifted to problem solving. Solution-focused partnerships began to identify and solve the "how-to" problems that plagued operations at every level. These partnerships were enhanced by the efforts of the Governor's Behavioral Health Action Committee, appointed October 7, 1991, the Ad-Hoc Joint Legislative Committee on Behavioral Health, and personnel at the Division of Behavioral Health. ("Ain't it awful," 1994, 1).

It should be noted that both the Arizona Council of Centers for Children and Adolescents (ACCCA) and the State Association of Behavioral Health Programs actively worked together toward solutions. Gayle Perrin, chair of the Governor's Special Task Force, did an outstanding job of assisting the provider community in resolving many of the payment and other problems. The Joint Legislative Ad Hoc Committee took many hours of public testimony and began to identify those issues that would need to be considered in formulating solutions. ACCCA worked closely with both governmental groups, becoming a technical resource on identifying issues and recommending solutions.

One of the major contributions that ACCCA would make would be the position papers it developed outlining a specific plan for reshaping the Children's Behavioral Health System. These papers were developed out of years of difficult learning experiences in system management and program development. The people who provided the services knew how to develop and implement a working system. Thankfully, not everyone agreed with Senator Ann Day who was quoted in the *Arizona Capitol Times* as saying, "Maybe too much say was being given to the providers . . . I think the legislature has to regain some control, rather than leave it up to the people in the field . . ." (*Capital Times* 1993, 45)

ACCCA's position papers recommended reform in the children's behavioral health delivery system. Their papers also recommended transfer of the Division of Behavioral Health Services (DBHS) to the state's Comprehensive Medical, Dental Plan (CMDP), and this recommendation was formally presented before the Joint Legislative Ad Hoc Committee on September 1, 1993. At the same hearing Dr. Jack Dillonberg, director of DHS, also presented a similar plan. Both recommendations would involve transfer of DBHS to AHCCCS. The latter move of DBHS to AHCCCS would be the plan that the committee would approve and which was incorporated into HB 2500.

Dr. Dillonberg's recommendation to the committee came as a surprise to many, including members of the ad hoc committee. In retrospect, it shouldn't have been a surprise. In a May 28, 1993, letter from Dr. Leonard Kirschner, then director of AHCCCS, to Mary Leader, the governor's executive assistant for health services, stated the following:

I believe that the federal Health Care Finance Administration (HCFA) was very accurate in its finding that the administration of the mental health program in Arizona is too diffuse, multi-layered and cumbersome . . . immediate steps should be taken to remove some of the layers of administration and the single state agency (AHCCCS) should take more direct responsibility. In essence, the HCFA recommendation was that mental health services should be bundled with the acute care services under the AHCCCS Health Plans . . . I strongly recommend that the Governor's Office seriously consider supporting HCFA and this agency's recommendation that a change in structure occur . . . The health plans are willing and able to take on this additional responsibility. (Kirschner 1993)

The HFCA recommendation referred to by Dr. Kirschner came as a result of an investigation by this federal Medicaid oversight body. There were a number of strong recommendations following the visit of six HCFA auditors to Arizona the week of November 29-December 3, 1993. One particular statement from the January 27, 1994, final report of the committee caught the attention of members of the legislature and bureaucrats alike:

Because of the serious lack of accountability that currently exists and the resulting lack of financial information to properly monitor the expenditures made for the program, HCFA management is giving serious consideration to withholding future payments for the Arizona Mental Health Program. (*Medicaid Review Report* 1993, 14)

This had to have an impact upon the ad hoc committee's decision to move DBHS to AHCCCS although this agency has played such a key role in the system's current problems.

Suggestions made by ACCCA were included in HB 2500, which was the legislative vehicle for implementing the results of the joint committee's work. Unfortunately, some of the suggestions were not used! A major concern was the bill's provision for moving the Division of Behavioral Health (DBHS) out of the Department of Health Services into AHCCCS. ACCCA's position paper had recommended transfer of DBHS to the Comprehensive Mental-Dental Program (CMDP), which is the state's medical insurance program for children in the custody of the state. That position was supported by Children's Action Alliance (CAA) in a September 13, 1993, letter to Senator Ann Day from its executive director, Carol Kamin, and the CAA's chair of the child-welfare committee, former state senator Jacque Steiner. The statement read,

"Moving the administrative functions of prior authorization, utilization review, and payment processing to CMDP will consolidate behavioral and medical responsibilities and accountability for these children and youth into one system." (Kamin 1993).

The final position of both ACCCA and the State Association was that HB 2500 should be defeated and that the DBHS be left in the ADHS at that time. The hope was then to work toward a system that would involve pulling all public children's services in the state into one: Department for Children, Youth, and Families, or Department for Human Services.

This dream of a unified behavioral-health agency was never realized as of this writing, but significant improvements were made in the Arizona Children's Behavioral Health System. One attempt at unity resulted in the development of a single purchase of care (SPOC) contract. Realizing that the children's agencies would not be combined, leaders in each state agency attempted to bring about some unity, at least in the contracting process. Eventual displeasure expressed by the attorney general's office resulted in a slow death of the new process.

Building an Associate Base

God's faithfulness to ABCS has been expressed in many ways. One of those ways is the qualified and dedicated associates he has provided. The early leaders like Rev. and Mrs. Wilson and Otis and Lucille Dickson

Diana Browning

will never be forgotten. Their lives were planted in this tender ministry, and the harvest of other gifted men and women would follow.

Don Cain was an innovator who caused quantum leaps to be taken in meeting the needs of troubled children in Arizona. Dr. Phyllis McFarland spent the majority of her thirty-year career developing programs and associates. Her expertise in special education and residential treatment was recognized throughout the state, and her ability in contract management both expanded services and garnered much needed dollars for the agency.

Jack Willis was the glue that held the agency together between administrations and provided business, financial, and administrative skills at a crucial time in ABCS's growth. Both he and Dr. McFarland were mentors to President Baker who received honors and was recognized for work, which these two giants made possible.

Diana Browning, executive assistant to President Baker, was a loyal and gifted lady who saved the president from many headaches and pitfalls. Her editing skills were awesome as was her ability to serve the board of trustees in every imaginable way. Her pleasant charm and wit were disarming and enhanced the morale of the office.

Quiet and almost timid, Shirley Cravens was nearly always in the background, but her work was always in the foreground. She provided continuity in the development office and saw one after another of the directors come and go until she was the director herself. She gave the terms "kindness" and "patience" new meaning. As explained in the earlier chapter, there are too many names to try and list them all. They are all important and deserve the gratitude from all who value the care of troubled children in Arizona.

It was never easy to say good-bye to associates you had grown to love and appreciate. The largest area of associate turnover was among the behavioral-health techs. This was an entry-level position, and the pay was minimal. In addition, the work of caring for troubled children on a day-to-day basis was physically and emotionally draining. Those who did stay would be promoted to supervisory and management positions in time.

It was difficult to lose associates for any reason, but losing them because of untimely death was difficult for everyone including the children. One of the saddest losses experienced by ABCS was the untimely death of Carlos Lewis, a behavioral-health tech at the Bunkhouse. He would have received his bachelor's degree in criminal justice from Grand Canyon University in December of 1993. Mike Heath was a maintenance assistance who died unexpectedly while on the job, January 8, 1988. Mike was best known for his willingness to allow the boys to work with him on simple jobs. He was active in his church, Iglesia Bautista Del La Fe, where he worked in Royal Ambassadors (*Footprints* 1998, 8).

Eric Taylor, a Bunkhouse mental-health tech, died in an incident with police, which may have resulted from a serious head injury or deep depression. Social worker Kaye Gutierrez was a popular associate with the foster parents in the ABCS Foster Care program. She died of cancer at the age of forty-four, and her testimony of faith in Christ was as strong in death as it had been in life (*Footprints* 1991, 2).

In spite of staff changes, the number of ABCS associates grew each year. In 1991 there were 133 associates; in 1992 there were 160; and in 1993 there were 178.

Building an Advocacy Base

Advocacy was not a formal program, although ABCS was involved in many activities that directly or indirectly advocated for children's rights. ABCS was a founding member, along with twenty-five other agencies, of the Arizona Council of Child Care Agencies, the predecessor of ACCCA. Representatives from these agencies met monthly to discuss problems and develop strategies to advance the quality of care for all children, particularly those who were clients and students in their agencies.

Adequate funding for children's programs was always a challenge. All of the council member agencies and the majority of nonmember children's agencies contracted with the state to provide care for the state's children. Council members became so acquainted with legislators and state department staff that they were on a first-name basis. The council identified those members of the legislature who

ACCCA members (L-R) Truett Baker, David Miller, and Dave Hitchcock attend legislative committee. Senator Debbi McCuen, lower left, was always a strong supporter of children.

210

supported children's programs and individually supported their election. Position papers were drafted, and countless meetings were held with state department leaders and members of the legislators. In turn, council members were invited to serve on legislative committees dealing with children's issues.

Representatives of the council would meet with the press to present their case for enabling legislation to increase funding for children. This was sometimes perceived as self-serving, which became an excuse for not appropriating adequate funding. The contracting process involved approval of agency budgets by state department staff, which became an odious matter when Regional Behavioral Health Agencies (RBHA) or state department personnel began to approve and disapprove line items in budgets. That practice was short-lived.

In spite of frequent disagreements and heated debate, there was mutual respect and a working partnership attitude that generally prevailed between the service agencies, state departments, and the legislature. There was a recognition that this cooperation must take place if children and families are to be adequately served.

The name of the council would change as needs and cultural circumstances changes. It was later called the "Arizona Council of Centers for Children and Adolescents." Later, the name would be changed to the "Arizona Council of Centers for Children and Adults." When the council merged with the Behavioral Health Association, the name was changed again to the "Arizona Council for Human Service Providers." With each name change, the scope of the council was enlarged to strengthen the unified voice for children in Arizona.

There were many fine directors of ACCCA. Only the last two will be mentioned. Maria Huffman was a tough advocate for children and a skilled administrator. She could go any day, face-to-face with a state legislator. She would rally the agencies in her association to support issues for children, but she was also a strong advocate for the agencies to receive fair reimbursement for their services from the state. David Miller took Maria's place when she resigned. David was a strong agency administrator from Tucson who had previously worked for the Department of Economic Security and knew well the state and legislative systems. David is a soft-spoken gentleman to whom people listened and respected. His testimony before legislative committees was always well thought out and forceful without being abrasive. David helped to steer the council during a critical time when it merged with the state's behavioral-health association and became the choice of the merged group to be its executive director.

Summary

Finances were strong in this period, but donated dollars were not as forthcoming as expected. This resulted in the first capital fund-raising campaign of the Baker administration, "For the Children." Counseling expanded as did group homes and foster care. The residential treatment center received the coveted accreditation by JCAHO. One hundred fifty-four children made professions of faith under the leadership of five chaplains who worked for ABCS during this time period: Paul Kinnison, Bill Helm, Dan Fosnight, Julie Blackshire, and Mike Ransbottom. Thrift World opened, and the children's services received the gifts of a guest ranch and a private residence. Administrative and corporate structures were changed, and offices were moved from the 400 Building on Camelback Road to a new office site at 8920 N. Twenty-third Avenue. The Barnicle Administration-Family Service Building was constructed on Little Canyon Campus, and day care started at First Southern Baptist Church in Phoenix. The "Circle of Champions" membership dramatically increased. This was a good time to be at ABCS and a good time for Arizona children and families. But greater days were ahead.

References

Ain't it awful' to 'what can be done. 1994. COMCARE Communicator. January 24, Phoenix, AZ.

Arizona Capitol Times. 1993. August 8.

ARS (Arizona Revised Statutes) 8-509 (B), State of Arizona.

Baker, C. Truett. 1989. Executive Director's quarterly report to the board. October-December.

Baptist Beacon. 1992. Children's Center Open to all Families. May 28.

Board Memo # 48. 1990. ABCS. December 21.

Board Resolution 88-PRO-3. 1988. Acceptance of Bell Property and Establishment of the Bell Group Home. September 23.

DES. 1997. Foster Family Care Licensing Requirements, R6-5-5825.A., State of Arizona.

Footprints. 1988. In Memory of Mike Heath. 7 (Spring): 4.

_____. 1991. Foster Care Staffer Kaye Gutierrez Dies. Spring.

Hedgecock, David. 2005. Telephone Conversation with Author, December 19.

Kamin, Carol. 1993. Correspondence to Senator Jackie Steiner. Filed in ABCS Correspondence Archives.

Kirschner, Dr. Leonard. 1993. Copy of correspondence to Mary Leader. Filed in ABCS Correspondence Archives.

Kull, Randy. 1992. Mental Treatment Bill Due. *The Phoenix Gazette*, October 14.

Littler, Debby. 1992. Fostering Growth. *Footprints*, Winter.

McClure, Jesse. n.d. Beat'um Up, Lock'um Up, Give'um Up. Division of Behavioral Health, Arizona Department of Health Services. Undated and unpublished reference sent to author by Mr. David Miller, Director of the Arizona Council of Human Service Agencies, Phoenix, AZ.

Medicaid Review Report. 1993. HCFA Region IX.

Merrick, Karen. 1991. A Look Back—ABCS Celebrates 30 Years. *Footprints*, Spring:1.

Chapter 8

New Programs, Buildings, and Rightsizing

The Period 1994-1999: "The Baker Years," Part 3

Introduction

Methods of meeting the needs of children and families is a changing process because needs change. In addition to that, the social climate changes, and the amount of resources that are available to an organization changes. Not all changes are good, but an organization that tried many different methods of improving itself is going to make mistakes in the process. This chapter will describe many successful efforts at strengthening its programs and finances in order to help children. It will also describe some attempts that were not successful.

This period witnessed the conclusion of a successful capital campaign, "For the Children." Ironically, it was also a period of financial crisis. Pledges did not bring immediate help to cash flow, and those pledges would take three years to be fulfilled.

Veteran staff retired, and "new blood" was infused into ABCS. Local programs were closed, but regional programs were opened. Two campuses were sold, and another campus realized its completion with two new buildings. (The two campuses closed were the Glendale Bunkhouse and Sunglow Ranch.) President Baker received a number of honors, which in turn brought honor and credibility to ABCS. Another staff member was killed. ABCS learned that its strengths were in raising donated dollars for children and contracting for services. Earning income from entrepreneurial ventures was not a talent of ABCS. This was a difficult and expensive lesson. Another hard lesson learned was that ABCS's skills were in programs with which it was familiar and which addressed the problems of troubled children and their families.

Spiritual Life Revitalized

The period of 1994 through 1998 was highlighted by seventy-four residential children choosing to accept and follow Christ. Mike Ransbottom was the director of the chaplaincy program and was assisted by Julie Blackshire, Aaron Norwood, Bill Gifford, and Bill Helm. Twenty-eight of the youth were baptized and always with the consent of their legal guardians. On one occasion, a baptismal service was conducted on a Sunday afternoon to allow the out-of-town family to be present. This was a special time for the family and for ABCS.

First Spiritual Renewal Week

The first Spiritual Renewal Week was conducted during the week of March 24-30, 1997. Services were held in the chapel of the Phoenix First Southern Baptist Church, and renewal activities were conducted each day. The March 29 activity that week was participation in a block party sponsored by the church for the entire community of which Little Canyon Center was a part. Services and activities were attended by students and associates. The Spiritual Renewal Week continued yearly during the duration of Mike Ransbottom's chaplaincy.

Visiting Youth Groups

Various youth groups would come to the campus and bring a picnic lunch and play games and sports with the children. In addition, the ABCS children would be taken to youth activities in the churches. Some of the younger children were invited to Vacation Bible School at Phoenix First Southern Baptist Church and had a great time (Baker, "A Time For," 1989, 25).

Food Share Program

To Chaplain Mike Ransbottom, ministry was more than teaching the Bible and sharing Christ with the youth, important as those ministries were. Chaplain Mike was also interested in families, including their physical needs. One occasion involved observation of the sister of one of the young residents at the residential treatment center when she came to visit her brother. Parental neglect had led to Jason's (not his real name) placement, and his sister Donna was the only family with whom he was in touch. She would drive up in an old truck that appeared to be falling apart at any moment, and she wore the same clothes during each visit. Staff took an interest in the older sister because of her obvious need and because of her devotion to her younger brother. Chaplain Mike learned about her impoverishment. They had little and sometimes nothing to eat when the brother went to her apartment for a visit.

Knowing that other family members of the treatment-center students probably faced the same problems, the chaplain started the ABCS Food Share Program in cooperation with St. Mary's Food Bank. Needy families of the residents were provided food boxes with the help of the food bank, ABCS associates, and church groups. Four to six large food boxes per month were distributed.

Associates provided other resources for Donna as well as the food boxes. They gave her clothing and provided transportation to work when her broken-down truck refused to run. In time she asked for a Bible and began attending every spiritual-life activity on campus. She began to help associates clean up after on-campus family activities. She later wrote Chaplain Mike, "God has worked and helped me through you; I never would have made it without the people at ABCS" (*Footprints*, "Sisterly' Love," 1998, 8). But ministry would go beyond the Little Canyon Campus.

Ministry to Juvenile Offenders

Rev. David Garza, the Arizona Juvenile Corrections unit chaplain, conducted weekly worship services for the youth in the Buckeye facility. At the time of this report, forty-two youths and one adult made professions of faith. Rev. Garza also did counseling and had a waiting list of boys wanting to talk with him (Ransbottom 1999). In a later report, Ransbottom revealed that a portable baptism pool had been donated, and thirty youths were scheduled to be baptized. At this time, seventy-two children and adults had made professions of faith through this program (Ransbottom 2000).

Buildings, Property and Programs

"For the Children" Campaign

This special fund-raising effort was started in 1993 with the help of Cargill and Associates of Fort Worth, Texas. The Cargill representative, Victor Varner, was always helpful and encouraging. Cargill was widely known for its success in fund-raising among churches and church organizations, and Baker had  known its leader and their success for many years. The campaign would be built around an organization involving the board, staff associates, and community leaders. The basic goal was $1.9 million, and the challenge goal was $2.8 million.

Jerry and Sarah Smithey

Mr. and Mrs. Jerry Smithy of Phoenix were the campaign chairpersons. Honorary chairpersons were Dwain and Beva Hoover. The Smithy's made a gift of four hundred thousand dollars for the chapel/educational facility. A major gift of $2.3 million in property was made by developer John F. Long, making the final total $3,617,318. This exceeded the overall challenge goal of $2.8 million and was an occasion of great rejoicing and thanksgiving to God.

Dennis Wilkins, board chairman, and his wife Marsha also made a significant pledge; and Mr. Wilkins led his company to make a matching gift. Not enough can be said regarding the board leadership of Dennis Wilkins and the full board whose leadership in the beginning set the tone for the entire campaign. Both the board and ABCS associates exceeded their basic goal, and the board exceeded its challenge goal.

The proceeds of the campaign would fund the construction of a dining/kitchen facility and a chapel-classroom building. Funds would go to various campus renovations, endowment, equipment, and developing a model for regional family-support centers.

Kitchen-Dining Facility

The long-range building plan on Little Canyon Campus was started by Don Cain. With some adjustments, the Baker administration continued the plan, which included a kitchen/dining facility. Proceeds from the "For the Children" campaign made it possible to begin the planning and construction for this critical need.

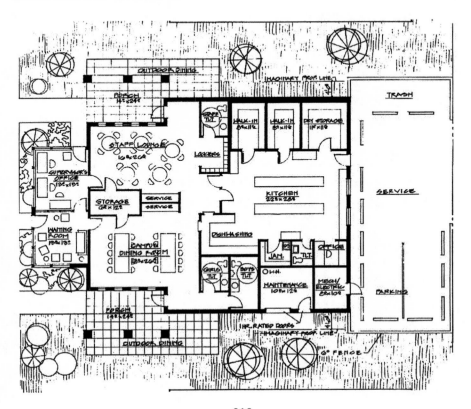

When the children's home opened in 1960, the only kitchen/dining room available was in the original cottage at 3101 W. Missouri. Pantry space was limited, and bulk staples had to be stored in an off-site facility. There were several old home-style refrigerators and freezers donated by generous friends. Children had to eat in four shifts because of the small dining area, which was dark and uninviting.

Groundbreaking was held November 2, 1993, on the Little Canyon Campus for the new kitchen/dining facility. Dean Glasco was the architect, and Redden Construction was the builder. Caliber Bank financed the balance needed to supplement campaign proceeds. Rev. Tom Wiles, pastor of First Southern Baptist Church in Buckeye, Arizona, was the board chairman. The project was completed and dedicated May 16, 1994. The 3,632-square-foot building was a state-of-the-art kitchen and dining facility. It could seat fifty people and contained a commercial-grade kitchen with walk-in refrigerator and walk-in freezer.

Stainless steel preparation tables and a large commercial-style dishwasher were but a few of the amenities. The building also had a large walk-in pantry, three offices, and four restrooms. One of the offices was designed as a campus evening/weekend supervisor's office in order that the large administration building could be shut down and locked evenings and weekends.

Smithey Chapel/Educational Center

For several years, Jerry and Sarah Smithey kept reminding President Baker that they wanted to do something for ABCS. They were strong supporters of Grand Canyon University and involved in other Christian-based projects, including a home for abused women in their former home town of Tulsa, Oklahoma. At lunch one day, while at Jerry and Sarah's favorite Mexican restaurant, they informed  Baker and his development associate, Ray Shelton, that they were interested in funding the chapel/educational center, which was a

220

priority in the "For the Children" campaign. This appealed to their strong interest both in education and the spiritual lives of children. They also agreed to be chairpersons for the campaign, which was in the beginning stage. Many dreams were realized and prayers answered that day. The new chapel with its bell tower rising above the Little Canyon Campus would be a reminder to all who passed by that this was a place that honored God.

After the plans were drawn and estimates made for the 7,330-square-foot structure, it was realized that the Smithey gift, generous and wonderful as it was, would not cover the full cost of this "campus centerpiece."

Jerry and Lora Railey

President Baker was familiar with the North American Mission Board Volunteer Builders program and the Arizona Southern Baptist Builders Program. The Baptist Builders group from Mississippi had made quite a positive impression on the ABCS family when they did so much to renovate the Glendale Campus and do repairs in other programs. They made this an annual event at the ABCS campuses for three years and, in the process, endeared themselves to the agency.

Baker talked with Ken Belflower, director of New Work Church Building and Support of the Arizona Southern Baptist Convention, to determine if the new chapel/education center could be considered for one of their projects. In addition to the cost savings, Baker saw the appropriateness for Arizona Southern Baptists in building the chapel. Mr. Belflower would later approve the project following his meeting with M. C. Chancy, associate coordinator of Projects and Volunteers for the Arizona Southern Baptist Builders. There was not only interest but also enthusiasm on the part of the Arizona Baptist Builders, but Belflower reminded Baker that this project would go on a priority list as earlier commitments had been made for other projects. The board had requested the Arizona Baptist Builders to do the construction, and it was granted (Board Resolution 95-ADMIN-6 1995)

The groundbreaking took place in December. Because the construction was done by volunteer labor, it took longer than expected.

When the time came for Builders to begin the chapel project, Jerry and Lora Railey, members of the Campers on Mission who tour the country to assist churches, were available and moved their RV onto the Little Canyon Campus. Jerry would supervise the volunteer builders; and his wife, Lora, would assist in the coed school program on campus and lead morning devotions for the staff and children.

The chapel would be equipped for audiovisual presentations and could be adapted to a variety of uses; however, there was never a question but that the main purpose of the chapel was to worship God. Never before had there been a place on the campus that was large enough and suitable enough for worship. Services had previously been held in the living rooms of the cottages. An attractive chapel would help in teaching the children what it means to "go to church" and would assist the chaplain and associates in helping the children understand how to worship and behave in church. There was also storage space and offices for the chaplain.

The earlier closing of Paradise Valley Conference Center in Prescott had been a source of sadness to Arizona Southern Baptists. It held a cornucopia of good memories of fun, food, fellowship, Bible study, singing, and worship. Young people had accepted Christ there; others had volunteered for missions, and all were inspired to live more Christlike lives. One of the daily rituals was the bell tones that rang across the wooded acres to call campers to eat and to worship.

When the conference center was sold, one enterprising supporter of the camp and ABCS decided that at least the bell should be kept and used somewhere else as a reminder of the camp spirit and the young people who created that spirit. As Providence would have it (the writer wasn't sure if it was appropriate to credit God with that recovery), the bell found its way to the bell tower of the new chapel on Little Canyon Campus. What more appropriate place could it have gone! The ABCS associates believed God was pleased, as once again, the bell tones called the young people to worship.

The Smitheys, strong supporters of the conference center, were very pleased that the bell would be placed in the chapel they had provided for the youth at Little Canyon Center (note to readers: no, the Smitheys weren't the ones who commandeered the bell from the camp, and the writer's lips are sealed as to speculation about the name of the individual!).

The chapel was one of two sections in this building. The second section was an educational center with four classrooms, a teacher's resource room, offices, and restrooms. The four classrooms were each equipped with a small "time-out" room where children could go when they were out of control or troubled. The door to those rooms did not have locks but had a window where the child inside could be seen by the teacher. In time, the doors were removed. Each classroom had its own restroom. In the center of the four classrooms was a teacher's resource and work room where equipment and materials were stored. The central location of this room, with windows on all sides, made it possible for monitoring all of the classrooms from this area. This was important when a teacher needed a break or was dealing with a difficult child and needed back-up help.

One of the classrooms was reserved for "community children." These were community children, not Little Canyon residents, who could not attend public school. The school districts contracted with the Little Canyon School to provide education for these children.

Dan Shufelt and Leonard Miller, representing Chimiarra Investments Limited, present a check to Truett Baker, President of ABCS, and Shirley Cravens, Interim Director of Development.

ABCS received a one-hundred-thousand-dollar gift from Chimiarra Investments Ltd. to equip the chapel and classrooms. This gift would provide audiovisual and sound equipment for the chapel, as well as seating and equipment for both the chapel and the classrooms. In addition, each of the four cottages would receive a color television and VCR and new furniture for the living room area. Twenty-five new mattresses were purchased and an irrigation system installed on the campus. This gift would also provide flooring for the chapel/classroom area and remodeling of the Carnes Building for use as an activity center for art, music, and recreation.

President Baker had been contacted earlier by Dan Shufelt and Leonard Miller, representing the trust, and they asked Baker to provide them with a wish list. He and development associate Shirley Cravens had no idea what the extent of their interest might be; so every need for equipping and furnishing of the entire campus, as well as the new chapel/educational center, was listed.

How often in a lifetime does one have the opportunity to make a list of everything one would like to have? Everything that could be imagined was placed on the list, hoping that one or two of the large items would be selected. Were they ever surprised when they were informed that the Chimiarra gift would cover *everything* on the list! To this day, ABCS does not know all of those who were involved in this gift, but their undying gratitude goes to the two men at Chimiarra Investments who represented the benefactors and made possible this very generous gift to ABCS. The following year, the same trust would fund the start-up of the ABCS adoption program with a seventy-five-thousand-dollar gift.

Steve Keipers, school principal, makes presentation to Dr. Sarah Smithey

On March 27, 1998, the building was dedicated. The only sad note was that Jerry Smithey had died during the construction period and didn't see the completed facility. Mrs. Smithey and her family were present at the dedication to celebrate this wonderful gift. There had been a time, years ago, when the Arizona Southern Baptist Convention *allowed* the birth of Arizona Baptist Children's Home but reluctantly supported it. Now the convention fully embraced it in many forms of support. Surely the early, persistent leaders who relentlessly struggled to birth a Baptist home for children in Arizona were celebrating all over heaven! The friends and family of ABCS will always remember with appreciation the convention leaders who "built the chapel" in the name of Arizona Southern Baptists. Only to name a few, they are Ken Belflower, Tim Willis, M. C. Chancy, Dr. Steve Bass, and Dr. Dan Stringer.

Finances

The 1997 financial year took a particularly hard hit with a deficit of $385,000. A good part of that was a "paper loss" because ABCS did away with fee adjustments in its method of setting rates for state agencies and private insurance. Also, state agencies were experiencing cuts in their budgets, which were passed on to those with whom they contracted.

Utilization was low because of cuts in funding. During this time, the ABCS fund balance took a drop that would take years to recover. The positive side must also be presented. It was during this 1994-98 period that the Little Canyon Campus was completed and refurnished; community-based group homes were started, and ABCS would extend its family-based programs to other areas of the state. New family-based programs such as Family Builders and Adoption would be started and expanded in the new statewide network. Capital expansion was a great success, but it was at the expense of diminished funds for operation and agency reserves.

The "resizing" that began in 1997 helped to stabilize the finances. Part of the diminished income undoubtedly was due to friends of ABCS who regularly made gifts to the general fund and who now diverted those gifts to the "For the Children" capital campaign

A Major Gift from Phoenix Developer, John F. Long

C. Truett Baker (left) and John F. Long

Mr. Long, well-known Phoenix area builder, is best known for building the Maryvale Community in West Phoenix, which he named after his wife, Mary P. Long. His reputation as a philanthropist was also well known. One Sunday in 1995, he was watching the North Phoenix Baptist Church telecast; and following the program, he called the church. He explained that he was interested in "giving a building" to be used for "a home," and the church personnel gave him the number of the Baptist Retirement Center. Soon after that, Dr. Dan Yeary, the North Phoenix

Baptist Church pastor; and David Jakes, director of the Baptist Retirement Center at that time, visited with Mr. Long. In the early course of their conversation, it was learned that Mr. Long wanted to give a building to a children's home. Dr. Yeary explained to the benefactor that he needed to talk to Truett Baker, president of Arizona Baptist Children's Services.

A meeting was set up with President Baker and the builder. Mr. Long spread out a map of an area northwest of Phoenix known as Tonapah and indicated that he would like to donate several pieces of property in that area to Arizona Baptist Children's Services, who in turn would sell the properties to fund a building. The appraised value of all the properties was $2.3 million—the largest gift ever given to the children's agency. The plan was for ABCS to sell the properties and the proceeds used to construct what would be called the "John F. Long Family Development Institute" (*Footprints* 1995). By February 1998, all the properties had been sold, except for one lot in the Tonapah area. An additional eighteen acres parcel of land at Sixty-seventh Avenue and McDowell Road had sold for eight hundred thousand dollars. It was time to begin preparations for building the John F. Long Family Life Development Institute.

Gifts Come in Many Forms

Over the years, ABCS had been given everything from horses to houses, and the agency was grateful for every gift! Some gifts were unusual but still valuable. Board member Kitty Robinson and her husband Robert gave ABCS a time-share in Sedona (Baker, Board Memo # 96-9, 1996).

The Bakers check out the 1926 Model A Ford

On another occasion Dwain Hoover, husband of trustee Beva Hoover, gave ABCS a 1926 Model A Ford, which had a 386 Corvette engine and a 400 "turbo something" transmission. It was a two-seat convertible painted bright orange. President Baker promised that he would give all board members whose pledges were up to date a ride in the souped-up antique car (Baker, Board Memo # 96-8, 1996).

Then there were the Betty Crocker coupons. One couple from the Baptist Retirement Center in Youngtown donated a doll collection that was displayed in the waiting room at the corporate offices on Twenty-third Avenue for many years. One of the most unique gifts were boxes of cereal donated by Doug Cooper, discussed elsewhere in this book. The endless list of goods included TVs, refrigerators, a pool table, a Hammond organ, furniture, lumber, school supplies, hygiene kits, clothing, and birthday and Christmas gifts. The ABCS volunteer coordinator estimated that "in-kind" and cash gifts were valued at $50,976 during the 1994-95 fiscal year. The following is a breakdown by category: $15,641 for Christmas gifts; $34,486 for hygiene and school supplies and activity tickets; $849 cash for Christmas gifts (Baker 1995).

Closings and Relocations

Sale of Sunglow Mission Ranch—1997
This wonderful gift came to ABCS October 28, 1987, through a trust governed by Mr. and Mrs. Richard Huff of Tucson, Casas Adobes Baptist Church of Tucson, and the Baptist Foundation of Arizona. When the ranch was accepted, it was done with the understanding that it would be operated by ABCS for two years, after which a decision would be made regarding its future use. If it could be operated to pay for itself and/or if it could be used to minister to children and families, the agency would probably

continue to use it. If not, it could be sold and the money placed in endowment (Baker 1987).

It was enjoyed as a retreat center for the board and associates and by individuals and groups in southern Arizona. A modest charge was made for its use by friends outside of ABCS, but it lost money

Ronanne—Dinning Room at Ranch

227

almost from the start. The realization that ABCS was subsidizing private use with money that people gave to help children led to the decision to sell the facility. This was one of the most difficult decisions the board had to make, but it had to be done, and the proceeds from the sale would help ABCS at a time when the financial picture was as bleak as it had ever been. The ranch loss in FY 1988-89 was $20,292. It simply was not working out.

The operation was undercapitalized from the beginning, resulting in a great deal of deferred maintenance. It was designed for a maximum of twenty-eight guests; and that, together with weeks that the ranch went unused, was not a cost-effective operation. Had ABCS been able to afford making major additions and improvements, it might have been different. This was not a reflection upon the managers who worked hard and creatively to make it a quality-resort setting. They just didn't have enough resources with which to work.

In addition to undercapitalization and small size, it was a disadvantage being four hours from Phoenix and not having an ongoing, broad, marketing plan. The board approved listing the ranch with Richard Huff on February 8, 1990, and then again on November 8, 1994 (ABCS Board Executive Committee 1995). The first offer was turned down. The second offer, which Richard Huff brought, came from Mr. and Mrs. Robert Paral of nearby Sunsites, Arizona. They planned to continue its use as a guest ranch. The executive committee of the ABCS Board approved the offer in a special called phone conference meeting on September 5, 1996. The new owners made a significant down payment and financed the remainder with ABCS for a two-year period.

It was sold for slightly more than its appraised value. The proceeds from the sale of the ranch were used to pay off the line of credit with the Baptist Foundation and repay money borrowed from the ABCS endowment. Money was used to pay for deferred maintenance on the campuses, and the remainder went into the ABCS endowment. What a blessing this gift was to ABCS!

Closure of Thrift World

In 1998, the board finally agreed to close the thrift industry (ABCS Board 1998). One of the overlooked benefits of the thrift industry was the resource it offered for the programs. It provided furniture and household goods, as well as supplies and equipment to all the ABCS programs, including the new, fledgling regional centers. Foster parents were able to obtain clothing and personal items for the children in their homes. However, even this financial advantage did not nearly offset the loss. With its closure and that of other entrepreneurial endeavors, ABCS would learn to "stick to the knitting"—that is, do what we do best! ABCS' forte was selling services to the state for its children, and fund-raising.

Little Canyon Campus Changed from Coed to All Boys and Capacity Was Reduced

Due to low census in the girls unit, it was closed, making the campus an all-boys facility. ABCS regretted not offering services to girls at this time, but the truth is that discipline on campus would be easier to manage with only one gender in residence (Baker, "Quarterly Report," 1996).

The residential-treatment center's capacity would be reduced from forty to thirty beds. The ten beds closed in the residential treatment program would be taken over by the Bell Group Home located across the street at 3118 W. Missouri at that time. This did not happen immediately as ABCS had to apply for this single ten-bed unit to be licensed as a therapeutic group home. This change became necessary because the referrals to the residential treatment center had greatly diminished, but referrals to therapeutic group homes had increased. This made possible a more cost-effective operation on the Little Canyon Campus and strengthened ABCS's finances.

The residential treatment center had also been underutilized due to severe cuts in state funding for residential beds. This would result in a $240,000 a year savings at Little Canyon Campus, which would still be operating in the red, but the loss would be greatly reduced. All of these measures together would again put ABCS in a positive financial position by 1998. Each of the four units could house ten children each, but administration chose to keep only eight children in each unit, except for the one unit that was used as a group home.

Bell House in Mesa Sold and Boys Moved to Old Journey Group Home in Phoenix

The 1,625 square foot residence at 318 E. Eighth Drive in Mesa was given to ABCS by Duard and Elladee Bell (described in chapter 7). This group home was used by the East Valley Behavioral Health Association (EVBHA) which initially purchased all eight beds. The first child was admitted May 19, 1989 (Baker 1989). Because of the high acuity of behavior, considerable property damage took place resulting in high-maintenance costs. In time, EVBHA withdrew its block purchase of beds and established a "fee-for-service," which means they paid only for the filled beds. These two factors, together with the small size, eventually led to the decision to close the group home and move the boys to the now vacated old Journey Group Home at 3118 W. Missouri in Phoenix. The move, made on February 27, 1997, would not increase the number of beds, but the house was owned by ABCS, and it was vacant. Its proximity to the Little Canyon Residential Treatment Center across the street made it less costly to operate and easier to supervise. In addition, this move would be temporary until a larger place could be found for the Bell boys. The Bell House in Mesa sold April 15, 1997.

Journey Group Home Move

The Journey Group Home for boys (the former Bell Group Home), ages eight through twelve, was opened at 3118 W. Missouri, on June 1, 1991 (Baker 1991). This house had been sold earlier by ABCS, but the buyer defaulted on the loan, and this house and an adjoining house were returned to the ownership of ABCS. It was then remodeled and well served its purpose as a group home, except that it was not cost-effective to operate. ABCS learned that a group home needed a capacity of at least eight residents to pay for itself. A search began for a larger house that could serve eight youth.

Obtaining a use permit for a group home in a modest to upscale Phoenix neighborhood is almost impossible, but the ABCS administration, with the help of maintenance coordinator Les Jennings, Jr., did find a very suitable home at the corner of Forty-seventh Avenue and Campo Bello. It was remodeled and the garage retrofitted into offices and storage space. On December 11, 1996, the Journey boys moved from their small quarters at 3118 W. Missouri to their new address in Northwest Phoenix. This was the only group home to remain at its present location when all other ABCS Phoenix programs moved to the John F. and Mary P. Long Family Life Development Center on Peoria in 2001.

Closure of Glendale Campus—1997

The Glendale Campus, located at 5115, 5125, and 5133 W. Myrtle, housed at different times the emergency shelter, group homes, independent living preparation program, and maintenance facilities. The first and largest of the three properties, 5125, was purchased February 1, 1982. It served as an emergency shelter for boys from that date until 1994 at which time it was divided into two group homes. This was due to the underutilization of the shelter. In addition, DES informed the ABCS staff that group homes would be more utilized.

The emergency shelter at 5125 W. Myrtle was also used as the site for the Wrangler Program, the ABCS independent-living program. It began with four beds and was enlarged to eight beds when the program was moved from 5125 to a newly purchased house at 5115 W. Myrtle in June 1985. This adjoining property, purchased from George Duff, added to the size of the Glendale Campus and allowed both the shelter and independent living preparation programs to increase their bed capacity.

A small maintenance building was constructed on the 5125 property and became the maintenance center for all of ABCS. A third house, also adjoining the 5125 property, was purchased from Nancy Spann in March 1990. This one-thousand-square-foot residence was too small and deteriorated to use for anything but storage; however, it allowed the Glendale campus property to be enlarged.

In 1996, it became apparent that the Bunkhouse campus buildings were deteriorating faster than ABCS could maintain them. This was in spite of enormous help from volunteers and the addition of staff to maintain the facilities. The troubled youth in the program expressed their anger and frustration by damaging the property.

The shelter was licensed for twenty-six boys, and in 1996 the average census was 18.3, which didn't pay the bills. The deficit in FY 1995-96 was $100,411 and $70,432 during the first six months of FY 1996-97. The underutilization was a direct result of the inferior and deteriorated physical condition of the facilities. In addition, DES had licensed forty new group homes in the past twelve months, and they were in far better condition than the ABCS facilities.

Another issue that cannot be overlooked was the needy condition of the youth being referred to the ABCS group homes at the Bunkhouse. The seriousness of their behavioral-health needs exceeded the ability of this program to appropriately serve them. DES was using the group homes as an inexpensive treatment center, and this was neither appropriate nor workable. The facility and the staff were being burned-out, and the 70.4 percent occupancy rate was insufficient to pay for the cost of care.

The decision was made to temporarily close the Glendale Campus by March 1, 1997 (ABCS Board Executive Committee 1997). A task force was appointed by President Baker to study the best use for the Glendale Campus (Baker 1997). President Baker wrote to the board:

This is our greatest challenge. This property houses three residential units in two buildings: The Bunkhouse, our former 16 bed shelter, is now two group homes—Bunkhouse and Challenger (both under one roof). The Wrangler House for Independent living preparation, is south east of that building but on the same campus. It is actually landlocked with access only by an alley. The Wrangler House is in the worst condition imaginable. It was not built for its present type of use. We have provided an enormous amount of repair and remodeling on the house, but we cannot keep up with the deterioration. The Bunkhouse has been studied by architects and a remodeling plan is being developed which includes the interior, exterior, landscaping, and the surrounding building on the property, i.e., the Spann House and Wrangler House. However, we are also studying the best use for this property and will certainly involve our board in that discussion. We do not have a funding source for the extensive remodeling that needs to be done. (Baker, Board Memo 96-8, 1996)

One of the early efforts to determine the "best use" of the campus was to have a study done to determine the feasibility of future campus use. A study was done and a report submitted by Searer, Robbins & Stephens Inc. The elaborate campus master plan, which the architects developed, was beautiful and included remodeling of the Bunkhouse and Wrangler House, as well as construction of a new shop and maintenance building. The estimated cost was $410,290 (Searer, Robbins, & Stephens Inc. 1997). Neither the administration nor the board believed that the use of the campus for the two group homes could support this investment.

The same resolution reflecting the decision of the Glendale Campus Future Use Committee recommended that the campus be sold. An appraisal had been done by Michael W. Housecraft & Associates in the preceding July. Their conclusion was "the existing improvements have no contributory value to the overall subject property value . . .," and therefore the appraisal applied only to land. The appraisal was 99,724 square feet at $1.50/square foot for an appraisal of $150,000. It was noted elsewhere in the report that if a similar use to the present use could be made, the value would be much greater (Michael W. Huscroft & Associates 1997). The property was sold to another children's services agency, which was able to use the buildings after remodeling.

AzCare

ABCS and two other local child and family service agencies formed a for-profit corporation on June 23, 1994, called AcurCare Group Arizona Inc. It was a franchise of AcurCare Group, LLP, of Houston, Texas.

The purpose of the corporation was to provide an employee assistance program (EAP) for businesses and agencies who wished to add this service to its employee benefits. The staff consisted of a director and several experienced counselors who were qualified to deal with many problems, including substance abuse, divorce, mental health, grief, housing, elder care, and a variety of other problems that affected the performance of employees in the workplace. If an employee was frequently late, appeared depressed, or upset, the supervisor in a business could refer the employee to the EAP at no cost to the employee. The employer paid a monthly fee based upon the number of employees that would be covered. The first meeting of the board took place May 3, 1994, and committees were formed, and officers were elected.

When AcurCare Group, LLP, was sold to PacifiCare Behavioral Health Inc., AcurCare Group Arizona Inc. had the choice of being a part of the acquisition or pulling out. It did the latter, and changed its name to AzCare Inc. on August 1, 1995. The program grew rapidly but so did competition. When the idea was first conceived, there were two EAPs in the Phoenix area. By 1997, there were ten. By 1996, the program had reached a crossroads.

Several solutions were explored that were not satisfactory to the board. ABCS made an offer to the AzCare Board to purchase the shares of stock owned by the other two partners. The offer was accepted April 2, 1996, making ABCS the sole owner of AzCare Inc. stock. The board met May 15 and approved the new directors and elected officers. The Amended Articles of Incorporation and Bylaws were approved. Mark Dickerson, an attorney serving on both the ABCS and AzCare boards, did the legal work, which was an enormous job. The reason behind this decision was that the EAP was compatible with other ABCS programs.

Plans were being made to develop a statewide network of services. This would mean that ABCS would have counselors working in many areas of the state, which would provide a counseling presence for AzCare as well as ABCS programs. The idea made sense. Archie Stephens, longtime board member of ABCS and board member for AzCare, representing ABCS, was asked to accept the position as the director for new ABCS

EPA (Baker, Board Memo #96-6, 1996). He accepted the offer and began immediately to solicit additional contracts. At the time of the acquisition, AzCare had twelve contracts covering 3,040 lives. The average per-person fee for the EAP services was $3.28, which participating companies paid monthly for each employee. One of the largest contracts was with the Tempe Elementary School District with 1,744 employees.

It became apparent in mid-1997 that it might be unwise to continue funding AzCare. The program was so close to the break-even point, which made the decision to sell very difficult. Mr. Stephens was asked to contact brokers and begin the process of divesting ABCS of its EPA business. Two companies had expressed a strong interest in purchasing AzCare. One was a local hospital, and the other was Blue Cross/Blue Shield of Montana. AzCare's days were numbered, and that was sad for all involved. The EAP received high marks from its customers and had an excellent service record.[5]

Americorps

Similar to the peace corps, Americorps is a federal program for youth who were willing to give a year of service to a nonprofit organization in return for a small stipend and help with college costs. The Arizona Council of Centers for Children and Adults (ACCCA) was the Arizona sponsor for the program. ABCS and eleven other member agencies of ACCCA chose to participate. Kerri Goncher-Cardenas was one of eighteen original Americorps members who worked in one of the eleven agencies. Kerri worked in the educational program of ABCS and received national recognition when the *New York Times* did an article on the program. She worked for two years in the ABCS program before being asked to coordinate the statewide Americorps program for ACCCA. She was a "natural" with the kids and her contribution to the ABCS educational program was described as "invaluable" (The Insider 1996, 4).

---

[5]   In time, the program was sold, but it was after the period covered by this history.

New Strategies for Excellence

Total Quality Management (TQM)

Since the onset of the Baker administration, quality as a principle and quality as an outcome have been an ongoing goal. ABCS was initially introduced to the concept of quality management through the JCAHO accreditation process. The culture developed from that eventually affected all programs, as well as the way associates thought about program development. Juxtaposed to that was the belief that quality facilities and programs were an expression of Christian commitment and were thus honoring to God.

President Baker reported in his quarterly report that Dr. Tina Olson, former dean of Nursing at Grand Canyon University, had been employed as chief quality officer for ABCS (Baker, "Quarterly Report," 1996). Prior to coming to ABCS, Dr. Olson was chief quality officer for Western HealthCare Alliance, a subsidiary of Samaritan Health Systems. She introduced ABCS associates to the W. Edward Deming system of quality improvement. Deming's "fourteen points" are legendary in the health care and business fields (Deming 1986).

Following Dr. Olson's introduction of this popular method of implementing quality management, the weeks and months were filled with making storyboards, flowcharting, creating Pareto charts and indicators. The total quality management (TQM) culture has its own vocabulary and symbols, and the associates picked these up quickly under the skilled leadership of the chief quality officer. Associates were taught the F-O-C-U-S-A-P-I-E acronym, which outlined the quality implementing process.

The Deming Quality Management Process

F   Find a key process to improve.

O   Organize a team that knows the process.

C   Clarify current knowledge of the process.

U   Understand causes of process variation.

S   Select steps in the process to measure, prioritize, and improve.

A   Assess identified steps in the process by trending measures.

P   Plan process improvement based upon trended measures.

I   Implement process improvement.

E   Evaluate process improvement.

After identifying a process that needed improvement, a team would be formed and a plan developed to improve the particular process. This process would be charted on what was called a "storyboard." Visualizing the process on the chart helped to identify weaknesses and cut out unnecessary steps in the problem-solving process. As various groups completed their problem-solving process, they would use their storyboard to explain the process to other associates.

1997 ABCS Quality Improvement Committee Structure

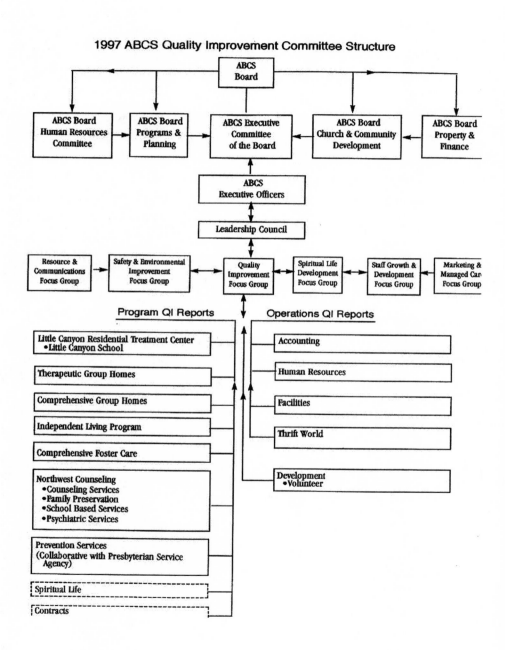

As associates gained skill in the TQM process, a plan was developed to guide future implementations, and this plan would be included in the agency's General Operating Procedures manual (Policy Manual 1996, ABCS). The TQM method became a part of the agency culture and would continue to be utilized in the JCAHO accreditation process. The impact was greater than merely creating a formalized method for TQM. The philosophy of excellence would be a part of all planning and implementation at ABCS. Who would have thought that the little house at 3101 W. Missouri would one day find expression in regional offices around the state?

The reach for excellence did not stop after Baker's departure. A recently employed associate and former trustee wrote the following memo to another associate in 2001: "Continue to communicate and promote with your staff, the elements of a 'value driven' approach to management, which includes changing to and maintaining our organizational culture as a continuous improvement, participatory culture . . ." (McDaniel n.d.).

The Focus Groups Network

The Staff Advisory Council was an early effort in the Baker administration to involve associates of the various programs in the total agency management. The associates' representative on the council, Barbara Hunter, wrote in the agency newsletter, "One of the main purposes of the Staff Advisory Council is to enhance communication between line staff and program coordinators" (Hunter 1985, 3).

In addition to "enhancing communication," the council developed a system of staff incentives. A list of incentives was included in a later agency publication listing everything from receiving an agency jacket or T-shirt, to use of the ABCS tent trailer for vacations (McFarland 1985). Although each program was represented on the council, all associates were invited to attend, depending upon their work schedules. This plan worked well but was later incorporated in a better organized and more focused plan of involvement and program implementation involving the associates.

This better plan, called the "Focus Groups Network," was started in 1996 during the formation of the strategic plan, "Building a Future for Children." The idea was to use this process to implement the goals of the campaign. It was highly organized and representative of the ABCS programs. The heart of the program was the "focus group" of which there were seven.

Focus Groups

1. Marketing and Managed Care
2. Safety and Environmental Improvement
3. Standards and Clinical Practice
4. Staff Growth and Development
5. Spiritual Life Development
6. Publicity and Communications
7. Resource Development

The various focus groups empowered the associates in the agency. In time, additional groups could be added, combined, or deleted, depending upon the needs of the agency. The groups were each made up of three types of members: (1) staff advisors, (2) program representatives, and (3) community advisors.

Recommended actions or policy would be developed at the focus group level, and then presented to the executive officers, who in turn would review and return the recommendation to the group, forward it on to the board, or reject it. Staff advisors were permanent members of each focus group, while program representatives and community advisors were asked to serve a minimum of one year, but their tenure could be extended.

The Leadership Council, composed of program coordinators, would continue to be a part of the network. The Leadership Council served as an executive committee for the network.

1. The purpose of the focus groups was to develop and implement quality standards for their specific focus in ABCS; to provide team leadership for implementing agency goals relative to the group's special focus; to be the primary component of the management

structure and make recommendations regarding plans in their specialty area.

An implementation plan would then be worked out for each task. The whole rationale was to involve associates in the planning, management, and operations of the agency using the synergy of creative ideas from the associates and from the community. The system worked well and created a great deal of excitement among the associates. The president was asked to present this plan to the staff of another agency who later adopted it as their management system.

There were at least two challenges, which this system presented. First, because of the shift system of caring for the children in the residential programs, it was difficult to schedule meetings that were convenient to all group members. Second, it was difficult for programs with smaller staff, such as foster care, to have representatives on each focus group. Other than this, the system was welcomed by associates and strengthened morale and investment.

FOCUS GROUP NETWORK
Leadership Enhancement and Goal's Implementation Process

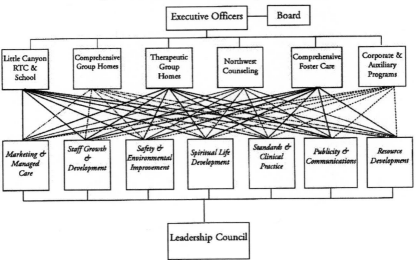

As the regional centers and adoption programs were added and other programs discontinued, adjustments would be made to the organizational chart. The chart represented the programs that were active at the time the Focus Groups Network was developed.

"Building A Future for Children"—Strategic Planning

Strategic planning has already been pointed out as a hallmark of the Baker administration. There were times when the administration was accused of "too much planning" and not enough "doing." The answer to this was always, "How much is too much?" Baker had a strong conviction that success didn't just happen—it was planned! Planning helps to identify resources, establish real needs, set reachable goals, assign focused tasks, and evaluate progress.

Planning was done in blocks of time from three to five years. Many believed that five years was too long for times that were changing as dramatically as they did in the past ten years. This led to a unique approach in planning. Long-range *directions* would be identified, and then annual goals would implement those major directions. In the "Building a Future . . ." planning model, the idea of *directions* was replaced with *principles* that were developed that kept planning focused upon the mission and specific priorities. These would be similar to the *goals and controls* later introduced by ABCS President David Jakes.

In 1995, the agency set out to develop a five-year strategic plan called "Building A Future for Children—1996-2000." The focus groups were involved in developing this ambitious plan. The first step in strategic planning was to define the mission statement. At that time the mission statement read, "The mission of Arizona Baptist Children's Services is to provide the highest quality services to children, adults, and families in the name of Christ and on behalf of Arizona Southern Baptists."

Ten principles were established that would guide all planning and goal setting:

1. All programs must offer the opportunity for Christian witness.
2. Funding must be diversified. Efforts must be made to minimize dependence upon any single source of revenue. Plans should call for a balance between purchase of care, insurance, fees for service, donations, grants, and endowment.
3. Programs must be developed in all regions of the state in addition to Maricopa County.
4. Programs should include long-term provision for children who cannot return to their own homes and are not suitable for foster care or adoption. This would include community-based group homes or a campus environment.
5. Major attention would be given to strengthening current programs and developing new programs that support families in their efforts to care for their children.
6. Every reasonable effort would be made to provide permanency for children and ensure that children remain in substitute care for as brief a time as possible.
7. Programs should be considered that support churches in their efforts to minister to families.
8. Programs must be of the highest possible quality.
9. There must be processes to measure quality and outcomes.
10. Programs must pay for themselves unless they are determined to be strategic in carrying out the mission of the agency or strengthening already existing programs. Such programs will then be subsidized with a capped limit.

When David Jakes began his work as financial/business consultant with ABCS in 1997, he introduced a unique system of planning that took the Baker planning model another step forward. It was a computerized program that he had previously used in his consultation work with other organizations. It was a more practical, utilitarian, day-by-day monitoring of "goals and controls" coupled with "operational indicators" that could compare current results with earlier established benchmarks in every area of agency life. It included specific assignments and time lines for getting goals completed. It was more pragmatic as compared with Baker's earlier theoretical and principle-based model. Everyone recognized immediately that this was what was needed. Every committee or group meeting would begin with a review of the "operational indicators" and "goals and controls."

Home-Based/Family-Based Services[6]

Two major directions were established that would give general guidance to expansion from 1996 to 2000. The first was a commitment to develop family-based services to help children remain in their own home. This would involve giving parents the tools to help their own children and being available to support them in their efforts to be effective parents. The second major direction was to establish regional centers throughout the state to make those family-based services more accessible.

As the needs of children and families changed over the years, so has the response to those needs. To summarize:

** In the 1870s to the 1940s, care was provided for the orphans.
** In the 1940s to the 1960s, care was provided for the "social orphans"—children whose problems required more help than their own parents were willing or capable of giving.

---

[6]   Home-based and Family-based Services are used interchangeably.

** In the 1960s, the importance of families was realized, and families were included in the treatment process, but it was still believed that the child was best served outside of his/her own home when the child's behavior was out of control.

Traditional services to neglected, dependent, or troubled children largely involved removing them from their homes as already pointed out. Home or family-based services are programs designed to help families remain together. Efforts could involve counseling, education, respite care, provision of resources, and referral to specialized services. The idea is to provide sufficient support to the parents and guidance in child management sufficient to allow children to remain in their own home.

In the late nineteenth and early twentieth centuries, single mothers, or even both parents, would place their children in orphanages simply because they could not afford to care for them. The First White House Conference on Children in 1909 declared that poverty should never be the sole reason for removing children from their homes. This was not fully implemented until the Social Security Act of 1931, which provided aid to dependent children (ADC), which later became aid to families with dependent children (AFDC). This was the first step in developing "family-based services."

Family-Based Services and Family Preservation would describe a variety of new programs initiated and funded by the federal government in the 1980s and 1990s. These programs were designed to keep families together and avoid, as much as possible, their removal except in instances of severe neglect and abuse.

The efforts of the federal government to support and keep families together got into high gear with the Adoption Assistance and Child Welfare Act of 1980, known as Public Law (PL) 96-272. It was a response to "foster care drift," which is the tendency of child-welfare agencies to allow children to remain for excessive periods of time in foster care. The law was enacted to reform the foster-care system. Two goals of the program were the "improvement of preventive services to avoid unnecessary removal of children from their homes . . . more efficient case planning and efforts to reunify families" (American Bar Association Juvenile and Child Welfare Legislative Report n.d., 167).

Congress approved, and President Clinton signed into law the Omnibus Budget Reconciliation Act of 1993. This act would provide one billion dollars in child-welfare funds to the states for the next five years for a variety of early intervention and prevention services designed to strengthen, preserve, and support families (Bourdette 1993, 1).

This early effort in family reunification and preservation was followed by the Adoption and Safe Families Act of 1997, PL 105-89. This bill was signed into law by the president on November 19, 1997. Both of these acts were designed to assist the states in their efforts to protect children and families. Within the perimeters of federal guidelines, states would develop a plan to provide permanency for children by supporting families. (Child Welfare League of America 1997).

The Adoption and Safe Families Act funding led to the development of numerous programs to keep children in their own homes and return children home from out-of-home placement. Some of the programs would be developed by state child-welfare agencies, and some programs would be purchased by states through private agencies.

In 1994, the Arizona Department of Economic Security began development of the first Five Year Plan to implement the act in Arizona. Two statewide advisory groups composed of community and agency representatives guided the yearlong task in developing the plan. [7]

Arizona Baptist Children's Services would be in the forefront of providing these special services to Arizona children and families while continuing to increase the effectiveness of its residential and foster-care programs. ABCS began to develop a "full continuum of care" with the exception of secure in-patient psychiatric care, and even that would be a strong possibility through contracting with an existing hospital. As the system and programs changed, ABCS continued to offer the same continuum of care, but those services that supported family-based

---

[7]   The writer served on one of those committees.

programs and permanency would be strengthened and expanded in a statewide network.

Family support can mean anything from financial help to counseling. This is a generic term that embraces the belief that the best thing that can be done for a child is to help the child's parents to be better-equipped parents. The distinction can no longer be made between caring for children and serving families. Every program at ABCS is now geared toward family support. The newer programs such as Family Preservation and Family Builders incorporate social technology that supported the earlier ABCS family-based philosophy.

It would be helpful to illustrate the concept of family-based services by describing several of those programs at ABCS. Readers will observe that each of these home/family-based programs have much in common, but they also have distinctive elements. The common elements include building on family strengths and supporting families in their desire to help their own children. Another common element is the availability and use of many community resources through collaboration with other community agencies. Several of the programs are described here.

> "The distinction can no longer be made between caring for children and serving families"

Family Builders

The history of this program goes back to the 1954 through 1959 St. Paul Project, a special initiative to help unmotivated and multiproblem families in St. Paul, Minnesota's public housing (Bart 1956). The Homebuilders program in Iowa and Washington was a similar strengths-based and family-focused program (Nelson and Allen 1989).

This new Family Builders pilot program was approved by the Arizona legislature in 1997, and services didn't require the usual eligibility requirements. The Family Builders' pilot program began January 1, 1998, in Maricopa and Pima counties, the state's two largest counties, and would sunset as a pilot June 30, 2000. The Family Builders program was an innovative alternative response system to reports of child abuse and neglect, implemented through a unique and exciting public/private partnership. Recognizing that not every report of abuse or neglect requires a full-fledged investigation by Child Protective Services (CPS), the program was designed to respond to selected low-risk reports of child maltreatment through a network of community-based providers[8]

ABCS was one of eight provider-coalitions to be awarded a contract. The coalition would serve thirty-eight zip codes in the northwest area of Maricopa County. ABCS organized approximately forty collaborators into the coalition, which was called Strengthening Arizona Families (SAF). The purpose of the collaboration was to provide resources, which were needed for the families to remain together. When CPS received a report of abuse or neglect in northwest Maricopa County, it was triaged[9]; and if not a high priority, it would be referred to the SAF response team. Acceptance of services was voluntary, and if the family consented to receiving services, they would receive an evaluation rather than an

Russ Yost, director, ABCS--SAF

investigation. They would be offered services that would diminish the circumstances that warranted the "hotline"[10] call.

The services offered to the family, through the collaborators, could be counseling, housing, parent skills training, parent-aid services, day care, food, transportation, respite services, utility payments, medical care, and other resources too numerous to list. The motto was, "Whatever it takes." It could include something as simple as paying a utility bill or something as complex as providing dental work to enable a parent to return to work. It could include repair of an automobile so the parent would have transportation to work. Case-management staff did the evaluations and served as "brokers

---

[8] The writer acknowledges the contribution of Anna Arnold, program manager for Arizona DES, for much of the Family Builders program language.

[9] Sorted according to priority.

[10] The term used for a child-abuse report

of services." ABCS would later form coalitions in other parts of the state through its regional centers. Russ Yost, a longtime counselor with ABCS, became the director of the ABCS-SAF program in Maricopa County.

The following is a true story, but the names have been changed to ensure confidentiality.

The ABCS SAF team attempted a home visit to Kerri and her family. She was not present when the team knocked at the door of her studio motel room. Kerri had five daughters living with her in the motel. She was also involved with an abusive man at the time. The team identified the boyfriend's vehicle, and made return home visit attempts when he was not present. Eventually, the team met the oldest daughter who relayed to her mother that a Family Builders team was offering to help the family. Kerri was hesitant at first to accept help, supposing that the offer was actually a clever ploy by CPS to get her children.

She arranged to meet the team at her workplace. Kerri told the team she had been married to a war veteran who treated her with anger and abuse when he returned from the battlefield. Kerri was punched in the mouth repeatedly which broke her teeth allowing infection to set in. She finally had the courage to end the relationship and her husband then took his life, leaving her alone with her girls. This was not the last abusive relationship for Kerri. She worked full-time but missed work due to toothaches for the untreated infections in her mouth. She qualified for AHCCCS (Arizona's Medicaid program), but had been unable to find an AHCCCS dentist who would pull more than one tooth per appointment. The SAF case manager located a dentist who agreed to pull all of Kerri's teeth and provide her with dentures at a reduced rate. Kerri had not been able to attend work regularly and provide for her children. She then ended her relationship with her boyfriend and paid a rental deposit on a two-bedroom condominium with assistance from her employer. Her brother provided funds to turn on her utilities. The SAF team provided the family with a washer and dryer, beds and clothing. An ABCS associate provided counseling. The SAF case manager was able to refer the family to a church that agreed to collaborate with the team and provide mentoring. When the case was closed, the church mentor would continue to provide support to the family.

Letters of appreciation were often received from former Family Builders' clients. One lady who almost lost her son because of her addiction to drugs wrote the following: " . . . appreciate everything you have done for me and my son and daughter. Instead of getting high on drugs, I can get high on the love for my kids . . . I will learn a trade so that I can make a living. I feel that finally my life is going to be all right . . . you really made a difference in my life. I thank God for sending you when I needed you. (*Footprints* 1998, 8)

Intensive Family Preservation (IFP)

The IFP program is similar in many ways to Family Builders; however, it is more focused upon intervention, training, and treatment when families are in crisis. The Family Builders program had a broader focus with emphasis upon providing tangible services, but the difference may only be one of degree since there is overlap. IFP associates are trained in cultural awareness, assessment, goal setting, parent education, techniques in defusing violence and anger among family members, short-term counseling, stress management, just to name some of the skill areas.

Restoring Arizona Family Traditions (RAFT)

RAFT is a home-based program of the juvenile court to help young offenders to live in their own homes. It is a multisystemic approach targeting those factors responsible for the young person's presence in the juvenile justice system. The treatment approach utilizes a psycho-educational and skills-oriented method of intervention. The RAFT therapist must have a master's degree in some area of human services and receive special training in the operation of this program, including training in the Homebuilders model of service delivery.

ABCS was awarded the exclusive contract for Maricopa, Yuma, and La Paz counties in 1999. Prior to that, RAFT services were available in Maricopa County. Jeff Evilsizor was employed as the RAFT therapist for

Maricopa County, January 8, 1996 (President's Quarterly Report, 1996). The intake process and program mechanics were much the same as the earlier described family-based services.

Abstinence Only

This Maricopa County program, to encourage abstinence, was an education program for schools, churches, and youth organizations. The contract to implement this program was done through a coalition of agencies including ABCS, Christian Family Care, and Catholic Social Services (Baker, "Presidents Quarterly," 1998, 2). While a good idea, unfortunately it was short-lived due to lack of participation and the program restrictions. It was closed the following year (Jakes 1999).

Parent Aid Program

The ABCS Parent Aid program began in July 2000, following the contract award from DES. During the first year of operation, fifty referrals were received. This was increased to seventy-three referrals during the second year. The number more than doubled in 2003. The overall purpose and process of the Parent Aid program are similar to the two programs previously described. It is more focused on teaching culturally sensitive parenting skills and empowering parents to provide a safe, nurturing, and resource-rich environment for all family members. Emphasis is upon preventing child abuse and neglect following children's removal from their homes by the court. In addition to teaching parenting skills, parents learn home-management skills and can take job-readiness training.

School-Based Services

School-Based Services was a program funded by ComCare, the Phoenix area Regional Behavioral Health Authority (RBHA), to help at-risk children in the early elementary grades. Joyce Willis, the coordinator, and six other therapists worked in seventeen schools in six school districts, serving children ages five to twelve (Gillespie 1996). The therapist worked with children in small groups and with the permission of the parents. Ms. Willis described the program:

We work with kids who have difficulties with anger management, oppositional defiance, and authority figures, as well as with ones who need to improve their social skills . . . the purpose was to help children learn different ways of coping and become more comfortable with themselves. (*Footprints* 1996, 3)

Counselors made monthly visits to the home of each child to review the child's progress in the program and support the parents in their efforts to provide the best parenting possible to their children.

This was one of the most effective programs in providing early intervention for children whose behavior could easily escalate in acuity and lead to serious problems later in their lives. The program was very consistent with the family-based model for helping children and families.

Summary

As the title of the chapter indicates, the period of 1994-1999 was a time of constructing new buildings, fund-raising, resizing, and beginning regional programs. New programs were started, and older programs were closed. This was all part of a steady growth that strained resources and nerves. Quality management and strategic planning overshadowed this period of unprecedented growth as ABCS moved from a primarily residential program to one that was family and home based. It moved from serving primarily in Phoenix to a statewide service ministry. The "For the Children" campaign brought wider recognition and support for ABCS and the Spiritual Renewal weeks started by Chaplain Mike Ransbottom kept the agency reminded of its true purpose and source of strength. The best that can be said was that lives were changed and families were strengthened.

References

ABCS Board. 1998. Closing of ABCS Thrift World. *Resolution 98-P&F-3* approved by the board, June 5.

ABCS Board Executive Committee. 1995. Offer on Sunglow Ranch. Board Resolution 95-E-1 approved by the committee, February 9.

_____. 1997. Temporary closure of Glendale Campus. Board Resolution 97-ADM-1 approved by the committee, February 6.

American Bar Association Juvenile and Child Welfare Legislative Report. n.d. Judicial and Administrative Case Law Under PL 96-272. Undated monologue sent to agencies by the Child Welfare League of America titled Implementing Adoption Assistance & Child Welfare Act of 1980, PL 96-272, 64 Irving Place, New York, NY 10003.

Baker, C. Truett. 1989. A time for every matter. President's annual report. June.

_____. 1987. Tentative Ranch Use Plan. Board Memo. August 26.

_____. 1991. Keys to success. President's annual report. June 30.

_____. 1995. Transitions. president's annual Report. June 30.

_____. 1996a. Board Memo #96-6. June 17.

_____. 1996b. Board Memo # 96-8. August.

_____. 1996c. Board Memo # 96-9. September.

_____. 1996d. President's quarterly report to the board. October-December.

_____. 1997. Best-Use-of-Glendale-Campus Task Force. Memo to board chairman Mark Dickerson. March 13.

_____. 1998. President's quarterly report to the board. October- December.

Baptist Beacon. 1996. Children's Services Ceremony Marks Start of Chapel Building. 57 (September): 19.

Bart, Charles J. 1956. Family-Centered Project of St. Paul. *Social Work,* vol. 1.

Board Resolution 95-ADMIN-6. 1995. Authorization to use Baptist Builders for construction of LCC chapel/classroom building. Approved December 1.

Bourdette, Mary. 1993. Victory on child welfare/family preservation initiative. Memo sent out to members of the Child Welfare League of America. August 9.

Child Welfare League of America. 1997. Adoption and Safe Families Act, PL 105-89. *Washington Social Legislative Bulletin* 35, no. 23.

Child Welfare League of America. 1997. The Adoption and Save Families Act, PL 105-89. *Washington Social Legislative Bulletin*, December 8. 35, no. 23.

Deming, W. Edward. 1986. *Out of the Crisis.* Cambridge: MIT Press.

Footprints. 1995. The Long Way.

_____. 1996. Reading, Writing and Therapy. Spring.

_____. 1998. Sisterly' Love. Summer.

_____. 1998. Thank-You, ABCS. Fall.

Gillespie, Jason. 1996. Northwest Counseling Services quarterly report. President's second quarter report to the board of trustees. October-December.

Hunter, Barbara. 1985. From the Advisory Council. *ATAT*. 2 (April): 4.

Jakes, P. David. 1999. President's Annual Report. June.

McDaniel, Don. n.d. 2001 Performance Plan and Evaluation. Memo sent to Senior Vice President, Operations, ABCS, Phoenix, AZ.

McFarland, Phyllis. 1985. Report From SAC. *ATAT* 2 (June): 6.

Michael W. Huscroft & Associates. 1997. A limited summary appraisal report of the property located at 5115, 5125, 5133 W. Myrtle Avenue, Glendale, AZ. Prepared for Arizona Baptist Children's Services, July 18.

Minutes 1992, ABCS Board, March 19.

Nelson, Kristine E. and Marcia Allen. 1989. Public-private provision of family-based services research findings. Unpublished paper presented at the National Association for Family-Based Services, Third Annual Empowering Families Conference, November, Charlotte, NC.

Policy Manual 1996, ABCS, C-1, GOP-V, 01/05/96

Ransbottom, Mike. 1999. Chaplaincy services report. Minutes, ABCS Board of Trustees, June 4.

_____. 2000. Chaplaincy. Minutes. ABCS Board Of Trustees, September 22.

Searer, Robbins & Stephens Inc. 1997. A place called home: a renovation of Glendale Campus for ABCS. January 7.

The Insider 1996, Americorps, September-October.

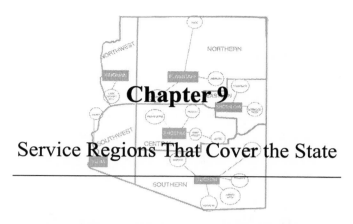

Chapter 9

Service Regions That Cover the State

The Period 1994-1999: "The Baker Years," Part 4

Into All the State

This is the second major direction, which resulted from the "For the Children" strategic plan. The first was developing home-based services. The second direction was the commitment to establish family ministry centers in the six areas of the state. The reasoning was that the services of ABCS needed to be available to all Arizona families—not just those in Maricopa County. For many years, the Baptist constituency that supported ABCS outside of Maricopa County has requested that services be available in their areas. More and more, the interest of donors was to support programs in their area of the state.

Equally as important as the interest of the Baptist Family were the changes created by a new understanding of what was best for children and families (referred to as "best practice"). When the primary programs for children were residential, children could be sent to the children's home or later to the residential treatment center in Phoenix regardless of where they lived. When their residence at Little Canyon Center was over, they could then return home or to another form of permanent care. However, the new direction was to provide services to keep children in their own homes. To achieve this, it was necessary to have the family-based services brought to the family in their own area. The earlier model was to take children to the services. The new model was to take the services to the children and their families. For this to be possible, there must be family-support centers nearby with the staff and resources to help those families. Those services must be available on a daily basis.

The early groundwork had been laid for work outside of Maricopa County (Minutes 1985, ABCS Board). The motivation for those early efforts was good, but the implementation was always undercapitalized. One of the guidelines in the new strategic plan required that regional centers have one year's operating expenses raised before a center could open. This involved developing a budget for the region, which was done jointly with the development council. When the council raised the needed amount, the ABCS president worked with the council in employing a regional director. The director would then implement the other plans necessary to open the center. The regional directors, who were members of the leadership council, would come to Phoenix for monthly council meetings.

Regional Development Councils (RDC)

The local Regional Development Council was at the center of the regional planning process. The following information describes the plan that was followed to implement the opening of each regional center.

Background

The 1996-2000 Strategic Plan for Arizona Baptist Children's Services called for a shift from being a strictly residential services program in Phoenix to a model that was family-based throughout the state. This was a time-consuming and expensive effort because of the complexity of developing programs that must pay for themselves through state-contracted services. A decision to begin a regional center was based upon the expressed desire and support of the Southern Baptist churches in a particular area. The ABCS president would initially meet with the directors of missions/ evangelism in that region to determine the extent of their interest.

Purpose of the Regional Development Councils

1. To further determine if there was sufficient interest and resources in the area to have an ABCS Regional Family Support Center and to develop a plan for opening the center
2. To cultivate interest in and develop resources for the total ABCS ministry
3. To identify potential areas of need that could be met by the regional center

The following programs were offered in Maricopa County by ABCS. The regional centers would rely on the experience of ABCS in developing their own program that would be unique to their area.

> Foster care
> Counseling
> In-home crisis intervention
> School-based services
> Parent education
> Prevention services
> Adoption
> After-school programs
> Family-preservation programs (Family Builders, RAFT, Parent Aid, etc.)

The early days of regional operation were critical and required strong support from the central office in Phoenix. It was necessary to have a director of regional programs to provide this support when the time came. Steve Hanna would later be appointed to this position, in addition to his Southern Regional duties. This director would also be the key ABCS staff member who worked with the regional directors and development councils.

Southern Regional Center in Tucson

Regional development would be a slow process. Don Cain first tried to start programs in Tucson. The Baker administration then started counseling centers in Tucson, Show Low, Casa Grande, and the East Valley. These lasted for only a short time, but it was a start. In 1985, the board was instrumental in beginning an advisory council in Tucson at the same time that a counseling program was started in the city's Emmanuel Baptist Church.

Rev. Joe Chan, ABCS Trustee
and Southern Regional Advisor

Having Sunglow Ranch in that area was an encouragement to start other work, and the ranch manager was involved in the development council meetings. The ABCS Board members from the Tucson area that served on the local advisory council were Joe Chan, Barbara Huff, Marvin Humble, and Steve Hanna. Mrs. Myra Calcote, who served as a volunteer and later as office secretary, was appointed regional representative for ABCS and faithfully supported ABCS in the Tucson area for many years. Marvin Humble served also as a regional representative; and he and his wife, Ginny, also worked as Sunglow Ranch managers.

Steve Hanna, Southern
Region Director

The development council continued to give leadership to regional planning when the decision was made to reestablish a permanent Tucson presence. This was a part of the larger ABCS plan to develop work in several regions of Arizona. Joe Chan was elected by the group as chair of the council. Committees were formed to carry out the work of initial implementation.

In the course of the planning, it was learned that Christian Family Care Agency in Phoenix had an office in Tucson, and they were interested in working with ABCS. A plan, involving collaboration with Christian Family Care, was submitted to the ABCS Board. It was approved with a beginning date of January 1, 1998.

This collaboration with Christian Family Care Agency resulted in making office space available to ABCS. Steve Hanna, an ABCS Board member, was asked to be the regional director of the Southern Arizona office of ABCS. He accepted and went to work setting up the new office and starting programs. Family-life education, counseling, and family-support programs were among the early programs offered by the center. Later, foster care and adoption were added. Steve was creative and successful in starting programs and, in time, developed a shelter program for abused women and children. The development council was always supportive and gave direction to the program. In time, the center would have its own offices at 1779 N. Alvernon Way.

By June 1999, Director Steve Hanna reported that over 150 people attended various family workshops over the past quarter; five churches were participating in the church counseling pilot program; two couples began the application process for becoming foster parents. (Hanna 1999). The Tucson Center started satellite counseling sites at Sierra Vista and Casa Grande. Steve's August 30, 2000, report to the board indicated that two young women were currently being served in the shelter for abused women (ibid.).

The southwest Regional Center in Yuma

President Baker visits with Mrs. Alma Carnes on her 100th birthday in Texas

The Yuma Development Council was organized April 9, 1998, with twelve people serving on the council. Rev. Rick Ogston, a local pastor, was asked to chair the council, which was held at West Yuma Baptist Church. Yuma has held a special place in the history of

261

Arizona Baptist Children's Services. The first major gift came from a Yuma couple, Mr. and Mrs. J. B. Carnes. The second major gift to ABCS also came from a Yuma couple, Mr. and Mrs. Dean "Barney" Barnicle. This gift would fund the construction of a badly needed administration and family-service building on the Little Canyon Campus in Phoenix. Mr. Barnicle served on the ABCS Board, and he and his wife, Betty, made office space available to ABCS when the time came to begin a regional center in Yuma. The writer spent many happy hours in Yuma visiting with this delightful couple. They never failed to insist that the writer stop by one of their gas stations and fill up his car at their expense.

When the required amount of $70,000 dollars was raised in Yuma, another board member, Charles Wesner, was employed to serve as regional director of the Southwest Regional Center.

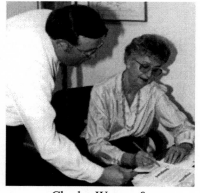

Charles Wesner &
Velma Graham

Office space was made available in the Thunderbird Plaza, 2855 S. Fourth Avenue, Suite 120. This was an office complex owned by the Barnicle family. The dedication took place October 2, 1998. Barney and Betty Barnicle continued to support the regional center and donated a fifteen-passenger van to assist in the job of transporting children, which was part of the regional program requirements.

The regional office in Yuma conducted an evening support group for adolescents, outpatient substance-abuse counseling, and parenting classes. A satellite office was opened in Parker, in La Paz County. Space was donated in the Baptist church there for regional activities. These included an adult substance-abuse outpatient group counseling and education for juvenile first offenders. In addition, substance-abuse education was offered in the local jail. The Renewing Arizona Family Traditions (RAFT) program was conducted in both counties.

The following true story [11] demonstrated the networking ability between the various regional centers to provide better services to children and their families.

> Jeremy grew up in the Yuma area and when he got into trouble, the local juvenile court turned to the ABCS Southwest Regional office. He was soon admitted to the ABCS Residential Treatment Center in Phoenix. Bob Garrett, the intake coordinator for the center, recalled how much easier it was for him to place Jeremy knowing that he had talked to therapists at the Southwest regional office. Jeremy made friends with another resident in the program who invited him to attend church with him at North Phoenix Baptist Church. Jeremy's new friend, Tom, was baptized that evening. Jeremy later attended camp with Tom and other youth at the church, where he accepted Christ. He asked to be baptized in a church in the Yuma area. Because of the regional office, associates were there when he returned to his home to help continue the treatment started in the treatment center and encourage him in his new spiritual pilgrimage. (*Footprints* 2000, 1).

There were so many wonderful people who worked toward getting an ABCS regional center in the area. Barney and Betty Barnicle have already been mentioned. Years earlier, Bill and Barbara Jewett had worked to begin work in their city. Both Bill and Barbara served on the ABCS Board at different times. Rev. Charles Tyson, Jim Buster, and Gilbert Taeger served as ABCS trustees from Yuma together with earlier local Baptists who are listed in the appendix.

Others who must not be overlooked are Pastor John Burley, Mary Taeger, Morrisa Heintz, Pastor Tyrone Jones, Teresa Ray (secretary for the center), Brenda Heke, Gary Maxwell, Pastor Bret Burnett, Pastor Stephen Fusilier, and Ann McConnell.

One of the grandest ladies of all was Velma Graham. Mrs. Graham was a member of the first group of Circle of Champions. She was a

---

[11]   The actual names of clients are not used to protect confidentiality.

faithful supporter as long as President Baker could remember. She served on the development council, and then served as a volunteer secretary in the regional center office. She did not have the resources of other Yuma friends, but she generously gave what she had of her money and time for many years to support the ABCS children's ministry. There were others.

Under Charles Wesner's leadership in both Yuma and La Paz counties, the program outgrew its Yuma office. Again, the Barnicles stepped up and constructed a larger building in the Thunderbird Plaza, which more than doubled the existing space and was better arranged for a counseling office suite.

In time, Wesner would leave the center to return to the pastorate, but he left a legacy of success and credibility for ABCS in the two southwestern counties of Arizona.

Eastern Regional Center in Show Low

This regional center was another product of the strategic plan, "Building A Future For Children," approved by the ABCS Board, March 15, 1996. An area dinner conference had been held there earlier, and there was strong support from the director of missions Rev. Jerry Purkaple and other area friends. Rev. Dennis Adams, pastor of the First Southern Baptist Church in Show Low, was a member of the board and gave early encouragement to starting work in that area and offered the church as a possible site for the offices. This offer would later be accepted, but Pastor Adams was by then pastor of a northwest extension of North Phoenix Baptist Church in Phoenix.

Several board members were from the White Mountain area who were always strong supporters of the idea of having an ABCS presence in their area. To name a few: Rev. Dennis Adams, Paul Barger, Martha Jane Storie, Louise Fuller, Doug McDaniel, Don McDaniel, and Stan Fuller. There were others.

As early as September 1986, plans were made to develop an advisory council made up of area pastors of all denominations. Seventeen people were present for the first meeting at which time a number of questions were raised about the credentials of the counselors and their Christian character. The group seemed pleased with the answers, and plans moved forward to establish a counseling center.

The work was started in November 1986. One of the ABCS chaplains, Eddie Kines, was chosen to travel to Show Low two times a month for two days at a time and provide counseling. Office furniture was moved from Phoenix, December 27, 1986, and an office was located in the Desert Pines Baptist Associational Office. Arrangements were made for the ABCS counselor to stay at the Apache Pines Motel for $20.14 per night. This early plan was supported by the local ministers' association, and they agreed to ask for financial support from their churches so that "Christian counseling" would be available in the area. This plan lasted for less than a year. It was simply too draining on counselors to make the long trip twice a month, and the effectiveness of the program was hampered by both the infrequency of the counseling and the fact than the counselor was not a part of the community. The program was eventually discontinued. Another more successful effort would later be made.

Council member Dr. David Daffern and director of missions, Rev. Matt Gaston enjoy a snack.

The Show Low Development Council was organized July 31, 1998, with eighteen people serving on the council. Rev. Doug McDaniel, an ABCS trustee, was appointed as chair of the council. By this time, the Desert Pines Baptist Association had a new director of missions in the person of Rev. Matt Gaston. Rev. Gaston, like his predecessor Jerry Purkaple, became very interested in the prospect of an ABCS regional center and indicated that First Baptist Church of Show Low would provide space for the offices.

The committee began its work of raising the amount for the first year's budget. Rev. McDaniel was approached about the possibility of serving as the regional director. He was completing his master of counseling degree from the University of Phoenix and could continue his education as well as direct the center. He accepted. The budget of $16,660 was subscribed, and nine hundred square feet of donated office space was remodeled at the Show Low First Baptist Church for use by the center.

The reason the budget was minimal in Show Low was because Rev. McDaniel offered to forego a salary the first year. An open house was held March 6, 1999, and the center began its work.

Truett Baker had stepped down as ABCS President as of January 1, 1999, but remained on the staff as a consultant with special responsibilities for establishing an adoption program and working with the regional programs. Baker was able to work with Doug McDaniel in setting up the center, writing the policies, and making contact with potential referral resources in the community. This was pure joy for him, remembering the dream of fifteen years earlier, that regional work for ABCS be started in Arizona.

The first programs were counseling and family-life education. Family Preservation, Family Builders, RAFT, Foster Care, and Adoption would later be added. One of McDaniel's strengths was in his interest and ability to work with the local juvenile probation authorities.

Northwest Regional Center in Kingman, Bullhead City and Lake Havasue City

An area dinner conference was held in Kingman in the first year of Baker's administration. There were other occasions when he would visit the pastors' conferences or preach in one of the area churches. There was less support from this region of the state, and therefore the idea of a regional presence there was not met with the enthusiasm that was encountered in other areas of the state.

Baker was contacted by Dr. Nelson Garrison, a psychologist in Florence, on March 24, 1997. He discussed with the ABCS president the idea of jointly sponsoring a counseling office in the Lake Havasu area. The two had discussed this possibility earlier. At this time Dr. Garrison was working in the Florence State Prison during the week and spending weekends with his son, Chad, pastor of Calvary Baptist Church in Lake

Havasu. Prior to his prison work, he directed a Christian Counseling Center in Phoenix. The next time Baker heard anything about Dr. Garrison was the announcement about his funeral.

His widow lived in Lake Havesu and was active in her son's church. Mrs. Garrison and her son, Chad, attended the first "Information Meeting" regarding the possibility of a regional center being started in the area. Prior to that, Baker met with the River Valley Baptist Associational Director of Missions, Tommy Thomas, who was enthusiastic about the idea of a regional center in the area. In turn, he invited Baker to speak to the pastors at their regular weekly meeting on May 21, 1998, at Golden Valley Baptist Church in Kingman. Twelve ministers were present, including the director of missions and Rev. Bill Purdue, a former trustee. The ministers were receptive to the idea and talked of their concern about substance abuse among their youth.

On September 10 and 11, 1998, development council meetings were held in Lake Havasu, Kingman, and Bullhead City. It was becoming apparent that competition was taking place in the three cities to have the regional office in their city. People in each city attended the council meeting very well when the meeting was held in their city, but then, the other two cities were not well represented. To deal with this, Baker ended up having development councils in all three cities. Thirty-eight people attended the three meetings, but only five were pastors, which was discouraging.

Another meeting was held November 5, 1998. Notices went out to twenty-three people, and only seven attended—all from Kingman where the meeting was held! Visits were made to the local departments of social services, juvenile probation, and the state behavioral health offices to explore area needs. Rev. Paul Temple, pastor of College Park Baptist Church in Kingman, offered space in his church for offices.

Baker discussed this situation with the new ABCS president, David Jakes. Soon after, Baker ended his consultation time with ABCS, and the future of the regional center was left in the hands of the new president and the development council. The good news was that in time, a regional center would be started in the area, with offices in all three cities. That dream became a reality in December 2000, when Bill Greco was employed as the director of the regional center. The new director worked for many years in the YMCA program and brought a wealth of experience and skill with him to the new task. He holds the distinction of being the first layman employed as a regional director.

Less than a year after opening, the director reported that forty-seven counseling sessions had been held; and programs were conducted for a charter school staff, juvenile offenders, substance abusers, as well as programs given to strengthen families (Greco 2001).

Northern Regional Center in Flagstaff\Prescott

The Northern Regional Center was the last new region to be developed. This area had the least activity in terms of preparation for a center, as well as having a history of providing the least support. It was difficult to find board members from the area. Dr. Evelyn Lewis of Flagstaff was one of the strong trustees. However, during this time of regional exploration, she would retire and move to Phoenix. The Yavapai and Grand Canyon Associations, which included the cities of Flagstaff, Prescott, Prescott Valley, Page, Winslow, and Sedona, initially comprised the area of the northern region.

Baker met with pastors in the Grand Canyon Association in Flagstaff and the Yavapai Association in Prescott. Rev. Arnie Sorrells, director of Missions for the Yavapai Association, invited Baker to talk to the pastors at the regular monthly meeting of their executive committee.

There was a positive reception for the possibility of a regional center in Northern Arizona. Rev Barry Hall, a former pastor in Sedona and an ABCS trustee, directed a counseling service and offered his services to help the center get started. Others that encouraged the opening of a center were Dr. Steve Daniel, a psychologist and son of Mark Daniel, director of Missions for Apache Association, and Eddie Christian, a psychologist in Flagstaff who was director of Eddie Christian Communications. As a parting reminder, Baker noted to President Jakes that Prescott Valley was the fastest growing city in Arizona and one of the fastest growing in the nation. Also, one of the greatest areas of need was in Yavapai County. The DES director for District III indicated to the author that 50 percent of her district's resources were spent in this one county.

After Baker's departure, President Jakes would meet with Rev. Al Campsen, director of Missions/Evangelism for the Four Corners Association, and this area would be included as part of the Northern Regional Center. This last regional center would be started in 2004 to complete the network.

The Central Regional Center in Phoenix

Since Phoenix is the home of ABCS, the idea of a "regional center" there seemed strange; nevertheless, home-based services in Maricopa County needed to be under a regional umbrella to be consistent in a statewide organizational plan for regional centers. Also the ABCS Central Regional Center programs needed to be separate from the corporate offices as were the other regional centers. The residential treatment center (formerly Little Canyon Center) in Phoenix would serve all six regions. As it turned out, all Phoenix ABCS programs, except for one group home, would be relocated to the newly acquired Charter Hospital building to be named the John F. and Mary P. Long Family Life Development Center.

Little Canyon Residential Treatment Center received JCAHO accreditation "with commendation." When the review team realized that there were other programs at ABCS in addition to the treatment center, ABCS was informed that all programs would now have to be included in the review for JCAHO accreditation. This was a new policy with the Joint Commission. A review was scheduled for the other programs in three months, and all agency programs were then accredited by the Joint Commission.

There are at least three possible accreditations for health and family service agencies such as ABCS. The Joint Commission on Accreditation of Health Organizations (JCAHO) is the most difficult to obtain and the most credible and well-known accreditation. It is the accreditation required for Medicaid reimbursement. It was granted to ABCS for three years. Built within JCAHO requirements is an ongoing quality-assurance component that requires constant monitoring and improving.

During this same period in 1998, the Little Canyon School received North Central Accreditation for which it had worked for several years. This accreditation would allow the school to accept public school children, in addition to those children who were diagnosed as emotionally handicapped. Steve Kuipers, principal of the school, led in this effort and deserved much of the credit for this significant achievement, along with the teachers in his program.

By the close of the Baker administration in 1999, regional development was well under way. The ABCS supporters in the regional offices that were in operation were pleased, and the word spread to other Baptist Family members across the state. Even in the northern area of Arizona where support had been slow in developing, enthusiasm for the work was growing.

Summary

The transition of Arizona Baptist Children's Services from a Phoenix-based program to one that was statewide represents the most dramatic change since the children's home became a residential treatment center in 1970. The success of this transition resulted from the vision of the board and the support of the people in the areas where the centers were located. Earlier attempts at establishing services in various areas of the state were unsuccessful but did contribute to the strategic knowledge base that later did result in success. Baker's experience at establishing regional centers in three other states was helpful in defining the strategy that was effective. Two major factors were responsible for the success.

First, the community had to demonstrate its interest and support for such a center. This was done through the dialogue that took place in the advisory council discussions. Not only did the Baptist churches need to desire the ABCS presence, but state social service and juvenile departments had to express the need for services, which ABCS could provide. Donated dollars and the availability of purchase of care dollars had to be a part of that expressed interest.

The second factor in the success of the regional centers was financial support. The advisory council had to develop a budget based upon the services that would be offered, and then raise the first year's budget. When the goal was reached, the center could begin its work.

With everything in place, the final criteria for success was the selection of the right person for the regional director. Such a person would need to have skills in fund-raising, program development, counseling, and working with state personnel and church leadership. This was a tall order, but the success of the center would depend upon selection of the appropriate person. The early selections of regional directors did prove to be good choices, and the centers would thrive because of it.

References

Footprints. 2000. Jeremy's Story. Fall.

Greco, Bill. 2001. Northwest Region Opens in Lake Havasu. *Footprints*, June.

Hanna, Steve. 1999. Southern Regional report to the board. ABCS Board Minutes. June 4.

Minutes 1985. ABCS Board, September 20.

Chapter 10

Purchase of Care
and
Church-State Relations

Introduction

The associates and the board have long believed that God had given this Purchase of Care (POC) resource to Arizona Baptist Children's Services (ABCS) to enable multitudes of children and families to be helped. The small struggling children's home blossomed into a large multiservice, statewide ministry because of its partnership with the state's children's services agencies. In so doing, ABCS has not violated its commitment to minister to the spiritual needs of children and families, and the state has not supported any particular faith. The state has fulfilled its statutory mandate to care for dependent and troubled children through ABCS and other faith-based agencies.

When the author joined the staff of ABCS in 1984, a large percentage of the budget income consisted of Purchase of Care (POC) funds from the state of Arizona. Although this was a cause for concern at the time, there was a strong conviction that it would be changed. It was not. What has changed is the size of the budget and large scope of services, which have significantly increased over the past several years. Approximately 85 percent of revenue came from POC. The board and administration were not comfortable with this high percentage for practical reasons. It was not believed, however, that this violated the historic church-state-separation ideal so cherished by Baptists and others in this country who value religious liberty. This realization came slowly out of the experience ABCS had with state agencies and POC.

Definition

Purchase of care is defined as "an organized procedure by which an entity of the government enters into a formal agreement with another entity: private for-profit, not-for-profit, or individual purveyor of services" (Demone and Gibelman 1989, 11). In the case of human services, this involved the outsourcing of mandated health and social services to private agencies. The state outsourced these services because it was more economical and believed that a higher quality of service could be obtained in this manner. Many believe that the state should not be in the business of providing human services itself because of accountability and quality management. The state is the licensing agent for services and should not be in the position of licensing itself to provide those services.

In Arizona, the following public agencies purchased services from private agencies through the process called "purchase of care."

* Division of Adult, Children, Youth, and Families (ACYF) of DES
* Regional Behavioral Health Authorities (RBHA), which contracts for behavioral health through the Department of Health Services
* Administrative Office of the Courts (AOC), County Juvenile Probation
* Bureau of Indian Affairs (BIA) and individual tribal communities
* Department of Education and individual school districts

ABCS and Purchase of Care

The practice of accepting POC began in the early years of the Baptist Children's Home history (See chapter 4). It literally "kept the dream alive" during days when there was no endowment and the only support came from some churches and individuals who believed in this young ministry. There was no regular financial support from the convention in the beginning. The practice of accepting POC was reaffirmed during the Cain administration and became the method by which rapid expansion of services would take place. The Department of Welfare and the courts saw ABCS as a children's agency they could trust, and that would provide quality care to the children in state custody.

The Baker administration would continue to accept POC although Baker himself believed that the agency would be able to move away from depending so heavily upon that source of income.

One of the concerns often expressed by church agencies regarding POC was that it would disallow religious practices. Accepting POC in Arizona by ABCS did not limit the freedom to teach the Bible or hold religious services on campuses. It did not prevent the agency from having chaplains or discussing matters of faith with the children and families in the agency's care. However, it should be noted that any expenses related to religious practices were not a part of the POC reimbursement.

Permission was obtained from parents or legal guardians before children were baptized. Permission was also obtained from parents for children to participate in the religious programs of the agency. Children were not coerced into participating in any of the religious activities. Very few children declined to participate. As a matter of fact, Arizona licensing standards for group care require that "each child shall be provided the opportunity to have religious training . . . A child shall be encouraged to attend the church of his faith or the faith of his parent(s), but attendance shall not be mandatory" (Arizona Dept. of Economic Security).

Another issue that the Baker administration faced was the points of view that church and state separation meant that the church should have nothing to do with the state. There are many who will agree with Chief Justice Rehnquist, who wrote in *Wallace v. Jaffree*, "The wall of separation between church and state is a metaphor based on bad history; a metaphor which has proven useless as a guide to judging. It should be frankly and explicitly abandoned" (*Wallace v. Jaffree* 1985).

There will be no argument about the importance of religious freedom and separation of church and state. However, separation does not mean alienation or isolation. The words of Jesus, "Render to Caesar the things that belong to Caesar, and to God the things that belong to God" (Matthew 22:21), have traditionally been interpreted by many to imply a distance between the two or, as Thomas Jefferson put it, "a wall." This "absolutist" view has been widely held and interpreted to mean that religious organizations should not accept funds of any kind from government. This was not the intent of the authors of the First Amendment of the Constitution. The religious freedom clause of that amendment states that government *shall not* do two things:

1. Establish any form of religion
2. Prevent the free exercise of religion

Accepting POC from the government by a church-related agency does not violate the establishment or free-exercise clauses of the First Amendment. Each agency, which accepts POC, must carefully examine the impact that relationship with government will have upon the mission of the agency and its ability to maintain its integrity as a private, faith-based organization.

The key to cooperation is to understand that church and state represent two authorities who can live side by side without either dominating the other. Each has a particular venue in which prescribed authority is exercised, but the freedom to exercise that authority is not absolute for either. A church congregation can worship God as it seems proper, but the congregation is not free to do anything it pleases, justifying its action as religious practice. It cannot build a new building or remodel an existing one without a building permit issued by the city or county. It cannot operate a kitchen without a health permit. The state has authority in health and safety matters, and the church has authority in spiritual matters. They need each other. The church needs the protection of the state, and the state needs the values, hope and guidance, which faith offers.

Supreme Court Decisions about Church-State Separation

There is also a larger issue that cannot be ignored. There is the issue of regulations resulting from public laws and policies that affect churches and their institutions. These regulations may have nothing to do with whether a church, or church-related institutions, accepts POC or any other government funds. Eligibility for property tax exemption, ERISA requirements, labor laws, and various reporting and disclosure rules have gradually eroded the absolute separation that religious bodies once experienced.

Allan Carlson, formerly the assistant director of the Office for Governmental Affairs, Lutheran Council U.S.A., wrote, "Religious organizations are seeing their activities and autonomy compromised directly by new or threatened state controls and compromised indirectly by governmental definitions that confine unrestricted 'church activity' to an ever smaller circle" (1979, 27).

Churches and their institutions are more involved with government today than ever before, and it is becoming increasingly more difficult to decide what areas belong to Caesar or to God. The intent of the law has been to bring about social justice and equality for all citizens. It has been the difficult task of the courts, and primarily the Supreme Court, to interpret those laws in such a way as to maintain a balance between justice for all and church-state separation.

The basic test for determining the constitutionality of a law involving church-state relations was established by the Supreme Court in *Lemon v. Kurtzman* (1971) and came to be known as "the Lemon test." A government program that benefited religion in any way would be determined as appropriate if it met the three parts of the test. First, the statute must have a secular legislative purpose. Second, its primary effect must be one that neither advances or inhibits religion. Third, the statute must not foster an excessive entanglement with religion (Sidler and Rolland 1996, 471).

Two approaches have emerged. The "absolutists" position would maintain a strict separation of church and state while the "accommodation" point of view would favor a position of cooperation and partnership between church and state. Supreme Court scholar D. P. Aiese points out that there is increasing public support for the accommodation position. "Absolutists are a dwindling group. Even some Baptists whose heritage forcefully bespeaks the wall of separation, are no longer certain that walls, like fences, make good neighbors. Many feel that cooperation is inevitable because of the mutuality of concerns of church and state. It is also believed that such relationships should be encouraged. To do otherwise is to bring hostility rather than separation" (1986, 186).

The inconsistencies in totally embracing a pure absolutist's interpretation are glaring. The strict absolutists interpret the "no establishment" clause to mean transportation to parochial schools should not be supported with tax money, but they do not object to government-paid chaplains serving in the military. Some church groups strenuously object to their institutions accepting POC for needy citizens. Those same church groups have no objection to tax exemptions for their church properties and their minister's housing allowances that are tax-exempt (Marus 2002).

Many believe the relentless effort to remove all vestiges of religion from the schools and public places have impinged upon the "free exercise" clause of the First Amendment. Samuel Hill, Jr., and Dennis Owen write, "The separation clause of the First Amendment prohibits the establishment of a particular religious group, not the removal of religion from the public arena" (Hill and Owens 1982). Religion is a part of all social orders of every civilization. There is a "crossing over" in many areas. Christians and people of other religious groups work in government, as well as involve themselves in their religious organizations.

The situation appears to be this: there is no absolute separation. In fact, "the Supreme Court has consistently stated, and most Americans generally believe, that there are some circumstances when the state may intervene to prohibit groups from exercising their religion" (Aiese 1986, 182). Examples would include the prohibition of polygamy by the Mormons and required immunization of the children of Christian Science practitioners. Chief Justice Burger wrote, "No perfect or absolute separation is really possible" (*Walz v. Tax Commission* 1970). In Lynch v. Donnelly, which drew upon the Lemon test, Chief Justice Burger later wrote about the court, "(It) consistently has declined to take a rigid, absolutists view of the establishment clause . . . in our modern, complex society . . . an absolutists approach in applying the establishment clause is simplistic and has been uniformly rejected by the Court" (*Lynch v. Donnell* 1984).

Civil Liberties:
Are We "Throwing Out the Baby with the Bath Water?"

In any discussion involving church-state separation, there are many viewpoints that should be heard. There are Christians, who hold strong convictions that any formal relationship between church and government is dangerous, regardless of how separately their functions are maintained. There are others who believe that all vestiges of religion should be removed from public life. Both of these points of view support the strict "separatists" interpretation of church-state separation.

In a *Wall Street Journal* editorial, U.S. senator William Armstrong of Colorado described a number of instances in which various states had taken action prohibiting the use of the services of religious organizations to the detriment of needy people. New York City, in conjunction with the ACLU, terminated its contracts with religious foster-care agencies, dumping four thousand children on the already strained resources of the city social services. The reason? The Jewish, Catholic, and Protestant agencies required their children to attend religious services, even though they could choose the particular services to attend. Senator Armstrong pointed out that in millions of households across America, parents require their children to attend church or synagogue. Why would foster children be treated differently? He also cited an example of a hospital in Baltimore that faced loss of accreditation because it refused to allow abortions to be performed. In commenting on these events, Senator Armstrong stated,

> The irony of this mistake is that the institutions most successful in dealing with social problems are those that foster a religious system of ethics—Alcoholics Anonymous; the Salvation Army; America's church-related charities such as orphanages, hospitals, homes for the elderly—are this country's most important social safety net. They were

helping the afflicted long before government became involved, and they do it much better than the public sector ever will. (1987, A14).

An editorial that appeared in the April 4, 1994, issue of the *Wall Street Journal* echoed Mr. W. J. Bennett's warning about this dangerous trend to "neutralize" religion in public life (Bennett 1992). "There are some realities that they ought to come to grips with. The United States remains one of the most religious nations on earth and by far the most religious country in the Western world. Nine out of ten Americans profess a belief in God. Yet we are also a nation, that in the wake of the school prayer decision, spent three decades actively expunging every vestige of the religious impulse from public life and discourse. It is hardly a coincidence that this same period saw the rise of much social pathology. A reaction from this country's religious tradition was inevitable. It has arrived" (*Wall Street Journal* 1994).

The increasing complexity of this issue is evident in that this has become both a serious political as well as religious issue. It is time for a new partnership between government and religious institutions (Sider and Rolland 1996, 468).

Pros and Cons

The major disadvantage in accepting public funds is that a church-related agency cannot discriminate in its hiring practices in regard to religious preference (with some exceptions). This has been a concern of Arizona Southern Baptists. Any issue that could affect the quality of spiritual life should be a concern. The federal laws involving discrimination in hiring practices should not be a problem since provision has been made in the past for religious organizations to employ only those who adhere to their faith.[12] The Bush administration's faith-based

---

12   While federal law permits this discrimination, the author is opposed to it.

initiative was very explicit about this provision (A Guide to Charitable Choice 1977, 7).

The problem is at the state level in Arizona. This involves an executive order issued by the governor. Former ABCS executive director Don Cain requested a legal opinion on this from the law firm of Ryley, Carlock & Ralston. The opinion was rendered January 19, 1983.

Impact of a Discriminatory Hiring Policy on Government Contracts

Section 3.07 of the DES contract states that the provider (ABCS), will comply with the provisions of Title VII and State Executive Order 75-5 (EO 75-5).

Section 3.01 states that the provider will comply with all federal laws, rules, regulations and executive orders which we interpret to include Federal Executive Order 11246 (EO 11246). The BIA (Bureau of Indian Affairs) contract is also subject to EO 11246. As discussed previously, ABCS is exempt from the application of Title VII insofar as religious discrimination applies; however, EO 75-5 and EO 11246 provide that the state and federal government contractors will not "discriminate against any employee or applicant from employment because of . . . religion." There are no exceptions to the Arizona Executive Order. If ABCS adopts a preferential hiring policy, it is possible that ABCS could be deemed in breach of its contracts with DES., The contract could be terminated and ABCS "blacklisted." To the best of our knowledge; however, the Arizona executive order has not been enforced in similar circumstances.

Conclusion

In summary, ABCS can implement an employment policy wherein it will hire only individuals who adhere to certain religious tenants; however, the implementation of such policy could endanger ABCS's government contracts (Ryley, Carlock & Ralston Law Firm 1983).

Non-preferential hiring does not have to be a major disadvantage unless the agency allows it to be. Christian agencies address this subject by explaining to prospective applicants their Christian foundation and the expectations that this carries. Most applicants who apply to a Christian agency do so because it is a Christian agency. They want to work with colleagues who have similar moral and ethical ideals. Those non-Christians who do choose to accept employment under those conditions are often receptive to spiritual matters and even turn out to accept the faith they previously ignored. This is a result of the positive Christian influence within their new work environment. The Gospel of Jesus Christ is more powerful and winsome than their unbelief.

There are other disadvantages. Contracting is burdensome and full of bureaucratic red tape. There is no guarantee that an agency will have its contracts renewed from year to year. There is the possibility of loss of donor support. Some donors feel that if an agency is receiving purchase of care, the agency does not need their money. Cash flow problems may result from accepting POC because the state does not always pay its bills on time. This is one reason a POC agency must not become too dependent upon government contract funds (Wedel 1976). Some strength in advocacy can be lost because government may see any advocacy on behalf of children by their vendors as arising from self-interest. Perhaps the major disadvantage is the risk a church agency runs in altering its religious focus, as pointed out earlier by Professor Garland, dean of the Baylor University School of Social Work.

Nevertheless, there are many advantages in the church-related agency accepting POC funds. The most obvious is the funding increase, which allows expansion of ministry. Ralph Kramer estimates that in many instances, it increases the range of services "sometimes as much as by a factor of 10." He adds, "Government funds may even be regarded as a more secure source of income than reliance upon the uncertainties of fund-raising events and public solicitations" (Kramer 1989, 103-104).

There was a time when church-related agencies felt secure with their annual missions allocations. That is changing. Church agencies are well advised to develop as many funding sources as possible and not depend entirely upon any one of them.

Another advantage, which must not be overlooked, is the opportunity church-related agencies have to be involved in the development of public policy. These public forums welcome the faith dimension, integrity and human compassion faith-based agencies bring to the table. It is an opportunity for the church to bring "light" and "salt" to the marketplace.

Summary and Implications

This chapter began with the stated purpose of reexamining the impact, which accepting POC by church-related agencies has upon traditional views of church-state separation. Much of the climate in which the doctrine of church-state separation has been formulated has been one of a hostile or controlling nature. Neither persecution nor control is effective because church and state each has venues of separate authority, and the authority of one must not encroach upon that of the other. This was clearly articulated in the teaching of Jesus when he said, "Render unto Caesar the things that are Caesar's and to God the things that are God's" (Mark 12:17). The "separation" was never intended to be interpreted as alienation. Quite the contrary is true. Two of the greatest interpreters of the Christian Gospel, the Apostles Paul and Peter, urged believers to "be subject to the governing authorities because they are established by God." (Romans 13:1; 1 Peter 2:13)

It was pointed out earlier that the first charity efforts both in Europe and the colonies were joint efforts by church and government. History has demonstrated that it is impossible for church and state to be isolated from each other. This issue is how can they work together and maintain the integrity of their respective roles? Others have said it best: "A successful partnership between church and state depends upon both institutions remaining true to their best nature" (Sider and Rolland 1996, 473).

For the past 230 years, this country has enjoyed a measure of religious freedom hitherto unknown in the history of civilization. Reaching this point has not been an easy or perfect journey. Even as an earlier hostile environment shaped an adversarial relationship between church and state, a climate of freedom today should reshape that relationship into one of cooperation and mutual respect. Local, state, and federal governments are not our enemies. Many good things are being done for people because of their government. That does not mean there are no abuses or huge gaps in services, but the state must be given credit for the good that it does itself and through its provider community.

While president of ABCS, the author received a letter from a parent whose children had earlier been removed from her custody. Her two girls had been taken from her for seventeen months because of drug abuse. Following this traumatic removal, the mother disappeared for several months but reappeared after she completed a drug rehabilitation program. While in the ABCS foster home, the foster mother took the girls to church and Sunday school. When the children's mother began visiting her girls, she joined the family in their church attendance and eventually accepted Christ and was baptized. Her life changed completely, and in a short time, the girls were back with their mother. The mother kept in touch with the foster mother and later wrote a letter to her. The foster mother showed the letter to ABCS President Truett Baker. It read,

I want to express my thanks to you. I owe you so much. The love and nurture you have provided has meant so much to me. The support you have given me since (after the children went home) has been more help than you'll ever know . . . thank you for showing me the Lord. I always knew he was there. I just didn't think he loved me. I feel so much love in my heart since turning my life over to Jesus. I have never felt closer to anyone in my life. Being saved was the best thing that has ever happened to me. I truly never believed that there was anyone in this world that loved or cared about me or what I did. That's one of the reasons I turned to drugs and alcohol in the first place. *Then, by the grace of God, my children were taken from me and placed in your loving care.* As I came to know you, your love spilled from my children over to me. I have been so blessed by your love. Thank you! (Baker 1995).

It must be remembered that it was the state of Arizona that removed the children for their protection, and the positive outcome was the result of the cooperation between the two agencies—ABCS and DES.

Every schoolchild has at one time learned the prologue to the U.S. Constitution, which states that one of the objectives of government is to "promote the general welfare." From the Elizabethan Poor Law of 1601 in England to the present day, British and American governments have assumed some degree of responsibility for the human welfare of their citizens. Church and state share this common goal—to meet the needs of people. They can do that together and yet maintain their respective roles as religious and civil authorities.

Meeting the needs of the homeless, the abused, the hungry, and disenfranchised of our society will call for more resources than any single social institution, including the government, can provide. It is going to take the cooperation of government, churches, schools, and the business and civic communities working together and pooling their resources to make a dent in the social and spiritual problems of our times. Jim Wallis, editor-in-chief of *Sojourners* said it best: "I believe the future will see a myriad of 'new partnerships' formed to solve many of our social problems. That's because the problems are simply too large for one sector of the society to be able to solve. It will take all of us . . ." (2000, 166).

ABCS has been an example, over the past forty years, that faith-based organizations can work together with government agencies and retain the integrity of their respective values.

[1]   Portions of this article originally written by C. Truett Baker, appeared in the *Journal of Family Ministry* 10, no. 3 (1996): 4-21. Used by permission of the editor.

[2]   The writer questioned the appropriateness of including this chapter after it was written. The book editing committee believed POC was such a vital part of the ABCS story that it should be included to provide a rationale for its acceptance.

References

Aiese, D. P. 1986. The Supreme Court and the Religion Clauses of the First Amendment. *Review and Expositor* 83 (2): 182.

Arizona Dept. of Economic Security. Group Care Agency Licensing Standards, article 74 (Rev.6/77), R6-5-7409.D.4.

Armstrong, W. 1987. Taking Religion and Common Sense Out of Foster Care. *Wall Street Journal*, January 14.

Baker, C. Truett. 1995. Mother Finds Christ After Children Are Taken Away. Baptist Bulletin Service, S-14-95, Baptist Sunday School Board, Nashville, TN.

Bennett, W. J. 1992. *The De-valuing of America*. New York: Simon & Schuster.

Carlson, A. C. 1979. Regulators and Religion: Caesar's Revenge. *Regulation*, May-June:27-34.

Demone, H. W., Jr., and M. Gibelman. (In Search of a Theoretical Base for the Purchase of Services). 1989. *Services For Sale*. New Brunswick: Rutgers University Press.

Guide to Charitable Choice. The Rules of Section 104 of the Federal Welfare Law.

Hill, S., Jr., and D. Owens. *The New Religious Political Right in America*. Nashville: Abington Press, 1982.

Lemon v. Kurtzman. 1971. 403 U.S. 602.

Lynch v. Donnelly. 1984. 103 s. ct. 1359.

Ryley, Carlock & Ralston Law Firm. 1983. Letter to Don Cain dated January 19. Filed in ABCS Correspondence Archives.

Sider, Ronald J. and Heidi Rolland. 1996. Correcting the Welfare Tragedy: Toward a New Model for Church-state Partner ship. In *Welfare in America*, edited by Stanley C. Carlson-Thies and James W. Skillen, 454-479. Grand Rapids: William Erdmans Publishing Co.

Wallace v. Jaffree. 1985. 105 s. ct. 2517.

Wallis, Jim. 2000. *Faith Works*. New York: Random House.

Wall Street Journal. 1994. Church and State. April 4.

Walz v. Tax Commission. 1970. 397 U.S. 669.

Wedel, Kenneth R. 1976. Government Contracting for Purchase of Service. *Social Work*, March:101-105.

Part V: Transitions, Challenges, a Bright Future

Chapter 11

A New President and a New Home

The Period 1999-2002: "The Jakes Years"

Crisis Leads to Consultation

The retirement of Executive Vice Presidents Dr. Phyllis McFarland and Mr. Jack Willis in 1996 created a vacuum in leadership that could not be filled by President Baker and his new administrators. These two giants were truly "the power behind the throne," and with their absence, much of the management strength diminished.

The 1996 fiscal year ended with the a record annual loss of $365,343. To make matters worse, the leadership deficit came at a time when the state of Arizona was having serious budget problems of its own, and that resulted in reduced referrals to private agencies. One program alone, the Glendale Bunkhouse shelter, lost $100,411 in FY 95-96. These losses in revenue could not continue.

The writer well remembers the look of relief that came over the faces of the board of trustees when the president recommended the employment of the former president of the Arizona Baptist Retirement Centers, P. David Jakes, as a consultant (Baker "Special Report," 1997).

His work with ABCS began in the middle of 1997. By September, Baker made a special report to the board outlining a plan for closing some facilities and revising the budget. With these closings and relocations in place (details follow), Mr. Jakes would work with Baker in revising the budget. This would mean eliminating several staff positions. Baker described this measure as the hardest decision he had to make while president of ABCS.

In retrospect, there were several factors that created the "crisis of '97." Much of this was due to the difficulty ABCS had in collecting money, which it was owed from the state for services rendered to state children. Aging receivables were running as high as 120 days and even longer, but there was another issue that was best understood in hindsight.

Experience had taught ABCS that private funding was the lifeline to the future. One of the principles in strategic planning was that income must become more diversified in the future. ABCS looked to its constituency, the Arizona Southern Baptist Convention, its churches, and individual members for support. So did Grand Canyon University, Baptist Senior Life Ministries, and the Baptist Foundation of Arizona. In addition, the convention and the churches believed that the first obligation Christians had was to support their local church with their tithes and offerings. The result was that there were more ministries to support than there were people to support them. Even still, many generous people supported one or more of these ministries in addition to their church.

In other states, nonprofit organizations had learned to *earn* money through various business ventures. ABCS saw this as a possible additional source of income and opened several businesses at various times. Thrift stores were first, then day care; next was Sunglow Ranch, and last of all was AzCare, an employee assistance program (EAP). All were great ideas, but all lost money with the exception of the ranch, which lost money in operations but made income for ABCS when it was sold. The skills of ABCS were in raising donated dollars and purchase of care programs. The staff was not highly skilled business people in the for-profit sector and learned over a five-year period that they needed to work with what the agency does best.

David Jakes's Consultation Begins

The first phase of Mr. Jakes's work with ABCS was to do a financial/management review and present a written report with recommendations to the board. President Baker and Mr. Jakes met on September 22, 1997, and discussed the challenges. Out of that meeting, four needs were identified.

1. A management audit of the agency would be done. This would involve:

    ** An analysis of the budget and spending system
    ** An analysis of the administrative costs of the agency

2. The agency would learn how to live within its budgeted dollars.
3. Decentralization of budget management within the agency
4. The agency would learn how to live in an environment where revenues were not predictable.

On September 30, October 1,5 and October 27, 1997, Mr. Jakes interviewed management associates, and studied policies and reports. He prepared a report, which was submitted to the executive committee of the board on October 29, 1997. The report was very detailed and recommended twenty-two areas in which he believed he could make the agency operate more efficiently.

To summarize the report, Mr. Jakes recommended that budget preparation and monitoring be "pushed down" to program coordinators who would become more accountable for their programs. Various indicators would be developed for measuring efficiency, and revenue-producing potential would be explored.

The second phase of the consultation involved regular meetings with associates to teach them the skills they would need to carry out the efficiency implementation, which Mr. Jakes presented. Following an agreement with Mr. Jakes in January 1998, it was decided that the new consultant would provide one day per week of consultation (Jakes, P. D. 1998).

As the new consultant began his work, program coordinators were brought into the problem-solving process. The coordinators were trained to develop and manage their own program budget, which was a new experience for them. They made reductions in their individual budgets eliminating nonessential staff positions, many of which were unfilled positions. In all, thirty-five positions were eliminated, and a new adjusted budget was effective for January through June, the last half of FY 1998. Some positions were combined, and responsibilities in others were reassigned. After all the shuffling had taken place, only 10 associates would be dismissed in the reduction in force.

President Baker gave the sad news individually to each of the ten associates. He also informed them of a generous severance package. Assistance was promised from the ABCS Human Resources office in locating new employment. At least two associates were later rehired when financial conditions were better. With Mr. Jakes's assistance, four hundred thousand dollars was cut from the budget resulting in a year-end positive financial position. President Baker wrote in his quarterly report to the board:

> In spite of the sadness of this process, I believe our staff felt that we were fair and that the unpleasant business was handled well. There have been no adverse repercussions of which we are aware. One of the positive outcomes of this is that we have decentralized our budget management and given this responsibility to the program coordinators. They feel empowered and challenged to operate their programs in a cost-effective way and still maintain quality. (Baker, "President's Quarterly Report," 1997, 2)

Based upon the Jakes' report, Baker submitted several recommendations at the September special meeting of the board.

1. The Glendale campus would be closed resulting in an annual savings of $250,000. In retrospect, there were several factors that created the "crisis of '97." Much of this was due to the difficulty ABCS had in collecting money, which it was owed from the state for services rendered to state children.
2. The sale of the Bell house would result in another fifteen thousand dollars. The Bell House in Mesa was sold April 15, 1997.

3. The Journey Group Home for boys, ages eight through twelve, would be relocated to an eight-bed group home at 17402 N. Thirty-ninth Avenue in Phoenix. This would result in a revenue increase of eighty thousand dollars annually.
4. The residential treatment center on Little Canyon Campus would be reduced from forty to thirty beds by closing a ten-bed unit due to low census in the girls unit. Thus, it was made an all boys facility.
5. The Bell Group Home at 3118 W. Missouri, across the street from the main campus, would fill the vacated ten-bed unit on the Little Canyon Campus. The added group-home beds would result in additional revenues of ninety-three thousand dollars. If implemented according to plan, this resizing would result in a savings of $690,000. The immediate steps had been taken, and with the beginning of consultation from Mr. Jakes, the long-range stabilization would take place.

The Transition

The Period:1999-2000

The Change Begins

The board of trustees was magnificent. They handled the losses of 1997 with courage, hope, and vision, always expressing their confidence in the ABCS staff and always expecting God to settle all the accounts in his economy of time. This does not mean they sat back and easily digested the setbacks. They held the administrative leadership accountable but also "held their hand" during this crisis. President Baker recalls a board finance committee meeting in which one of the trustees asked him what he planned to do to deal with a particularly bad financial situation. Baker's reply, "I don't know," was a mistake that would haunt him for the rest of his career at ABCS. The exasperated trustees immediately replied back, "What do you mean, you don't know. It is your job to know." In a choked voice that was breaking, he replied, "We'll find a way."

From that moment forward, Baker said he believed that it was time for new leadership at ABCS. He had taken the agency as far as his ability would allow, and it was time for more skilled leadership to step up to the challenges of managed care, the new financial complexities, and changing needs. When he tendered his resignation to the board, it was with this explanation that he had outrun his ability, and it was time for new more capable leadership. This was not the sentimental confession of one who was wallowing in self-pity and defeat. It was an honest and grateful recognition of a wonderful and successful past and a belief that new leadership would bring vision and new energy to a place and people he deeply loved.

The Announcement

Baker gave the following formal statement to the board on March 27, 1998:

One of the deepest convictions of my life was the call of God, through this board, to become the third President of ABCS on January 1, 1984. This coming January, 1999, will mark the completion of fifteen wonderful years as president of this agency. The following September 12, 1999, will be my 65th birthday and will mark the date of my retirement from regular full-time employment with ABCS. That is seventeen months away which will give the board abundant time to make plans for appointing the fourth president.

For the past year, I have expressed to various members of the board that I believed the agency needed a different type of leadership. I do not believe it should wait seventeen months to take place. This is in no way a reflection of my waning interest or desire to be a part of ABCS. Quite the contrary! I love this agency, its people, its friends and everything about it. I love this convention and the warm, sustaining support I have felt from the agency and the convention these many years.

I feel good about what we have done together. God has blessed me and he has blessed this agency and I believe we are at a point when a change of leadership will only enhance the continuing growth. It is a good time to make this change; however, I do need to continue to work for a short period of time, and I believe I still have a great deal to offer.

I want to take the liberty of making a recommendation which I believe will be in the best interest of ABCS and its current president. I have discussed this with our board chairman and vice-chairman who believe it is worthy of presentation to you. I am recommending that the board appoint a search committee for the new president and proceed with the recruitment and appointment of this individual. At such time as this appointment is made, my resignation as president will become effective, and I will continue in the employment of ABCS as a "consultant" until I reach my 65th birthday. Any continuing role I might have as a consultant after that will depend upon the needs and desires of the board, and its new president and my personal circumstances.

The extent and nature of our continuing journey together is known only to God and is in your hands and his. However long this journey may continue, it has been a joy and privilege to this point. It has been the most satisfying work experience of my career. I am so grateful to God and to Arizona Southern Baptists for the opportunity I have had, and I look forward to seeing greater things in the future as ABCS continues its leadership role in serving the children and families of our state in the name of Christ and on behalf of Southern Baptists. (Baker, "Retirement Plans," 1998, 1-2).

Baker wrote to his staff, in the agency newsletter, a similar announcement that was much shorter and specifically for them.

ABCS Has a New President

The Search
The dilemma Baker faced was that his sixty-fifth birthday was a year and one-half away, and the agency needed new leadership then. At least he thought it did. He worked it out with the board to begin their search immediately, and this way, they wouldn't be rushed and could do a broad and thorough search.

The board accepted Baker's recommendation, and board chairman, Joe Chan, set in motion the process of leading the board in a national search for the next president. The board had authorized the executive

Donna and David Jakes

committee to serve as the search committee; and the board chairman, Joe Chan, would chair the search committee. A profile was developed describing the qualities and skills the board wanted in the new president. Notices were placed in newspapers, Baptist state papers, and sent to all the Southern Baptist child-care agencies in the Southern Baptist Convention. Applications were received and reviewed by the search committee until August 15, 1998, the cutoff date for accepting applications.

During this time, it was evident to Baker and the board that their consultant David Jakes, not only met the qualifications, but greatly exceeded them. President Baker encouraged him to submit his name for consideration. He was a well-known leader in human services in Arizona having served as president of the Baptist Retirement Centers and chief operating officer, years earlier, for the Baptist Foundation of Arizona. His father was an Arizona pastor. Mr. Jakes was trained and experienced in health care administration and more than a little familiar with health care accreditation, which was under the same umbrella as was ABCS' accreditation. Mr. Jakes eventually submitted his name for consideration although that had never been his thought in consulting for the agency.

At the Baptist State Convention, in November, Joe Chan, ABCS board of trustees chairman, introduces David Jakes (far right) as the new president of ABCS. Also pictured are (from left) Carolyn Baker, former president Truett Baker and Donna Jakes.

On November 3, 1998, the search committee recommended to the full board that P. David Jakes, now an ordained minister, become the fourth president of the Baptist agency (ABCS Board of Trustees, November 3, 1998). Two issues were discussed by the board. The first was an inquiry as to the need for Mr. Jakes to start in January 1999 since Truett Baker would remain on the staff until September. The explanation given by the search committee was that Mr. Jakes was needed in establishing the regional centers, and this would give time for Baker to introduce Mr. Jakes to government leaders, members of the legislature, and other agency directors. This would help with a smooth and thorough transition in leadership.

The second issue had to do with Mr. Jakes's consulting business. He had asked to continue a very small consulting practice in exchange for taking a major cut in salary by accepting the ABCS presidency. The board believed this was fair and President-elect Jakes agreed to abandon the practice should it interfere with his new commitment to ABCS.

President Baker had developed a deep appreciation for Jakes and his commitment to ministry and his business ability. Baker's strengths had been in developing programs and the ability to communicate with the Baptist Family. He built contacts in the community and was active in local and state organizations, as well as a strong advocate for children in the legislature. He was a successful fund and friend raiser. However, he was not a strong business or financial planner, and that was badly needed. Baker saw in David Jakes the person who could meet that need. Jakes was a well-known leader in Arizona Southern Baptist life and a popular speaker and preacher. It was his leadership as a consultant that had turned ABCS around in its worst financial hour, and he would encounter other challenges during the first two years of his presidency.

Former President Baker moved out of his office at ABCS during December 1998, and on January 1, 1999, Jakes moved into the president's office. Formal announcements were then made to the public.

A Reversal in Roles

David Jakes was now the president, and Truett Baker was the consultant; however, the relationship between the two friends did not change. Baker's consulting role would involve taking hands-on responsibility for several ABCS programs.

First, he would assume the role as coordinator for foster care. The position was vacant, and this was a service area in which he was most experienced. He would lead in hiring a coordinator for that program and developing an operational manual for foster care.

Second, he would continue developing the new adoption program and employ a coordinator to direct it. He and the coordinator would work toward meeting the requirements for licensing, and expand both the new adoption and the foster care programs to the regional centers.

Third, he would continue the work of developing the regional center network. During his presidency and the consultation period, centers would be started in Tucson, Yuma, and Show Low.

Fourth, he would continue representing ABCS on the Special Children's Ad Hoc Advisory Committee in the Arizona legislature and representing ABCS on the Arizona Council of Centers For Children and Adults (ACCCA), which would soon become the Arizona Council of Human Service Providers. This name change would occur with the merger of ACCCA with the state's Behavioral Health Association.

Fifth, he would assist the new president in an orientation process to help him become familiar with all aspects of agency life. Mr. Jakes was already familiar with much of the culture, finances and operations; but there would yet be much for him to learn.

Quality and Accreditation

The quality management program, introduced in earlier Joint Commission preparation and refined by Dr. Tina Olsen continued to be the centerpiece of accreditation preparation. The residential treatment program on the Little Canyon Campus first received Joint Commission Accreditation in 1974. In 1980, reaccreditation was received, along with full member status in the Child Welfare League of America. There is no record of reaccreditation following 1980 until 1992. Child Welfare League membership was lost, apparently due to increase in quality of standards and decrease in quality of facilities at ABCS. But again in 1992, the residential treatment center received full JCAHO accreditation. By that time, the boys and girls had state-of-the-art cottages in which to live, although, other facilities on the campus were less than acceptable, and this was noted in the 1992 report from the Joint Commission.

In 1998, the residential treatment center received accreditation with "commendation," which is the highest level of accreditation granted by the Joint Commission. In addition, all ABCS programs were accredited in that same year. An added achievement for the Little Canyon Center in 1998 was the accreditation of the Little Canyon School by the North Central Association. The school had prepared several years for this achievement and was able to obtain it following the construction of the new Smithey Chapel and Educational Center. This accreditation from the North Central Association qualified the school to accept other children in addition to those who were in special education. This opened up new opportunities for serving community children who were not residents of the treatment center.

Completion of Regional Expansion

Earlier chapters described the formal openings of the Southern, Southwest, and Eastern Regional centers. Some changes would take place in those centers after 1999. Charles Wesner resigned from the Southwest Regional office to accept a pastorate in the Yuma Association. His successor was Kurt Wesolowski who began his duties July 1, 2001. Kurt had a BS in Psychology from California State in Fullerton and a graduate degree from New Orleans Baptist Theological Seminary. He was a former pastor (*Footprints* 2001).

Bob Seymour filled the director's position following the resignation of Doug McDaniel in the Eastern Regional Center. The 2002 annual report noted that "the Adoption program in the Eastern Region is moving along with two children who have been placed and two more ready for placement. The center is initiating a program called 'Bridges' which is a tutoring program for children in the community. The goal is for the Eastern Region to eventually become a child advocate center."

Three more centers would be added to complete the statewide network—Northwest, Northern, and Central Regions.

Northwest Regional Center—Kingman, Bullhead City, Lake Havasu City

Early groundwork for this center is described in chapter 8. During former president Baker's final consulting days, a development council was organized with people from the three cities. President Jakes began working with the development council and the director of the River Valley Association. Tommy Thomas, as were all the directors of associational missions (DOEMs), was most supportive and helpful. President Jakes continued the fund-raising efforts for the area. It was clear from the beginning that offices would need to be established in each of the three cities for work to be effective in that region.

The projected cost for the first year of operation was $54,790. The interested Baptists in the region were able to raise $11,971; the Arizona Southern Baptist Convention contributed $25,000, and an individual donor from the region pledged $20,000 for a total of $56,971—more than enough to begin the program. Bill Greco was employed as regional director, with offices in the three major cities in the region: Bullhead City, Lake Havasu City, and Kingman (*Footprints* 2001).

Northern Regional Center—Flagstaff, Prescott

This would be the last and most difficult regional center outside of Phoenix to begin. This was due to the absence of earlier financial support and interest from this area. Few trustees had been selected from the area that comprised the Yavapai, Four Corners, and Grand Canyon Baptist Associations. The area dinner conferences, held in the early to mid-1980s, helped to raise the awareness of northern Arizona Baptists about ABCS.

This is a large land area and much of it sparsely populated, particularly on the Indian reservations where Baptist work in general was not as strong as in other areas.

Soon after the announcement of the regional centers network, ABCS was contacted by Rev. Si Davis, director of Missions/Evangelism (DOEM) for the Grand Canyon Baptist Association, and Rev. Arnie Sorrells, DOEM for the Yavapai Baptist Association. Both were interested in supporting ABCS work in their areas. Baker met with the DOEMs and the pastor's conferences in both associations and presented the plan for developing children and family services in their areas (the Northern Regional Center would open in March 2004, with Jim Maynard as the director).

Central Regional Center—Phoenix

To have a consistent and comprehensive statewide network, it would be necessary to connect the earlier work in Phoenix to the new network of regional centers. It was therefore determined that Maricopa County, which included three Baptist associations, would make up a regional center. It would include the residential treatment center, counseling, special education school, foster care, adoption, group homes, and family-based services.

The corporate office, separate from the regional centers, would consist of administration, accounting and payroll, human resources, development, facilities, and public relations. The corporate office would then be in the position to equally support the six regional centers. The original idea was to designate the planned John F. and Mary P. Long Family Life Development Center as the Central Arizona Regional Center, and its functions would then be separated from the corporate office, which would remain at the 8920 North Twenty-three Avenue location. While this arrangement made sense, a better plan would emerge when the purchase of the Charter Hospital became a reality.

Openings and Closings Continue the Transformation

AzCare (EAP) Stock Is Sold

The antecedences of this ABCS wholly owned for-profit corporation is found in chapter 8. Like Thrift World, the employee assistance program seemed to be the perfect fit for ABCS. Counseling resources were available, and the agency had a strong history of success in behavioral health. It was a great idea, but the weakness lay in the agency's EAP inexperience and lack of capitalization. What is of more significance is the fact that in the beginning, there were two or three EAPs in Arizona. That number would rapidly grow, and the larger well-financed organizations could maintain themselves through the lean start-up period. In 1998, the *Phoenix Business Journal* listed eleven of the major EAP in the Phoenix area (1998). There is no question but that AzCARE

could have survived if it had remained in business for six more months. It was too far in debt, and the "ghosts" of Thrift World hung like an ominous cloud over the entrepreneurial efforts of ABCS.

Archie Stephens, the president and CEO of AzCare, was authorized to begin a marketing process to sell the AzCare stock. However, he would continue to search for potential clients in the event that the profit threshold could be reached before ABCS had to divest itself of the company. The stock was sold July 1, 1999, to Viad Resources Inc. of Montana. The eighty-thousand-dollar net went into the ABCS endowment (Minutes 1999. ABCS Executive Committee, August 12).

The Impact of the Cease and Desist Order on ABCS

The history of ABCS would not be complete without the sad saga of the Baptist Foundation of Arizona bankruptcy. The writer did not believe that he could improve on the explanation President Jakes gave at the ABCS Board in a memo regarding the cease and desist order impact on the agency. While rather lengthy, the following information succinctly pulls together the complicated threads of this tragic event.

BACKGROUND INFORMATION

On Monday, August 9, 1999, ABCS received a letter from the Baptist Foundation of Arizona, which was sent to all investors regarding the current status of the investigation by the Securities Division and the Attorney General's Office. The letter indicated that BFA had frozen all funds and business investments, and furthermore, listed several actions taken by the Board of Directors for BFA. The letter requested that all questions concerning the letter be referred directly to BFA.

While facts of the investigation are still under consideration and being disclosed to the BFA Board of Directors, it is important to remember that this matter is a BFA issue and not ABCS. Arizona Southern Baptist Convention (ASBC) agency has a different mission statement and purpose, but we do work with sister agencies within the ASBC in a cooperative manner. It is my sincere prayer that there will be quick and successful resolution to the BFA crisis within the near future.

ABCS has funds currently invested at the Baptist Foundation of Arizona. We have a total of $240,000 in short or long term investments, of which $180,000 is discretionary and not designated for a specific purpose. The absence or loss of these discretionary funds will not cause immediate financial distress to ABCS because we do not routinely use these funds for operations, but rather use our bank line of credit to manage cash shortfalls resulting from timing fluctuations on the payments on accounts receivables. In addition, we have $1.2 million in a (restricted) endowment fund. It is our understanding that the Management Oversight and Operations Committees of BFA are determining the effect on endowment funds.

As I reflect upon the potential impact of the BFA situation on ABCS, there are several possible categories for impact. These are as follows:

* Faith, Integrity, Credibility and Trust
* Fund-Raising Potential
* Separate Corporations vs. Single Corporations
* Cooperative Program Giving
* Future Litigation
    (Jakes, Minutes, ABCS Board, Memo, 1999, 37-38.)

The endowment fund consisted of small and large gifts made by friends of ABCS who wanted to ensure the future of the agency through their bequests. It represented the proceeds of estate planning largely encouraged and guided by BFA from its beginning. Tragic as that was, the greater tragedy was the loss of credibility and trust, which would emanate from the BFA closure to other Arizona Baptist institutions including ABCS. The foundation had been supportive of ABCS in many ways and wanted the children's services to have the financial strength in the future that it had not known in the past. To that end BFA wanted and encouraged the growth of the ABCS endowment. The writer believes that none were more devastated than the BFA leadership, now that those plans were in serious jeopardy, if in fact not destroyed. The children's services was born in faith and had learned to live by faith. There was never a doubt that the God who had given life would continue to meet her needs.

A New Program—Adoption Is Born at ABCS
Provision was made for providing adoption services in the bylaws.

> The object and purpose of this Corporation is to carry out the purpose and actions of the Baptist General Convention of Arizona, providing for the establishment and operation of homes for the care and training of orphan and needy children and the placement and adoption of children when proper . . . (ByLaws and Rules of Decorum 1958. Article I.1, ABCS)

The dream of ABCS having an adoption program began with George Wilson, its first leader. However, that time was not right (Flint 1986). Little more was said about an adoption program since the administration was advised against this because of lack of children available and the high cost of adoption. (Note to readers: It would be helpful to understand that this was a period of time before the "permanency movement," and children were allowed to stay in foster care until their majority without hope for return to their own home or adoption.)

When Baker was appointed Don Cain's successor, starting an adoption program was among his early goals. Baker had always believed that the best thing a Christian family-service agency could do for a child was to help the parents. If the child had no parents, or could not live with them, the next best move was to find the child a new permanent home. Adoption could be the answer.

An adoption program would not be started in 1984 nor even soon thereafter, but the need for permanency could still be met. Mr. Baker became acquainted with Mrs. Kay Ekstrom, the executive director of the Christian Family Care Agency in Phoenix and Tucson. They became good friends and served on a number of committees together. Mrs. Ekstrom and Mr. Baker had an informal agreement that Christian Family Care Agency would give priority to all children referred to them for adoption by ABCS. They would also work with Baptist families interested in adoption who were referred to them by ABCS. This worked well for a number of years; however, as child welfare moved more toward a managed care system, it was becoming increasingly important that those agencies, which provide the best service for children, will be those that offer a full continuum of care. In the case of ABCS, that would include adoption. Also it was becoming increasingly clear that permanency for children must become their highest priority. To be as effective as possible, ABCS must be able to offer all permanency options *directly*, including adoption. To understand the importance of providing adoption, one must be aware of the changing "best practice" permanency philosophy.

President Baker's career spanned the years of transition in which the federal government moved from supporting foster care to supporting adoption and family preservation. Prior to coming to ABCS, he possessed a strong conviction that children belonged in their biological family, except for cases of abuse and neglect. Even then, the placement of "least restriction," such as foster family care, was preferred over institutional care. One of the early strategic plans called for establishing "pregnancy counseling and adoption" (Board Resolution 85-PRO-4, 1986, 1). While the goal was not achieved in the early days of the Baker administration, it was on his heart and mind and on the front burner of the strategic planning process (Board Resolution 96-E-1, 1996, 22). The agency newsletter reported, "By 1998, ABCS plans to have an adoption program in place to respond to the needs of children who cannot return to their biological parents" (*Footprints* 1996, 2).

There had been so many delays in starting the program, and Baker shared the urgency he felt with the board, which was reflected in the board minutes.

"Two issues are in the forefront for ABCS in the near future and Dr. Baker spoke to each of them. The agency will become involved in adoption very soon as the state is preparing to privatize this program state-wide. Secondly, ABCS must accelerate the development of its planned regional centers, to be in operation within the next three to six months. The urgency is due to the state's plan to privatize adoption and other child welfare services, and to issue other 'Request for Proposals,' (RFP) throughout the state for bids by agencies that have a presence in that area . . . ." (Minutes, ABCS Board, 1998, 3).

In 1998, ABCS received a seventy-five thousand-dollar gift from Chimiarra Investment Ltd. to begin an adoption program. These were the same friends, who, the year before, had made a gift of one hundred thousand dollars to provide furniture and equipment for the new Smithey Chapel/Educational Center and the Little Canyon Center campus. This recent gift was in keeping with the strategic plan for 1996-2000, "Building a Future for Children."

The board approved a business plan for adoption at its December 1997 meeting (Minutes 1998. Board Resolution 98-PRO-6). Mrs. Angela Cause, who was finishing her master's degree in social work at the time, was employed to direct the program under Baker's leadership. Baker had extensive experience in adoption, which included counseling birth parents, preparing home studies, and supervising placements; however, every state has different adoption policies and regulations. It was believed that some

of the funds from the Chimiarra Investments' gift would be well spent in purchasing consultation from an experienced Arizona adoption agency.

Rachel Osterle, director of Aid to Adoption of Special Kids (AASK), was a colleague and good friend of Bakers. They had served on committees together and shared an interest in placing children in permanent homes. Mrs. Osterle agreed to provide the consultation, which involved giving technical assistance in the adoption process and the development of policies. They would assist

Angela Cause

ABCS in completing the requirements for an adoption license. Over the next several months, both Baker and Mrs. Cause studied the Arizona licensing requirements and court severance procedures and, in the process, completed the documentation necessary for the license.

The adoption license application was submitted March 18, 1999, and two days later, it was approved, and ABCS received its license. The application consisted of forty-four policies and the development of eighty-four forms. Credit was given to Angela Cause who did a careful and professional job in putting the application together. (Note to readers: After the ABCS adoption program was in full operation, DES hired Mrs. Cause to direct the state's adoption program). Credit was also given to Mrs. Rachel Osterle and her staff who held nothing back in seeing that ABCS was well prepared for providing quality adoption services.

The program consisted of two parts, for families who qualified to adopt. The first would be to complete the adoption home study and assist the family in the certification process. The second part of the program would be working with birthparents who needed help in deciding what future role they wanted to have in the lives of their children. This was called "birthparent counseling." It must be clearly understood that this counseling was not an attempt to convince parents to give up their children but to help them decide what they wanted and were able to do. The strength in an adoption has always been in protecting the rights of the birthparents.

The ABCS adoption program would begin by serving those children in its foster-home program whose case plan was adoption. The next group that the program would focus upon would be families who needed help with an unplanned/unwanted pregnancy.

In January 1999, Alice Thornton, the director of Foster Care and longtime ABCS associate, resigned for health reasons. Since the new president, David Jakes, began his duties as president at that time, former president Baker agreed to supervise foster care on a temporary basis as well as develop the adoption program. Kristin Henricksen had been employed as foster-care clinical supervisor in December 1998. She was promoted to director of Foster Care April 9, 1999. With both Mrs. Cause and Mrs. Henricksen now appointed as directors of their respective departments, Baker, in consultation with President Jakes, relinquished his responsibilities

First Adoption: L to R: David Jakes, ABCS President; the new family; Rae Wharton, CPC Director of Adoption; Angela Cause, ABCS Director of Adoption

in those areas (Baker, "Plans For Departure," 1999.)

As the adoption program grew under Angela Cause's leadership, preparations were made to involve the regional centers outside of Maricopa County. In addition, ABCS Adoption would join a coalition within the county. The following statement appeared in one of Mrs. Cause's reports to the ABCS Board:

The Adoption program will begin operations in Maricopa County; however, the response from our regional areas has also been positive. Efforts are currently being made to establish services in the regional communities. Since receiving our adoption license, ABCS has become a participant in the "Children First" collaboration. Children First is a joint effort by several Maricopa County adoption agencies to address the permanency needs of children in the foster care system. Children First recently responded to a Request for Proposal (RFP) issued by DES for the recruitment, certification, and supervision of adoptive families. (Cause 1999, 49).

By September 2000, President Jakes reported to the board that "ABCS had entered into a cooperative agreement with Crisis Pregnancy Centers, and several clients were expected to give birth over the next several months. Adoption services have been expanded to the eastern and southern regions" (Jakes 2000. Board Memo, 42).

Moving closer to the anticipated time for the first adoption placement, Mrs. Cause reported the following to the board:

The adoption program completed its first series of adoption parent training classes involving four families. The program is currently serving sixteen families in varying stages of the adoption application process. This includes foster parents who desire to adopt, private applicants and families who have been referred by the Department of Economic Security. (Cause 1999, 49)

The first adoption was completed July 5, 2001, in the Central Regional Office (Maricopa County). The adoptive parents completed their training and certification through the new ABCS adoption program. The adoption and foster care associates were present for the happy occasion (*Footprints* 2001).

The first ABCS adoption completed outside of Phoenix took place in the Southern Regional Office in Tucson and was reported in the Arizona Southern Baptist Convention news journal, *Portraits* (Carlson 2001). By way of background on this adoption, a family in Mountain View Baptist Church in Tucson learned about the new ABCS adoption program and contacted their pastor. He in turn contacted the ABCS Southern Regional Office in Tucson. That started the journey for a couple who would be the first to adopt through ABCS outside of the central region. Soon afterward, the next adoption took place with a couple from the ABCS Eastern Regional Center. The placements continued as did a new era in services to children and families through Arizona Baptist Children's Services.

A Family of Ten Children Are Adopted

When an entire family of ten children (all siblings) are adopted by a couple, it makes headline news, and so it did all over the United States. Retired chief petty officer Van Hughes and his wife Shirley were ABCS foster parents who were licensed as a regular foster home February 10, 1995.

The first of the ten children were placed with them in foster care, with the other eight following over a period of time. They had to update their license to a group foster home, which was granted April 21, 1997. This may have

The Hughes Family

been the largest group of children in one family to be adopted in U.S history, and it made headlines everywhere. Two major publications that told their story were the *Air Force Times* (1999) and the *Dallas Morning News* (1999). Some of the statistics that characterize daily life in the Hughes home are listed in these articles:

** They use two gallons of milk a day
** Six loads of laundry are done each day
** They have a fifteen-hundred-dollar food bill each month
** It takes four hours to open presents on Christmas, and that's just for the children
** Several are straight-A students, and several excel in sports

Van and Shirley Hughes have two biological sons, and also helped raise a grandson. They both work in the preschool department of their church, which says a great deal about their love for children. Their pastor told the author, "Any child would be blessed to live in this home. Their patience is outstanding . . . they love each other . . . I can't think of a finer couple and more loving family" (From the personal notes of the author regarding the Hughes Family, during their home study for foster care. Used by permission).

The family appeared on the *Rosie O'Donnell Show* and received thousands of dollars in gifts (*Footprints* 1999). ABCS did not do the adoption as the agency was not yet licensed to do so, but ABCS associates did licensing and supervised the Hughes couple as one of their foster parents. One of the reasons ABCS felt strongly about starting its own adoption program was the fact that foster care and adoption work together as a team. Many children in foster care become available for adoption, and the permanency process is expedited when one agency can do both.

Foster Care and Adoption Work Together

One of the best examples of this relationship was found in a *Footprints* article about Mike and Tami Peterson.

Beth was one of many "throw-away" kids removed from her home due to parental abuse at the age of three. Angry, aggressive, and violent, she made no connection with any who tried to help her. At the time Beth was moved into a shelter, Tami Peterson was diagnosed with cancer.

Following surgery and three chemotherapy treatments, Tami and her husband Mike made the decision that the treatments were too painful and must stop. Doctors gave her three years to live. Mike, Tami, and many Christian family members and friends prayed for healing and their prayers were answered. The doctors were amazed. Tami made a new resolve to "make a difference" and began volunteering at the shelter where Beth was placed. The child who could "never bond" saw something in Tami and there was an immediate connection

The caseworkers also noticed the connection and inquired of Tami about her interest in adopting Beth. After much prayer and soul-searching, Tami and Mike decided to adopt her. They were licensed as foster parents through ABCS and Beth was placed with them for the duration of the adoption process. One day while riding in the car with the couple, Beth expressed her desire to accept Christ. It was a day that no one would forget. Tami commented, "They were right about one thing: no one could save this child. It took a much greater power." Weeks later, she began talking to her new adoptive parents about, "being a missionary." Beth's adoption was finalized in February, 2000. The "Throw-away" child now has a forever home and family" (*Footprints* 2000, 6-7,19).

This experience represents the essence of the goal ABCS has for children and families. The story of ABCS foster care would not be complete without remembering an event regarding two four-year-old Russian girls, whose story appeared on front pages of newspapers across this country. The girls, allegedly abused by their adoptive parents on a flight from Moscow to New York, were removed from the parents and placed in a foster home in New York. Later they were moved to another foster home in Phoenix, home of the adoptive parents (*Arizona Republic* 1997).

The Phoenix home in which the girls were placed was an ABCS foster home. The initial stories about the incident did not reveal which agency had physical care of the children, but the writer well remembers the day when the foster-care coordinator and the foster parents drove to the airport to receive the children upon their arrival. Their car was escorted out on the tarmac, and the children and their New York caseworker were taken in a dramatic move from the plane before it reached the gate, avoiding the press, who somehow knew they were on the plane. The children's division of DES (ACYF) insisted on confidential placement to protect the children. They called on ABCS for this special assignment as they had done so many times in the past, because of their confidence in the agency.

Retirement Begins

In September 1999, Baker reached his sixty-fifth birthday and completed his consultation period. Because of some unfinished tasks, he remained for a few more weeks to work on a Family Builder's contract for DES Districts III and IV, as well as work with Children First, the adoption coalition in Maricopa County.

Closure to President Baker's retirement process came to an end with an elegant dinner held in his honor at the Embassy Suites Phoenix North Hotel on Friday, September 24, 1999. Opportunity was given to friends to honor Baker with a contribution to the Baker-Scott Trust, set up in honor of his and his wife Carolyn's parents. The trust was designated to supplement associates' salaries. A commendation from State Senator Brenda Burns, President of the Arizona Senate, was read. Senator Burns was a former ABCS trustee and a personal friend of Baker. The evening of fellowship, roasting, and fine dining was topped by a generous expression on the part of the board of trustees—the gift of a new fully equipped 2000 Ford F-250 pickup truck. The board, with guidance from the new president, had outdone themselves in generosity, and Baker was at a loss for words (well, almost). In retrospect, this was one more example of the board's thoughtfulness and generosity expressed so many times through the years.

A New Corporate Office Site and the Central Regional Office

Part of the leadership transition process involved an introduction by outgoing President Baker to reacquaint incoming president David Jakes with Mr. Long, whom he had first met when president of Arizona Baptist Retirement Centers. Mrs. Long had died prior to this time, but Rev. Jakes had the opportunity to meet both Mr. Long and his son Jake Long, whom he had not previously met. The continuing process of developing the John F. Long project would now be the responsibility of President Jakes and his board.

P. David Jakes

One of the early goals of President Jakes was to "evaluate needs for future space for the corporate office (Minutes 1999. Jakes, "ABCS Short Range, 29). Former president Baker had discussed with the staff and board ways in which the John F. Long Family Development Institute could be used, and Rev. Jakes became a part of this ongoing dialogue when he began consulting with the agency. The original idea was that it would contain day care, day care training, foster care, adoption, counseling, and other family-based services. The corporate office would remain at its present location and would have more space after foster-care and adoption services were relocated. When the day care possibility was dropped, some thought was given to selling the corporate offices at 8920 North Twenty-third Avenue and combining all nonresidential programs, including corporate, under the John F. Long Family Institute umbrella. An additional reason for relocating was the increasing expense for maintaining the Twenty-third Avenue site.

The site for the new building became a serious search, and in September 2000, President Jakes submitted a resolution to the board recommending a building site at Fifty-first Avenue and Peoria. Prior to this time, forty-six possible locations had been explored. The resolution revealed that this building, to be constructed, would only contain the nonresidential service programs in Maricopa County and would constitute the Central Regional Office of ABCS. The corporate office on North Twenty-third would remain in that location (Jakes, "Revision of JFL Family," 2000). This potential site was eventually ruled out due to its proximity to underground fuel tanks at a nearby gas station, which created health and environmental risk. The exploring was not yet over.

The administration learned of the impending sale of Charter Hospital of Glendale on July 26, 2000, and began exploring this site and its buildings, while keeping open the option at Fifty-first and Peoria. A letter of intent was submitted to purchase the facility from Crescent Real Estate Funding VII, LP, with closing to take place on or before December 31, 2000 (Jakes 2000. Purchase of Charter, July 27).

This very attractive facility was built on eight plus acres in 1987 for the purpose of providing hospital and inpatient residential treatment (secured and nonsecured) for children and youth. The fifty-nine-thousand-seven-hundred-square-foot building included patient rooms, classrooms, outpatient counseling rooms, kitchen/dining facilities, large administrative and clinical areas, swimming pool, tennis courts, a gymnasium, basketball/volleyball courts; and it was completely furnished (Jakes, "ABCS Conceptual Narrative," n.d.) It was large enough to house all residential and nonresidential programs for ABCS in Maricopa County, as well as the corporate office. The final move would bring all of these programs and services under one roof with the exception of the Journey Group Home, which would remain at its current location in West Phoenix. The Charter Hospital had been licensed for ninety hospital/residential beds.

John F. and Mary P. Long Center

Mr. John F. Long was quite pleased with this Glendale site, and the decision was made to name it *the John F. and Mary P. Long Family Life Development Center.* The funds given by Mr. Long earlier would be used to purchase the property, along with proceeds from the sale of the Little Canyon Campus and the Corporate Offices Building. In addition to discussing this with Mr. Long, President Jakes discussed it individually with the families that had given funds to build the Little Canyon Campus. Their endorsement would be very important, and it was given. Their generous and thoughtful gifts would be remembered wherever ABCS facilities were located.

Two major problems stood in the way of acquiring the facility—funding and zoning. Funding for the new $3.5-million-dollar Charter Hospital property would be the next challenge. The cost of the facility was three million dollars. In addition, approximately five hundred thousand dollars would be needed for replacing carpet, air conditioners, and other renovation. The greatest expense would be remodeling a portion of the second floor for classrooms. An estimate was made that it would have cost in excess of eight million dollars to purchase the land and construct similar facilities.

Help From the California Baptist Foundation

The Golden Gate Seminary in Phoenix was now a vital part of Arizona Southern Baptist Convention work, and the California Baptist Foundation (CBF) had assisted the convention in various ways since the loss of the Baptist Foundation of Arizona. President Jakes was familiar with the California Baptist Foundation and contacted CBF officials regarding the possibility of interim financing for the purchase of Charter Hospital. The children's services had cash on hand from the sale of the John F. Long properties but would need the proceeds from the sale of the Little Canyon Campus and the corporate office building to fund the hospital purchase. Even with the sale of the other ABCS properties, there would be a shortfall in meeting the $3.5 million needed to purchase the hospital and making the necessary renovations and remodeling. Not only would the

CBF provide interim financing of $3,341,500 for the property purchase and remodeling, but they agreed to establish a line of credit for ABCS in the amount of $510,000 (Minutes 2001. ABCS Board Resolution 00-ADMIN-04). As in so many instances in its history, God's hand was again at work to protect and grow the Arizona Baptist children's agency. This time he used the California Baptist Foundation.

At the same board meeting, approval was given to sell the former corporate office to the Presson Company for $725,000, to close on January 31, 2001. The offer would be nonbinding because the purchase would be subject to the approval by the ABCS Board of Trustees. The purchase would also be contingent upon favorable zoning conditions at the proposed Charter Hospital property (Jakes 2000. "Purchase of Charter Hospital).

During this same period when financing arrangements were being made, the agency was experiencing some zoning difficulty with the City of Glendale. Use permits for buildings expire after twelve months, and the building had been vacant for two years. ABCS was required to get a text amendment approval to the zoning statutes to allow for the presence of the special education school. The Planning and Zoning Commission and the City Council of Glendale had to approve the special use permit. It took four to five months to obtain all the required permits and approvals. Neighborhood meetings had to be held and notices published regarding the proposed use of the property (Jakes 2005).

Although the building was furnished, it would take extensive repairs to put the various systems in working order. Also the two-year vacancy made it necessary to have extensive cleaning. The mechanical systems had to be serviced and some replaced. As the Baptist Family had done so many times in the past, they stepped forward in the form of the Campers on Mission (COM) to again assist ABCS. The timing was perfect because the COM were having their Southwest Regional Annual meeting in Phoenix. This organization, sponsored by the North American Mission Board, was looking for needed projects in the state. The president of the Arizona Chapter, Jim Creekmur, contacted President Jakes to offer their services. For several weeks in October and early November, ten COM volunteers cleaned bathrooms, walls, desks, chairs, and carpets in the administrative area of the building and checked out the building's mechanical systems. Commenting on this in the agency's newsletter, President Jakes was quoted, "We can't even begin to measure the dollar value of the effort that these volunteers put forth . . . but from the day we moved in, we could see the evidence of their efforts and feel the results of their prayers" (*Footprints* 2002, 3). Following the cleaning of each room, the group would pause and pray that the use of that room would be for the glory of God as children were served.

A New ABCS Campus in Glendale

On December 20 and 21, 2001, five large moving vans would transfer the furnishings, equipment, and records from the Twenty-third Avenue Corporate office in Phoenix to the new Charter Hospital facility at 6015 W. Peoria in Glendale. In addition to the corporate office, the move would bring ABCS service programs from other leased sites to the new facility, which would include foster care, adoption, family builders, parent aid, and outpatient counseling *(ibid.)*.

The remodeling of the classrooms, which would be on the second floor, was completed June 19, 2002; and three days later, June 21, the Little Canyon Campus and Bell Group Home children, staff, equipment, and records were moved to the new campus (Jakes 2002. ABCS Board Minutes, June 7).

April 14, 2002, was a day of celebration and dedication. ABCS associates and trustees joined volunteers and other friends to dedicate the John F. and Mary P. Long Family Life Development Center. Mr. Long and his family were present. He was quoted as saying,

> God is so good and his timetable is perfect . . . it would have been a mistake to purchase property and construct a new office complex when the former Charter Hospital of Glendale was perfect for your use and it was fully furnished. The purchase price was one only God could bring to ABCS. (ibid., 2)

A New Ministry: Crisis Pregnancy Center

An open house followed, and tours were given to all who wished to see the facility. As part of the relocation and fitting programs to available space, several opportunities for additional ministries were presented to ABCS. The Crisis Pregnancy Center (CPC) in Tucson had worked closely with the ABCS Southern Arizona Regional Office in Tucson, sharing many of the same values. The interest and experience of this fine organization was in helping young women with unexpected, and often, unwanted pregnancies. When babies became available for adoption, CPC referred the parents to licensed adoption agencies. President Jakes describes how the relationship between ABCS and Crisis Pregnancy Centers of Arizona (CPC) in Phoenix came about:

> ABCS was licensed as an Adoption agency about the time that CPC was strategically contemplating whether or not to start an Adoption program for themselves and learned of our new program. I met with Darryl VanderHaar, Board Chairman, privately at first, and then met with their full Board of Directors to talk about ABCS and our Christian Adoption program. As a result, their Board decided not to duplicate our new service, but rather to partner with us. CPC's responsibility in the partnership was to perform the birth parent counseling and refer infants for placement. ABCS' responsibility was to recruit and license adoptive families, make and supervise child placements through finalization of the adoption. The partnership has worked well . . . (Jakes 2005, 1)

The east wing of the John F. and Mary P. Long Family Development Center was available and an ideal place for CPC to locate its office. The space wasn't immediately needed by ABCS, and the close proximity of the programs made working together much more convenient and cost effective.

The ABCS administration also made an agreement with the Arizona Southern Baptist Convention (ASBC) to provide nine hundred square feet of space on the second floor of the new building for two of the ASBC programs—Baptist Senior Life Ministries and the Arizona Baptist

319

Historical Commission. ASBC needed extra space for its programs, and ABCS made the space available to the convention. Both of these programs of ASBC moved into their new home on June 15, 2002.

Little Canyon Campus is Sold

Prior to the relocation of the residential treatment and school programs to the new John F. and Mary P. Long Family Development Center, President Jakes had discussed possible interest in the purchase of the ABCS Little Canyon Campus by Grand Canyon University (GCU). Negotiations for a sale began in earnest in November 2001 and escrow closed July 5, 2002, with the university paying ABCS $1,713,000 for the campus and buildings, where its birth and dramatic growth had taken place. The former Little Canyon Campus would be used by the GCU Department of Education, and that use would include a charter school, which would also serve as a lab for student teachers.

"Caring for Kids Inc."

Securing adequate funding for operations and capital expansion was a challenge for all four ABCS presidents. Each of the presidents led fund-raising campaigns, and Baker began a support club called the "Circle of Champions." Also during the Baker administration, a subsidiary corporation, "ABCS Endowment," was chartered to hold, invest, and manage funds and property in the endowment. Sadly, these funds were reduced during the BFA bankruptcy.

President Jakes and the board took another step forward in promoting fund-raising. They established a new corporation for fund-raising—"Caring for Kids Inc." This new 501 (c)(3) nonprofit, tax-exempt program is an affiliated corporation of ABCS. Its goal was to raise financial support for ABCS and other Christian organizations. The new corporation would be in place by January 1, 2002 (Minutes, ABCS Board, 2001). Jakes appointed Rev. Shannon Martin as the executive director. The first chairman of the board was Todd Stottlemyre, former pitcher for the Arizona Diamondbacks.

Foster Care and Counseling Changes in the Central Arizona Regional Office

In chapter 10, the disadvantages of accepting purchase of care (POC) were listed. One of those disadvantages was the uncertainty of contract approval and adequate funding. Both foster care and counseling depended almost entirely on purchase of care by various state agencies. For several years, the outpatient (counseling) and foster-care programs ran a yearly deficit. It reached the point in 2001 that the administration and the board believed they could no longer offer those services in Maricopa County. This was not the case in the other regional offices. The subsidy burden became too heavy in spite of the fact that foster care is foundational in child welfare and outpatient counseling is foundational in behavioral health. On August 30, 2001, President Jakes called a special meeting of the board via telephone, and the approval was unanimous to *temporarily* close both programs in Maricopa County, "with regrets" (Minutes 2001. ABCS Board, August 30). This was the first time in almost forty years that ABCS did not provide foster care and counseling in Maricopa County.

The writer had made a point in the previous paragraphs about the important link between foster care and adoption. This principle is not diminished by the action, which the administration and board had to take. It was a decision that was commensurate with the risk that goes with contracting with the state. The rates paid by the state were simply not sufficient to continue those two quality programs. The state rates remained the same year after year, while agency expenses increased year by year.

The unhappy decision was made with the understanding that efforts would be made to reinstate these important programs at a later date when funding was more realistic. Dr. Willcoxon, ABCS executive vice president, would report in the following month that the agency was in the process of transferring eighty-five foster families to other agencies (Minutes 2001. ABCS Board, September). This closure involved only the central regional office. The other regions would continue their foster-care programs.

A New Relationship Emerges between ABCS and ASBC

The relationship between the Arizona Baptist Children's Services and the Arizona Southern Baptist Convention had been one of "limited ownership," since the birth of ABCS in 1960. The ownership was expressed through the election of ABCS trustees by the convention. The relationship structure began with the ABCS administration, which was accountable to the ABCS Board, which was accountable to the ASBC, generally acting through its executive board. This was a typical management paradigm for Baptist state conventions and their agencies throughout the Southern Baptist Convention. There was at least one exception where "child care" was a department of the state convention (Oklahoma) and did not have a separate board.

Concerns began to emerge in the 1980s and 1990s about descending liability as litigious winds swept the country. Churches, church agencies, and other religious bodies were not exempt from this storm. For Arizona Southern Baptists, this became an existential concern of great magnitude with the BFA bankruptcy. Would the tentacles of liability reach out to garner assets from the convention and its other agencies? While it is questionable as to its responsibility in law, the ASBC did pay a settlement to the BFA Liquidation Trust. This thin connection of potential liability was established as a result of the convention-elected BFA Board of Trustees.

This would have implications regarding ABCS's relationship to the ASBC. If a child died while in the care of ABCS or if a troubled parent sued ABCS and the State of Arizona over a child custody matter, including adoption, would the ASBC also be held accountable and be subject to a financial judgment? Other questions were raised. Can the churches carry out their mission of benevolence without owning the institutions that provide those services? Should a state convention directly own any ministry other than church planting, church growth, missions, and evangelism? Caring for widows, orphans, the sick, the troubled, and the poor are all vital Christian ministries that Jesus affirmed. Churches support many such benevolent ministries without having to own those ministries. Examples are Crisis Pregnancy and World Hunger Relief.

All of these issues were discussed with the ABCS and ASBC boards. As a result, on July 1, 2001, the ASBC voted to divest itself of its agencies, and Arizona Baptist Children's Services began a new relationship with the Arizona Southern Baptist Convention. Ownership of the children's services would belong to the ABCS Board who would elect its own trustees. The ASBC would continue to contribute to the work of ABCS through a "cooperative agreement." This would include regular financial support and continued observance of the Mother's Day offering in the churches. The convention had a similar agreement with the Baptist Senior Life Ministries and the Arizona Campus of Golden Gate Baptist Seminary.

In addition to removing any possible threads of liability for the convention, this action would open up new doors of opportunity for ABCS. It would remove the concern some had that church-state principles may be violated by ABCS accepting purchase of care from the state for its children. The scope of fund-raising could be enlarged. ABCS has valued its relationship with the ASBC, and the new transfer of ownership would not diminish that appreciation.

Summary

Each of the four ABCS presidents had unique contributions to make to the strength of child and family services in Arizona. These contributions were progressive, and each built upon the accomplishments of the earlier administrations. Even the nomination of trustees would reflect the presidents' agendas and be complimentary of the direction the presidents planned for the agency to take. But this was always a two-way process with the board influencing the president as much as the president influenced the board. A brief summary of the contributions of the various presidents will enhance the understanding of these statements.

George Wilson—Rev. Wilson shepherded the start-up process having served as an Arizona pastor; a member of the convention's executive board; a member of the Children's Home Board; and lastly, the first superintendent of the home. He loved children and was a well-liked and respected leader among Arizona Southern Baptists. He led in the successful effort to birth this new ministry.

Don Cain—Rev. Cain brought experience and knowledge of child-care technology to the children's home. He led in its transformation from a small group home for children to a multiservice agency that addressed serious, current children's needs in the state. In addition to being a minister, he was also trained in behavioral science. He knew how to work with state leaders and develop funding sources that would exponentially enlarge the small program. He developed the first programs outside of the Phoenix area.

C. Truett Baker—Rev. Baker, also an ordained Baptist minister and a professional social worker, had broad experience in child and family services and in developing regional programs. Baker's legacy would be twofold: First, he was knowledgeable about the importance of permanency for children provided through home-based services. Second, his experience in establishing regional programs would enable him to move ABCS beyond the Maricopa County borders to all areas of the state. While Rev. Cain would move ABCS toward special services for children, Rev. Baker would carry that a step further in offering specialized services to children and families through statewide home-based programs.

P. David Jakes—The fourth president of ABCS would have the technical business and administrative ability to give long-range stability to growth. His background in health-care administration, Joint Commission Accreditation, and managed care was a perfect fit to move ABCS into the fiscal complexity of the twenty-first century. He, too, is a Baptist minister and a sought-after speaker and preacher. He understands how to work with boards, Baptist polity, and develop and manage resources. One of Rev. Jakes's many strengths is his experience and ability to do strategic planning, which is vital to planned growth and stewardship of resources.

The first three years of the Jakes administration were characterized by adjustment, changes, relocation, and growth. This was the fallout period from the BFA bankruptcy. Adding further to the challenge was an internal financial crisis resulting in the discharge of a senior staff member. The programs were reaccredited; and a major new program, Adoption, started. The regional network was completed, and all Maricopa County programs but one were moved into the John F. and Mary P. Long Family Development Center in Glendale. New friends were made, such as the California Baptist Foundation, and a new relationship was developed with an old friend, the Arizona Southern Baptist Convention.

Secret of Success

Throughout the years, the boards of trustees have been the backbone and strength of ABCS. These faithful friends have stood by the agency in good times and in less than good times. They have attended countless meetings, raised dollars, advocated for children in the legislature, and constantly prayed for the ministry they served. They loved children, supported the associates, and above all else have seen their board service as a Christian ministry, serving God by caring for his children.

Alongside the board, the ABCS associates have served God in their own way by caring for the children on a day-to-day basis. They have endured insults and assaults in ministering to the physical, mental, social, educational, and spiritual needs of the troubled children in their care. They have often been unappreciated and always underpaid. Some have stayed a few weeks and others for over twenty years. There are not enough words of praise to give proper credit to these heroes of children. However, some of the best rewards have been that of former students who have returned in later years to say "thank-you" to a special associate in their life while they were at ABCS.

ABCS Trustee L-R Dennis Adams, Ron Riemer, Les Jennings, Jr.

325

This was also the period when President Baker turned over the reins of leadership to a new president, David Jakes. This was a time of celebration for the great things that God has done. But God is not done with ABCS, and the future is as bright as the promises and faithfulness of God.

Bunkhouse Associates

Truett Baker continued to serve as a consultant during the transition period until January 2000. He had left his "footprints" alongside the pioneers of earlier years. But equally as important, ABCS had left its "prints" on him, and that impression would be a source of joy in his modest achievements and in happy memories for years to come.

References

Air Force Times. 1999. Room in Their Hearts. October 4.

Arizona Republic. 1997. Four Year-Old Russian Girls Placed in Foster Care. July 31.

Baker, C. Truett. 1997. Special report to the board. ABCS, September 26-27, Phoenix, AZ.

_____. 1997. President's quarterly report to the ABCS Board. October-December: 2.

_____. 1998. Retirement plans. Filed in board minutes archives.

_____. 1999. Plans for departure as interim directors of foster care and adoption. Memo to P. David Jakes. April 7.

Business Journal. 1998. Top Employee Assistance Programs in the Valley. January 30.

By-Laws and Rules of Decorum, Article 1.1. 1958. The Object and Purpose, Baptist Children's Home of Arizona.

Cause, Angela. 1999. Adoption services report. ABCS Board of Trustees Report. June 4.

_____. 1999. Adoption services report. ABCS Board of Trustees Report. December 3.

Carlson, Donna. 2001. Adopting A Passion. *Portraits* 5, no. 1.

Dallas Morning News. 1999. Keeping it in the Family. August 9.

Flint, Gerald D. 1986. The building blocks of the ABC'S: The Arizona Baptist Children's Services. An independent research project conducted through the Department of History at Grand Canyon College, Phoenix, AZ.

Footprints. 1996. Agency Gears Up For Statewide Expansion. Summer.

Footprints. 1999. The Perfect Ten. Winter.

_____. 2000. The Miracle of Healing. Winter.

_____. 2001. A Match Made in Heaven. October:1.

_____. 2002. A Moving Time. March.

Jakes, David. 2002. Minutes of the ABCS Board of Trustees, June 7.

_____. *2000.* Memo to the ABCS Board of Trustees, September 22.

_____. 2000. Quarterly major budget variance and unbudgeted FTE Report. ABCS annual board report. September 22.

_____. *2000.* Purchase of Charter Hospital. *Memorandum to the Executive Committee,* ABCS Board of Trustees, July 27.

_____. 1999. Impact of BFA cease and desist order on ABCS. Special report to the ABCS Board of Trustees, September 24, 37-38.

_____. 2000. Revision of JFL Family Development Institute Plan. Board resolution 00—P&F-5. In Board Minutes, September 22.

Jakes, P. D. 1998. Letters to C. Truett Baker dated January 24 and 29. Filed in ABCS correspondence archives.

_____. 2000. Purchase of Charter Hospital. Memorandum to Executive Committee, ABCS, July 27.

_____. 2005. Email to C. Truett Baker dated June 09. Filed in ABCS correspondence archives.

_____. n.d. ABCS conceptual narrative—purchase of Charter Hospital of Glendale. Unpublished and undated paper in ABCS Archives.

Minutes. 1986. Strategic planning process and goals for 1986-87. ABCS Board Resolution 85-PRO-4. June 7.

_____. 1998. Approval of business plan for adoption program. ABCS Board Resolution 98-PRO-6. Phoenix, AZ, September 26.

_____. 1998. Special called meeting of the Executive Committee, ABCS, November 3.

—1999. Executive Committee, ABCS Board, August 12.

_____. 1998. ABCS Board of Trustees, March 27.

_____. 2000. Approval to purchase Charter Hospital of Glendale. ABCS Board Resolution 00-ADM-4, December 1.

_____. 2001. Adoption of management plan and closure of the outpatient and foster care programs. Board Resolution 01-ADMIN-04. August 30.

_____. 1986. Board Resolution 85-PRO-4.

_____. 1996. Board Resolution 96-E-1.

_____. 2001. ABCS Board of Trustees, September 28.

_____. 1999. ABCS short range goals. Quarterly report to the board of trustees, March 19.

Chapter 12

Welcoming The Children—Tomorrow

Introduction

There is a certain amount of arrogance when one presumes to forecast the future, unless the individual is a weatherperson. However, that must not be used as an excuse for not doing long-range thinking, which results in some kind of future predictions. With the best of long-range plans, yearly adjustment must still be made to allow for changing times, new technology, available resources, and other new information.

Arizona Baptist Children's Services is less than fifty years old, but she is well beyond those years of maturity in developing innovative and effective services | The stewardship of the past will be treasured and become the capital of the future. CTB

for children and families. Not having expensive campuses and buildings has given her a flexibility to move about in adjusting to changing needs, which older, more monolithic agencies have not had.

While being the last existing state Southern Baptist child/family service to begin, she has provided better coverage of the entire state than most of her other Baptist state counterparts. Her size, in relation to her constituency, is among the largest, if not the largest, of the child/family agencies affiliated in some way with a state Southern Baptist Convention. All of this is to say that ABCS has an honorable and productive past. That stewardship of the past will be treasured and become the capital of the future. So how will the future of ABCS appear? We know one thing. It will not look like the past, except for the values and Christian legacy that will be carried over into whatever new forms of child and family care seem best. The substance remains the same, but the forms or applications change. The application in the first century took the form of homes provided for the orphans by widows. In the eighth century, the application was a foundling hospital started by Datheus, archbishop of Milan. In 1740 in Savannah, Georgia, the application was an orphanage started by Evangelist George Whitfield. In more current times, these forms of care were children's homes, foster homes, adoption, and counseling.

No doubt, those past expressions of "welcoming children" will not all vanish in the twenty-first century. It is important to use those tools that have been effective in the past, and at the same time, be open to new ways to "welcome the children" consistent with the new challenges and helping technology that God has given.

And so . . . we think and dream and envision what could be.

There is no time frame on the implementation of the various directions that are suggested, if in fact they are embraced at all by ABCS. By suggesting these future directions, the writer is not implying that the current programs are unimportant or out-of-date. It was the writer who led in the beginning of some of the programs and developed all of them. Suggesting these directions is a recognition that needs change, and our tools to address those needs are refined and updated based upon new technology and understanding. The writer believes that the following directions and the methods for implementing those directions reflect changing public policy, increasingly scarce resources, and a better understanding of how children and families are best helped. It also recognizes the great potential that churches have in re-inventing their own role in family ministry.

> ABCS must develop resources that tie its methods more closely to family and church-driven ministries than that of state contract-driven services. CTB

The following ideas, new and old, must be understood in that light and recognized for what they are—one person's experienced projections about possibilities and opportunities, which ABCS may face. It must be understood that these comments are solely the thoughts of the author and do not necessarily represent the opinions of the ABCS administration and board, nor establish a mandate for their implementation!

This noble history of the untiring efforts of men and women and the faithfulness and blessing of God would not be complete without this explanation. The extraordinary growth of ABCS became a reality because of contracting with state agencies that cared for children. During that time, the mission of ABCS and that of the state were much the same. The future will be different. ABCS must develop resources that tie its methods more closely to family and church-based ministries. However, it would be a mistake to ignore the opportunities for continuing to cooperate with government agencies in serving children.

The following headings name the projected directions, and the numbered statements that follow each direction describes implementation methods for reaching those directions

Home-Based and Least Restrictive Services

1. Counseling and family-life education are fundamental to all child-welfare and behavioral-health services.

They are also cost-effective, portable, and instrumental in preventing the need for other services. Premarital counseling and parent education are far underutilized and undervalued as prevention agents. (Counseling is also referred to in this book as "outpatient services"). Training "lay counselors" in churches has unlimited potential as are support groups for various common family needs.

Affordability is a challenge that must be faced if we really want to help children and families. The ABCS Southern Regional office has a shared-cost method they call "Church-Supported Counseling" program. This is a plan where a church or association may contract with the ABCS center to provide counseling for their families, and the church/association subsidizes the program. The cost is shared three ways between the church/ association, ABCS, and the client.

The marketing of counseling programs will make this resource known to churches and the general public. There can be an educational component to the marketing, which will hopefully break down some of the barriers that keep people from seeking help.

A toll-free telephone service available to families all over the state can bring potential help and guidance for those seeking help with their children. Families that need extensive help can be referred to the ABCS Regional Center in their area. There may be grants available from Christian foundations to fund a pilot program to determine the effectiveness of such a program. It might be possible to use trained volunteers to answer the phones in much the same way as the Crystal Cathedral in California provides this service nationwide.

Jesus went about healing the sick, both in mind and body. Is not this a part of the mission of his church?

2. Children's services will continue to be family-based and permanency oriented.

This is not a new role for ABCS, but it is a young role. There are those who have difficulty in getting the "orphanage-image" out of their mind when they think of caring for children. The orphanage is an anachronism, and it will not be returning. Children's homes, for the most part, are a relic of the past. The children's home is a part of the Southern culture, and it will not go away soon, but it will go away. The few remaining children's homes in the north continue for a different reason. Professor Jones explains this: "Nevertheless, all these institutions have been marginalized; all exist on the periphery of the child-welfare mainstream where they manage to survive only because they are bulwarked on great wealth or backed by powerful veteran's organizations" (Jones 1994, 12). Best practices in child welfare recognize that children should not be reared in institutions but in families.

There may always be a role for group care for short-term emergency services or specialized services, such as for the developmentally disabled. Children should have the permanency and the security of belonging to a family. In addition to the "best practice" motivation, home-based services provide good stewardship of scarce resources as this focus puts money into programs rather than buildings.

The principle of "least restrictive" placement will continue to guide decisions regarding out-of-home placement. Child-welfare and family services are best understood as a "continuum of care" beginning with the "least restrictive" and extending to "most restrictive." The term "restrictive" refers to the proximity a child is to his/her own home on the "continuum of care" scale, and the intensity of care the child/family receives. The following are but a few of the child/family services, and their position illustrates the progression of acuity from the "least" to the "most" restricted care (Dore and Kennedy 1981).

The following programs must be seen in a downward continuum beginning with the *least* restrictive, "Family-life Education . . .," to the **most** restrictive, "Closed Unit Psychiatric Hospitalization.

Least Restrictive	Family-life education and school-based services In-home services Outpatient counseling Day treatment Family foster care
More Restrictive	Treatment foster care (Professional foster care) Group foster care Group home care Children's home care Therapeutic group home care Residential treatment (open campus)
MOST RESTRICTIVE	Residential treatment (closed unit or campus) Closed-unit Psychiatric hospital

The "restrictive" factor must always take into account the acuity of a child's needs and the child's permanency plan. One would not put a child who was seriously mentally ill in a foster home simply because it was nearer his family's residence; however, if the child was symptom free, a nearby foster home might be the placement of choice if the parents were ill or incapacitated, and the plan was for the child to return home following the illness. Many factors go into whether or not a child should be removed from his/her own home, and if removed, what type of placement is best. When all factors are considered, it should be in the "least restrictive" place.

3. Foster care, in its various levels, will continue to be the out-of-home placement of choice for most children.

The Central Regional Office (Maricopa County) of ABCS will develop a way to once again provide foster care and outpatient services. This may be done by using voluntary foster homes, which has proved successful in the Southern Region, or redesigning the program in such a way as for it to be cost effective. The appeal that voluntary foster homes have would be that they would not be state contract programs. Some combination of support may be used, such as voluntary homes for regular foster care and state contracted Professional Parent homes.

Foster care is the oldest form of out-of-home care (an example was baby Moses) and the most utilized. Here are some of the advantages that simply don't go away, regardless of the times:

(1) It is most like a child's own family.
(2) A child can receive individual and specialized care.
(3) It is flexible in many ways. A foster home can be located almost anywhere, and it can be specialized in any number of ways, such as custodial care, emergency care, shelter for unmarried pregnant women, therapeutic care, care for the developmentally delayed, care for children awaiting adoption, respite care to give exhausted parents a break, to name a few.
(4) The foster parents can provide parent training and modeling for a child's parents and even provide support for those parents after the child has been returned to them.
(5) It is less expensive since money is spent for services instead of buildings.

Professional Parenting (PP) is a specialized form of foster care that is a resource for very troubled children in a small-group setting. The agency may own the home, or it may be owned by the parents. It is usually a large home whose parents can care for six to eight children, depending upon the acuity of the children's needs. PP is a career for couples who want to provide care for children as full-time employment. Usually, the husband and wife both work in the home with the children and receive a salary as an employee of the agency. Sometimes this is done on a contract basis. They may even have help with the housekeeping and cooking. Professional parents work closely with the mental-health care professionals who are counseling with the children and their parents. The children may be seen individually and as a group by a social worker, psychologist, or psychiatrist; and they may be on psychotropic medications.

Dr. Robert Snodgrass, founder and director of People Places in Stanton, Virginia, has demonstrated for over thirty years that even the most disturbed children in institutions can be cared for in those skilled Professional Parent homes. The Jewish child care program in New York closed out their institutional programs in the 1940s in favor of specialized group homes and foster homes (Barnard 1973). These parents are highly trained and are salaried by the agency for which they work.

In the ABCS program, parents could be regular, as well as specialized foster parents. PP homes in every region could provide for most specialized out-of-home care needed by children and families under the supervision of the regional office associates. The important thing to remember in establishing a PP program is that there must be sufficient support for the parents so that they are not burned out by the severity of children's problems.

Diversity

4. *Diversity in support.* There should be a new openness to embracing diverse support.

Like the last recommendation, this emphasis is not new, but it is one that should continue to be developed. Baker was not successful in several entrepreneurial ventures—to earn money—but others could succeed where he failed. Investing in related for-profit businesses can successfully be done. It requires experienced business people on the board and in the administration to successfully make this happen. The thrift business and employee assistance programs were good examples that would work with the right leadership and adequate funding. ABCS shouldn't limit its possibilities to past ideas but look at business opportunities such as franchises of various types. Fast foods would be a possibility not only because of their earning potential but because of the training opportunity this would offer young people in the programs.

Donated dollars are shrinking in Arizona, as well as purchase of care dollars. There are skillful business people who have made millions for themselves who would be willing to share that knowledge with an agency like ABCS. In the past, our boards have given almost all of their attention to service programs. Depending upon any single source of funding is dangerous in this day and time. ABCS would be wise to develop many sources of funding in addition to the present sources of gifts, endowment, purchase of care, and fees for service. Future sources could include additional endowment, grants, earned income by business ventures, and special events. Donor acquisition must be an ongoing effort led by an experienced planned giving director. Without BFA, the children's services must offer assistance with estate planning and charitable life insurance. The California Baptist Foundation may be a resource for technical assistance in these areas. Whoever provides the hands-on estate planning, the agency must give public attention to encouraging inclusion of ABCS in wills and estate plans.

The Circle of Champions giving club has been a very helpful resource in increasing ABCS visibility and encouraging support. This emphasis should be promoted through the regional centers and perhaps lead to an annual recognition banquet for Circle of Champion members. The newly formed "Caring For Kids Inc." is a big step in the right direction to encourage corporate and foundation giving.

Obtaining government grants for specific child/family programs will be more easily pursued now without ownership ties to the ASBC.

This is one reason that Baptist hospitals and colleges have developed new relationships with their state conventions over the past thirty years. Grant writing is a specialized skill, and ABCS would be wise to retain the services of an experienced grant writer who would be constantly searching for opportunities to locate funding sources for meeting the needs of children and families, and then preparing proposals to garner those resources. When done properly by qualified, experienced people, there will be scores of grant applications going out each year to scores of foundations and businesses. Since grants are closely attached to specific projects, the grant writer must have a knowledge of child/family programs and be able to work closely with the program staff. The greatest challenge of this effort is recruiting the right person.

5. *Diversity in board membership.* Board member diversity must be considered.

It was a difficult decision for the ABCS administration and the ASBC to change their structured relationship, but it was a necessary decision for both groups. The change, which allows the ABCS Board to elect their members, is a step in the right direction, but a broader policy is needed. As it is now, ABCS Board membership is restricted to Southern Baptist Christians.

While ABCS is not currently a member of the Child Welfare League of America (CWLA), such membership requires that board composition reflects the characteristics of the population it serves. The CWLA consultant, James R. Mann, made the following observations in his report to the ABCS Membership Committee of the Board following the 1979 membership survey:

> It seems imperative that there be thought given as to how the current board can work with the ASBC in not only developing a new blueprint for board composition, but in allowing the ABCS Board full partnership in the nominating process. This is further complicated by the fact that funding is currently 86.3% public purchase of services . . . ABCS'

funding and clientele are predominantly non-Baptist. Thus, there exists a significant conflict with the community seeing the agency as too doctrinaire, and the Baptist Convention perceiving the agency as being too secular . . . *the league believes that board composition should reflect the clientele it services.*" (Child Welfare League of America 1979, 3-4)

Opening the door for board membership to non-Baptist Christians would greatly broaden the support and respect of the religious community. It would bring in fresh ideas, new advocates, new expertise, and other resources that are going to be vital to the agency's fiscal health in the future.

A shift needs to take place in the thinking about the role of the board as raising resources for those service programs. The board must become a "beehive" of entrepreneurial thinking about ways to increase endowment and operating revenues.

6. *Diversity in programs.* There is a future for group care in specialized services.

Several children's homes that are experiencing a decline in referrals are converting their group-care space to units for homeless mothers and their children. Mothers can receive job training and life-skills training while their children are cared for on the campus. Other campuses are converting their child-care space to care for the developmentally disabled. Virginia Baptist Children's Home and Family Services and North Carolina Baptist Children's Homes have done this for many years (Blackwell 2002). Detoxification and substance abuse treatment is another need that is growing, which can be met in group-care facilities.

Group care will always be needed for large sibling groups who wish to remain together and for children who have difficulty with the intimacy of relationships that characterize foster family care. Nevertheless, this should be short term as permanency options are planned. Children should not be reared in institutions unless they require lifetime care in the case of severely impaired children and youth who require children's nursing home care.

The diversity spoken of here is not limited to group care. Various new opportunities in counseling and family-life education have already been mentioned. An entrepreneurial opportunity exists for making use of a full or part-time person to do research and development (R&D) in Christian child and family services. This would be a wonderful way to use a social work doctoral student in a field-placement setting from the Baylor University School of Social Work. The writer is aware of no one doing this type of R&D work.

6. *Diversity in area served.* Into all the West?

At one time, Arizona Southern Baptists supported the child-care ministry of New Mexico because there was no such ministry in Arizona. In turn, the New Mexico Baptist Children's Home would accept children referred by Arizona Baptist pastors. Could a similar thing happen again? Arizona Southern Baptists, particularly ABCS, have been greatly helped by the California Baptist Foundation. At one time, other states were part of the ASBC, and the ASBC helped to start the Colorado Baptist Convention (Pair 1989). Could ABCS extend its regional network to include states that do not offer Christian social ministry, i.e., California, Utah, Nevada? ABCS would not want to duplicate services already being offered, but if resourcing churches that wish to extend Christian social ministries to their families included churches in other states, this might be a worthy possibility. ABCS could sponsor and be a part of a Western States Coalition of Christian Family Ministries. A dialogue could be set in motion for Arizona, California, New Mexico, Utah, Nevada, and Colorado to share ideas and resources to minister to the needs of children and families. Dr. Diana Garland, in her book *Church Agencies*, states that family breakdown may be the greatest social problem of our time (Garland 1994). Who better to address this tragedy than the church? (more to be said about this in recommendation 8.)

Prevention and Education

7. Regional programs will be expanded and strengthened.

Regional services are a corollary to the "least restrictive" principle.

For services to be "home based," and "least restrictive," they must have local expression and support. As long as the emphasis was upon group care, a child could be transported from any place in the state to a Phoenix facility or to any other large group facility.

There is another issue of a more practical and tangible nature for supporting a local presence. People are more interested in supporting a local ministry than one which is in another part of the state. For years, people outside of Phoenix would ask this writer, "When are you going to have services for children in our area?" The answer was always, "some day," and that day came. Program planning must now be done in six areas rather than one, and all six areas should have equal attention. This does not mean that all areas should have the same programs. Quite the contrary! Area programming should fit the indigenous needs and resources of the area. Traditional programs such as counseling, foster care, family preservation, adoption, and in-home programs should probably be regular fare for all regions. Specialized programs such as RAFT, addiction counseling, pregnancy counseling, maternity homes, and group homes should be developed as needed and as wanted by people in each area.

8. ABCS can be a resource to churches in helping their families.

Dr. Diana Garland, dean of the School of Social Work at Baylor University, has advocated for what she calls "church social work" (Garland 1994).[13] Her emphasis is upon equipping churches to provide social ministries to its families and to advocate for the needs of at-risk children and families. Such a ministry would connect families to resources where they can find the help that they need. Christian social ministries is a specialized

---

[13] Dr. Garland also wrote the foreword to this book.

field of social work offered at Baylor University in Waco, Texas. It would be an exceptional opportunity for ABCS to offer an internship to a Baylor social work student that would be mutually beneficial. The student would receive the practical experience required as part of his/her training, and ABCS could learn about ways that churches can be equipped to better minister to the total needs of their families. Dr. Garland has been a guest of ABCS in the past, and perhaps additional consultations could provide useful ideas and strategies to support this goal.

The church social worker is a broker of services. Part of the needed expertise is in knowing how to access resources to meet specific individual and family needs. There is no better place to go for help than to the church and people know about that. Many churches have a benevolence committee that provides funds to help with utilities, gas, groceries, and a myriad of other short-term emergency needs. Those funds are often managed by well-meaning people who give out resources without attempting to address the deeper needs of the family. The greatest need of all is spiritual, and this door is often opened by meeting the very immediate and physical needs of families.

One of the most needed ministries in churches today is family-life education. This could be combined with day care, after-school programs, and other family ministries to meet a critical need that many communities are facing, as families experience more and more deterioration brought on by poverty, drugs, violence, and child neglect. As resources are available, ABCS could have a day care specialist who would consult with churches about how to set up their own day care programs. This is a wonderful way to meet unchurched people in the community who are looking for all the help they can get for their children and themselves.

Advocacy

9.   Advocacy is a major force for helping children and families.

Advocacy is the term used to describe standing up for children in the public forum. It costs money—lots of money—to help needy and troubled children and their families. This expense is not always one that public officials want to embrace. When this happens, those who love children and value families must step forward and express their concerns. This may be at city council, the state legislature, or in the Congress. This advocacy may take the form of formal testimony before these government bodies or a letter or phone call to the officials of the government body.

ABCS has a rich history of joining with others in insisting that government shoulder the financial responsibility for dependent families. ABCS was a founding member of the Arizona Council of Centers for Children and Adults—now the Arizona Council of Human Service Providers. This advocacy partnership brought strength to the voice for children in the halls of the Arizona legislature. This positive voice for children was also joined by many members of the legislature in providing resources for children and families. ABCS can serve thousands of children each year through its service programs. It can serve tens of thousands of children and families by working with others in insuring that adequate resources are available to meet their needs. Children can't vote and must depend upon others to support them in the legislatures and in Congress.

Churches need to understand that they cannot lobby, as a church, for any issue in government. That will endanger their nonprofit status with the IRS. *Individuals* in churches can advocate for issues that affect the welfare of children and families.

10. Coalitions will replace competition.

ABCS has a history of working with other agencies in the community through its Family Builders and Family Preservation programs. As the regional programs grow, there will be opportunity for ABCS to form networks and coalitions with other agencies to respond to the needs of children and families for which the state wants to provide services. If the behavior and testimony of ABCS associates are Christ-honoring, they will have a wonderful opportunity to be "salt and light" in the marketplace of human suffering and need. Determination of need is like a coin with two sides. One side is need—is there a need in the community for this service? If a need is being met by others, ABCS should not duplicate that service. Gone are the days when the prevailing mentality is that, if Baptists don't do it, it won't be done right!

The other side of that coin is the call of ministry. In light of the mission and Christian commitment of ABCS, should this program be done? A need or needs may well exist, which are not appropriate for ABCS to address, nor are they consistent with its mission. ABCS should not try to meet every need.

11. The role of nonprofit family services organizations must be protected.

Nonprofit organizations (NPO), or not-for-profit organizations, as they are sometimes called, began as a loosely organized group of volunteers who gave their time and resources out of love and commitment for the cause they supported. One example of these roots goes back to Hamburg and Elberfeld, Germany, in the 1800s. A process for administering charity came about with the organization of a bureau and the apportionment of the cities into districts. Each district had an overseer who supervised volunteers. The volunteers called upon the poor in their district to see if they could render help. The volunteers did "friendly visiting," which was the forerunner of the social work profession.

The Charity Organization Society (COS) of London, which followed many of the Hamburg-Elberfeld methods, was born in 1869 and later started in Buffalo, New York in 1877. The early associates were volunteers who would later be trained. The training led to the professionalization of the "friendly visitors" in 1898. The occasion was the beginning of a training school for these "friendly visitors," sponsored by COS. This is the date given for the beginning of social work. It was called the Training Class in Applied Philanthropy and was held from June 20-July 30, 1898. It would later be called the New York School of Social Work and today is called the Columbia University School of Social Work (Baker 1998).

Over the years, society has idealized the work of charity. So highly did society regard these organizations that the government established special protection from taxation to promote and encourage private charitable initiatives to benefit those who were unable to care for themselves (Kluger and Baker 1994). With the emergence of block grants to the states in the 1980s, the federal government began a slow transfer of responsibility for charity to the states, but in the process, failed to adequately fund those transferred responsibilities (ibid). The states have used their federal money, matched with state money, to fund federal initiatives, such as Medicaid and Family Preservation services. Both NPOs and for-profit organizations have applied for those funds creating an environment of competition for the government dollars.

Many states have totally or partially "privatized" their human services. That is, they are relinquishing operational responsibilities for those services by contracting them out to private agencies (vendors), which may be for-profit or NPOs (Demone and Gibelman 1989).

Foster care is an example of a program that many states have turned over to the private agencies through the purchase of care (POC) process. As this begins to happen, the for-profit and NPOs flocked to "feed at the public trough" (Baker 1996, 13-14). Competition then becomes fierce, and the for-profit organizations complain that their NPO colleagues have a tax advantage over them, and the bidding process for contracts is not on a level playing field.

In addition to the NPOs and for-profit organizations, a third sector has slowly developed almost solely operating on government funds. For lack of a better term, they can be called "nonprofit vendors." Because of the near proximity to their funding source, they have also embraced the culture and stringent regulations of the state to the point that it is becoming difficult to separate them from their government funding source. When NPOs become this enmeshed with their government funding source, they begin to forfeit their distinction as an NPO. Their advocacy voice is smothered, and they can lose sight of the charitable or religious spirit that characterized their beginning. In addition, former supporters are discouraged from continuing their support because the government is "taking care of their needs," and they will give to other causes that truly need their support.

This writer believes that these are the strongest arguments for not becoming excessively dependent upon purchase of care revenues. As one of many resources, the income can be very helpful and enhance the growth potential of the agency. "The nonprofit organizations that will survive into the twenty-first century will be those that can thrive on competition, effectively read community needs and priorities, deliver the right services at the right time and right price, and be able to document their effectiveness" (Kluger and Baker 1994, xii).

Summary

The Christian Church has been "welcoming the children" in every generation since Jesus's earthly walk. They had a special place in his heart. His compassion reflected the strong sense of justice preached by Isaiah and Jeremiah.[14] God spoke to the early church through James to make it clear that faith in Christ was more than adherence to a system of beliefs. Faith produces good works, and among those works was the care for the widows and orphans. "Pure religion and undefiled before God and the Father is this, to visit the fatherless and widows in their affliction, and to keep himself unspotted from the world."[15] In every generation since the Old Testament prophets, God has made provision for the children, and Jesus only reflected the heart of God in this tender subject. The early church and generations of Christians since would find an expression of care, appropriate for their times, to help needy children.

ABCS followed in that tradition by providing a home for children in 1961. In 1970, the needs of children and families were different, and ABCS adjusted its services to fit those changing needs. Another adjustment was made in the 1980s and 1990s. It is the task of ABCS to prayerfully look again in 2006, and later in 2010, to see if there are better ways to serve children and their families.

---

[14] References are to Isaiah 1:17 and Jeremiah 7:6.
[15] James 1:27

Only God knows what ABCS's future will be, but the potential for outstanding leadership in Christian social ministry and child/family services is unlimited! If this sounds like a dream, remember the past.

Every good idea or dream will not be turned into a reality, but the dreaming and visioning must go on as long as there is a child who has no place or a family who has no hope. ABCS will not solve all the problems of Arizona's children, but by the grace of God, some will be solved. We will always be reminded that a service to children is a ministry to God: "In as much as you have done it unto one of the least of these, you have done it unto me." [16]

---

[16]   Matthew 24:45

References

Baker, C. Truett. 1998. 100 Years and more of social work. Unpublished paper presented at the District I, NASW Awards Dinner, Phoenix, AZ, March 3.

_____. 1996. A New Paradigm for Understanding Church-State Separation Issues as They Relate to Serving Children and Families in Need. *Journal Of Family Ministry* 10 (Winter): 3.

Barnard, Jacqueline. 1973. *The Children You Gave Us*. New York: Bloch Publishing Co.

Blackwell, Michael C. 2002. *A Place for Miracles*. Boone, NC: Parkway Publications Inc.

Child Welfare League of America. 1979. Report to the Membership Committee of the Arizona Baptist Children's Services for provisional membership, New York: CWLA, April 16-19. Filed in Program Archives of ABCS.

Demone, Harold W. Jr., and Margaret Gibelman, eds. 19989. Services for Sale: Purchasing Health and Human Services. New Brunswick: Rutgers University Press.

Dore, Martha M. and Karen G. Kennedy. 1981. Two Decades of Turmoil: Child Welfare Services, 1960-1980. *Child Welfare* 60 (June): 6.

Garland, Diana. 1994. *Chuch Agencies*. Washington, D.C.: Child Welfare League of America.

Jones, Marshall B. 1994. The Past and Future of Child Welfare: Voluntary Benevolence: America's History of Caring for Children in Need, Part 4. *Caring*, Summer.

Kluger, Miriam P. and William A. Baker. *Innovative Leadership in the Nonprofit Organization*. Washington, D.C.: Child Welfare League of America.

Pair, C. L. 1989. *A History of the Arizona Southern Baptist Convention: 1928-1984*. Phoenix: Executive Board of the Arizona Southern Baptist Convention.

1948 to 1955

Interest began to grow rapidly to open a Baptist college in Arizona. Grand Canyon College was founded in 1949 in Prescott, Arizona. The debt of the college in 1955 concerned Arizona Southern Baptists, and interest in the children's home decreased (Minutes, BGCA, November 2-4, 1948, First Southern Baptist Church, Chandler, AZ,).

1950

The convention approved a plan to supplement all funds designated for the children's home, up to one hundred dollars per month. The fund had now reached $8,305.67. No action was to be taken toward building a children's home until Grand Canyon College was on its feet [*sic*] financially. (Annual, BGCA, October 24-26, 1950, First Southern Baptist Church, Tucson, AZ; Pair 1989)

1951

The messengers of the BGCA directed that the children's home funds be invested in ten-year Grand Canyon College bonds (Annual, BGCA, Trinity Baptist Church, November 6-8, 1951; Pair 1989).

1952

The Baptist Foundation of Arizona (BFA) was organized, and the children's home funds were placed in their hands (Annual, BGCA, November 4-6, 1952, Calvary Baptist Church, Glendale, AZ).

1955

A resolution was passed by the convention to open a Baptist children's home (*The Baptist Beacon*, November 24, 1955).

1956

A gift of twenty thousand dollars was given for the first building on the children's home campus by Mr. and Mrs. J. B. Carnes of Yuma, Arizona (Annual, BGCA, November 14-16, First Southern Baptist Church, Yuma, AZ).

1957

The executive board of the convention appointed a committee to take steps necessary to begin the children's home project. The chair of this committee was Rev. George R. Wilson, later to serve as the first superintendent (*Baptist Beacon,* January 9, 1958).

1958

May 9. The Baptist Children's Home of Arizona was granted a charter to operate as a child-caring, child-placement, and child-adoption agency of the Baptist General Convention of Arizona from the State Corporation Commission, (*Baptist Beacon*, September 8, 1960)

1959

March 3, 1959. The executive board authorized all children's home funds that were held in the Baptist Foundation to be transferred to the board of the Baptist children's home (Annual, BGCA, November 16-18, 1959, First Southern Baptist Church, Winslow, AZ).

Land was purchased from the BGCA Trust and Memorial Fund from funds received from the sale of property donated by Lester and Marie Jennings of Laveen, Arizona (*Baptist Beacon,* November 5, 1959).

The children's home was granted a 501 (c)(3) Internal Revenue Service status.

1960

February 29. Rev. George Wilson, pastor of Central Baptist Church, Phoenix, and chairman of the children's home board, was appointed the first superintendent for the home beginning June 1, 1960 (Annual, BGCA, November 16-18, 1970, First Baptist Church, Winslow, AZ).

Final plans for construction of the home were approved August 5, 1960, at a cost of twenty-six thousand dollars. Groundbreaking was held August 29 at 3101 E. Missouri, Phoenix (*Baptist Beacon,* September 8, 1960).

1961

January 12. A child-care license was granted to the home for nine children. The first child was admitted to the Baptist Children's Home in January (*Baptist Beacon,* January 26, 1961)

The children's services was scheduled to receive ten thousand dollars from the State Mission Offering if their goal was met (*Baptist Beacon*, October 19, 1961).

Mr. and Mrs. Otis Dickson were appointed the first houseparents. Five children were in the home one month after opening (Annual, BGCA, November 14-16, 1961, First Southern Baptist Church, Phoenix, AZ).

BCHA Board approved setting Mother's Day to be a day of emphasis and prayer for the children's home (*Baptist Beacon*, March 30, 1961).

From this point forward, the name of the Baptist General Convention of Arizona references (BGCA) is changed to the Arizona Southern Baptist Convention (ASBC).

November 17, 1961. The Baptist General Convention of Arizona's name was changed to Arizona Southern Baptist Convention (ASBC) (Minutes,

Executive Board, Arizona Southern Baptist Convention, September 5, 1960; *Baptist Beacon*, November 30, 1961).

The children's home license is increased to twelve children (Annual, BGCA, November 14-16, 1961, First Southern Baptist Church, Phoenix, AZ).

1962

On September 10, 1962, approval was given to accept reimbursement from the State Welfare Department for expenses incurred in the care of children placed in the home by the state (Minutes, ASBC Board, September 10, 1962)

1963

The home was licensed to provide foster family care for six children ages six to fourteen. (*Baptist Beacon,* February 7, 1963; Annual, BGCA, November 13-14, 1963, Central Baptist Church, Phoenix, AZ).

1964

The board approved a fund-raising campaign to raise fifty thousand dollars for a new cottage and increased staff salaries, which was started February 14, 1964 (Minutes, BCHA, August 26, 1963). The campaign was discontinued after five months.

1964 to 1969

Care was provided to children in one campus cottage and six foster homes under the supervision of Superintendent George Wilson. These years were plagued by constant financial challenges for the struggling program (Annual, ASBC, November 17-19, 1965).

1966

The convention requested that the children's home develop goals for the next seven years. Six goals were established (Flint 1986).

Love in Action, a newsletter about the Children's home, began.

1969

Houseparents Mr. and Mrs. Dickson retired (*Love In Action* 1969, 11:4, August, 1).

Ms. Phyllis McFarland was employed to take the place of social worker Bill Johnson. (Minutes, ASBC Board, May 16, 1969).

1970

Rev. George Wilson retired on July 1 (Annual, ASBC, November 10-12, 1970, First Southern Baptist Church, Tucson, AZ).

Mr. Don Cain was interviewed for the superintendent's position on August 4 following a search led by Lester Jennings, Sr. The board approved his employment at a special called meeting on September 1, to be effective January 1, 1971 (ibid.). The children's home board approves purchase of care with state agencies for a second time and authorizes Mr. Cain to look for a "Southern Baptist" social worker (Minutes, Executive Committee, BCHA, September 24, 1970).

November 12. The ASBC bid farewell to its first superintendent, George Wilson, at the annual meeting (Annual, ASBC, November 10-12, 1970, First Southern Baptist Church, Tucson, AZ).

1971

January 1. Don Cain began as the second superintendent of the Baptist Children's Home of Arizona.

September 24, 1970. The name of the Baptist Children's Home of Arizona was changed to Arizona Baptist Children's Services (ABCS) to reflect the new direction of multiple family services instead of just residential and foster care. This is subject to ASBC Executive Board approval, January 1, 1971 (Minutes, ABCS Board, September 24, 1970)

From this point forward, the name of the Baptist Children's Home of Arizona references (BCHA) are changed to Arizona Baptist Children's Services (ABCS).

January. The Satellite Home program started, which was a continuation of the earlier foster care program. Eleven children were cared for in the first nine months (*Love in Action*, September 1973, 1).

February 22. A Group Home for Adolescent Girls opened at 309 W. Almeria, Phoenix. Fifteen girls were cared for in this home in 1971 (Minutes, Executive Committee, ABCS Board, January 4, 1971; Minutes, Ad Hoc Committee of ASBC Executive Board and ABCS Board, March 29, 1971).

March 4. Temporary shelter care for children was first opened at 1225 E. McDowell, Phoenix. It was later moved to 1480 East Bethany Home, Phoenix (Cain, "A Brief History of Arizona Baptist," unpublished).

April 1. The ABCS administrative offices were moved from 316 W. McDowell Road to a mobile office building at 3115 W. Missouri, Phoenix, on the West Missouri campus. (Jennings, Early Beginnings & Growth of Arizona Baptist Children's Services, given at the regular monthly meeting of the Arizona Baptist Historical Society, March 15, 1977. Filed in ABCS Archives; Minutes, ABCS Board, March 5, 1971).

November 1. Counseling services began with offices located in the new campus modular units at 3115 W. Missouri, Phoenix (Minutes, Executive Committee, ABCS Board, January 4, 1971. Filed in ABCS Archives).

November 15. A temporary shelter was opened at 3801 N. Swan Rd, Tucson (*Love In Action* 1971, 10:5, November, 1).

1972

May 18. A Group Home for Adolescent Boys was opened at 2018 N. Ninth Street, Phoenix (Minutes, ABCS Board, May 18, 1972).

July 20. The Papago Indian Children's Home was opened in Sells, Arizona. The program served both as a group home and an emergency shelter. Approved by the ABCS Board February 28, 1972 (*Love in Action* 1972, 11:1, March).

1973

The ABCS budget is now four hundred thousand dollars (Minutes, ABCS Board, March 1, 1973)

June 1. Property at 3118 W. Missouri, Phoenix, was purchased for a girls' group home. This property is located across the street from the Little Canyon Campus. (Minutes, ABCS Board, April 14, 1973; Jennings, "Historical Review," 1970).

June 1. The property at 5915 W. Laurie Lane, Glendale was leased as an overflow unit for the boys' shelter and later a boys' group home (Minutes, ABCS Board, September 6, 1973).

November 1. The leased Tucson emergency shelter was closed due to sale of the property. A long series of unsolvable zoning problems with the City of Tucson and Pima County prevented reestablishing the program (Minutes, Executive Committee, ABCS Board, November 29, 1973).

A group home for girls was started at 3741 W. Hazelwood, Phoenix (Jennings, "Early Beginnings," 1997).

1974

February 28. ABCS was given property located in Chandler, Arizona, consisting of a house, in town, and forty acres of farmland on Pecos Road. This came as a bequest from the "Rucker will." It was later sold with proceeds going to ABCS (Minutes, ABCS Board, February 28, 1974).

Little Canyon Residential Treatment Center receives its first of accreditation by the Joint Commission on Accreditation of Health Care Organizations (JCAHO).
(Jennings "Historical Review," 1970). ABCS was the first children's agency in Arizona to be accredited as a Children's Psychiatric Facility (Baker, "A Time For Every Matter," 1988-89).

A major financial campaign to be directed by Welch & Associates was reviewed (Minutes, ABCS Board, July 17, 1974; Minutes, Arizona Southern Baptist Convention Executive Board, November 12, 1974). Their proposal was approved by the board on December 16 (Minutes, ABCS Board, December 16, 1974).

July 22. Eighteen thousand dollars was requested from the ASBC Cooperative Program to fund a chaplain's program. ABCS was already receiving three thousand six hundred dollars from the Cooperative Program (In a letter addressed to Dr. Roy F. Sutton from ABCS executive director Don Cain dated July 22, 1974. Filed in ABCS Correspondence Archives).

Office space for ABCS administration was rented at 400 W. Camelback Road, Phoenix, Arizona (Minutes, Executive Committee, ABCS Board, May 30, 1974).

1975

A part-time chaplain was appointed (Flick 1985. Filed in the history archives of Arizona Baptist Children's Services).

August. The poor campaign results were discussed and the campaign cancelled. (Minutes, ABCS Board, August 28, 1975).

An ASBC study committee was appointed to make an in-depth study of ABCS and its operations (Minutes, Executive Board Meeting, September 9, 1975).

The offer of a one-hundred-dollar matching gift by Dr. Virginia and Mr. Vernon Furrow of Tucson was made for a children's home building in Sells, Arizona (Letter from Executive Director Don Cain to the ABCS Board, December 17, 1975).

December 15. ABCS accepted the responsibility for the Camelback Girls' Group Home and School located at 3324 E. Camelback Road, Phoenix. (Letter from Don Cain to Attorney Grady Gammage, Jr., dated February 21, 1979. Filed in archives of ABCS).

A second mobile building for the special education school was added to the Little Canyon Campus. The students that would attend were moved from Camelback Girl's residence (Jennings, "Early Beginnings," 1977).

1976

April 25. The board approved closing of the Papago Indian Children's Home in Sells, Arizona (Minutes. ABCS Board, March 26, 1976).

January 10. JCAHO accreditation is received for two years (Letter from Don Cain to ABCS Board, May 7, 1976).

1977

November 16. The study report of ABCS was presented at the annual meeting of the Arizona Southern Baptist Convention with instructions to ABCS for corrective action (Pair 1989, 341).

A full-time chaplain is appointed for ABCS (Flick 1985, 3; Annual, ASBC, November 15-17, 1979 at Trinity Baptist Church, Casa Grande, AZ).

1978

December 1. A receiving home program was started to provide emergency care for children. Twenty-nine families were licensed to provide this service during the first year (Annual, ASBC, 1979, 136).

October 27. Whiteaker feasibility study completed (Feasibility Study, Arizona Baptist Children's Study, Missouri Avenue Campus Expansion, 1978. Copy of study is in the ABCS archives).

1979

A therapeutic foster care program was started to meet the needs of handicapped children (Cain, Executive Director's Annual Report, 1980, Arizona Baptist Children's Services).

1980

ABCS becomes a fully accredited member of the Child Welfare League of America (ibid.; Annual, ASBC, November 11-13, 1980, First Southern Baptist Church, Tucson).

A film *Someone Who Cares* was produced by ABCSs to inform the community and churches about the work of ABCS (Cain, Executive Director's Annual Report 1980, ABCS).

The Emergency Receiving Home program is cancelled by DES (Minutes, Executive Committee, ABCS Board, October 28, 1980; Minutes, Annual Report of ASBC, 1981, 134).

1982

Dedication of the Jennings Boys' Cottage on Little Canyon Campus, September 24, 1982 (Annual, ASBC, 1982, 139). The cottage would be named in 1985 in honor of Lester and Marie Jennings, Sr., early founders of ABCS.

February 21. Property was purchased at 5125 W. Myrtle Avenue in Glendale, Arizona, for boys emergency services, which would be called the Glendale Bunkhouse. Boys formerly in the Bethany Home Road shelter were transferred there (Cain. Annual Report, Arizona Baptist Children's Services, 1982).

ABCS begins *Footprints*, a quarterly newsletter (Cain, Annual Report, Arizona Baptist Children's Services, 1982).

July 1. Program for independent living preparation for boys is opened in the Glendale Bunkhouse (*Footprints* 1982, 2:4, Fall, 2).

An ABCS advisory council was established, made up of members from the community, to create more visibility and raise funds for ABCS (Cain, Annual Report, Arizona Baptist Children's Services, 1982).

December 3. The childrens' residential facility at Thirty-first Avenue and West Missouri was officially named the Little Canyon Campus (Minutes, ABCS Board, December 3, 1982).

1983

ABCS administrative offices are moved from the second floor of 400 W. Camelback Road (2080 s/f) to the first floor (2560 s/f). (Minutes, ABCS Board, February 11, 1983).

Paul Kinnison is employed as director of Religious Activities/Chaplain (Minutes, ABCS Board, February 11, 1983).

May 31. Executive Director Don Cain's resignation was effective. Board member Jack Willis was appointed interim executive director (Pair 1989; Annual, ASBC, 1983, November 8-10, 1983, First Southern Baptist Church, Phoenix, AZ).

1984

January 1. C. Truett Baker from Virginia began as executive director (Minutes, ABCS Board, December 2, 1983; *Baptist Beacon,* December 22, 1983).

Approval is given for ABCS Goals for 1984-85 (Minutes, ABCS Board, September 20, 1983).

A volunteer program was started (Baker, C. Truett, President's Annual Report, 1984 Arizona Baptist Children's Services).

1985

January 22. The board approves the establishment of Division of Family Ministries with its own director to oversee counseling, family-life education, foster family care, and family ministry centers in various areas of the state (Minutes, Executive Committee, ABCS Board, January 22, 1985; Resolutions 83-PCR-5 approved June 22, 1884; Resolutions 84-PRO-1 and 85-PRO-2).

Employment of Dr. Ron Wilcoxon to direct Division of Family Ministries (*Baptist Beacon* 1985, March 28, 3).

The goals for 1985-86 were developed (Minutes, ABCS Board, 85-PRO-1, approved by the board September 26, 1985)

The following two sources will be abbreviated in their respective references to reflect the full reference below in "1" and "2".

1. 1985 Annual. Arizona Southern Baptist Convention, 57th Annual Session, November 12-13, 1985, North Phoenix Baptist Church, Phoenix, AZ.
2. Implosion '85. Executive Director's Annual Report of the Arizona Baptist Children's Services. Filed in the agency archives.

June 22. Dedication of the girls' cottage and lighted sports court on Little Canyon Campus, June 22, 1985 (Annual, 1985, 138-139; Implosion '85, 40).

The Carnes Building (the original building) on the Little Canyon Campus was remodeled after the girls vacated it for their new quarters. The building was renamed in honor of Mr. and Mrs. J. B. Carnes, who donated the money for its construction (Annual 1985).

The kitchen and dining room of the newly named "Carnes Building" was enlarged and the remainder of the building used for the school (Baker, "Executive Director's Quarterly Report," July through September 1985).

The Circle of Champions was started. These were friends who pledged to pray and support ABCS (Annual, 1985; Implosion '85). This support club was originally called the "Triple S" Club (*Baptist Beacon* 1985, February 14, 2).

The Glendale Bunkhouse was remodeled, and the independent-living program was moved July 1, 1982, from the Bunkhouse to a recently purchased house on adjacent property, 5115 W. Myrtle *(Annual 1985, 138-139; Implosion '85, 3-4).*

The first computer system is installed for business, accounting, and development *(Implosion '85, 4).*

The first of eight area dinner conferences was held throughout the state. These were dinner meetings held in churches to entertain, inform, and encourage support for ABCS.
(Annual 1985).

The board approves establishment of regional family service centers with the first center opened at the Emmanuel Baptist Church in Tucson, Arizona (85-PRO-2; Annual, 1986, 142; Victories, etc., 1-2).

1986

The following two sources will be abbreviated in their respective references to reflect the full reference below in "1" and "2".

1. 1986 Annual. Arizona Southern Baptist Convention, 58th Annual Session, November 11-12, 1986, North Phoenix Baptist Church, Phoenix, AZ.
2. Victories and Visions. The 1986 Executive Director's Annual Report of the Arizona Baptist Children's Services. Filed in the Agency archives.

Foster-care licensed beds were increased from ten to twenty beds (Annual 1986).

The first workshop for pastors was conducted in Phoenix and Tucson (Annual 1986.

The first long-range, (a three-year cycle) planning process was started, which was called Strategic Planning (Annual 1986).

1987

The following two sources will be abbreviated in their respective references to reflect the full reference below in "1" and "2".

1. 1987 Annual. Arizona Southern Baptist Convention, 59th Annual Session, November 10-11, 1987, North Phoenix Baptist Church, Phoenix, AZ.
2. Past Debts and Present Opportunities. The 1987 Executive Director's Annual Report of the Arizona Baptist Children's Services.

A development department was established and a full-time director employed (Annual 1987; Past Debts, etc., 6).

A documentary, *A Place Called Hope*, an audiovisual presentation, was shown at the ASBC annual meeting and in churches across the state (Past Debts, etc.).

A Family Ministry Center was opened in Show Low (Annual 1987; Past Debts, etc.).

Counseling Office were opened in Valley Southern Baptist Church in Mesa, Arizona (*Executive Director's Quarterly Report to the Board*, July-September, 1987, 2).

Nine Area Dinner conferences are held throughout the state (Past Debts, etc).

A gift of three hundred thousand dollars was made by Mr. and Mrs. Dean Barnicle of Yuma for construction of the Administration and Family Service Center on the Little Canyon Campus (Past Debts, etc.).

October 28. Mr. and Mrs. Richard Huff of Tucson, longtime supporters of ABCS in partnership with Casas Adobes Baptist Church and the Baptist Foundation, make a gift of Sunglow Mission Ranch to ABCS. (*Footprints* 1988, 7:4, Spring, 1,5; Annual 1988).

1988

The following two sources will be abbreviated in their respective references to reflect the full reference below in "1" and "2".

1. 1988 Annual Arizona Southern Baptist Convention, 60th Annual Session, November 1-2, 1988, Casas Adobes Baptist Church, Tucson, AZ.
2. New Beginnings. The 1988 Executive Director's Annual Report of the Arizona Baptist Children's Services, Phoenix, AZ.

A thrift industry was started November 28, 1988, at Nineteenth Avenue and Dunlap, Phoenix, to earn funds for ABCS (Board Resolution 88-P&F-2, Annual, 1988; A Time For Every Matter, 1-2).

Mr. amd Mrs. Duard Bell made a gift of a house and its furnishing in Mesa, Arizona. It was converted into a group home for younger boys. (Board Resolution 88-PRO-3 approved September 23, 1988; A Time For Every Matter).

The ABCS East Valley Counseling Office was opened at Valley Southern Baptist Church, Mesa, Arizona (Annual 1988).

ABCS was licensed to provide special services by the Arizona Department of Health Services, Division of Developmental Disabilities (New Beginnings, Annual, ASBC, 1988).

1989

The following two sources will be abbreviated in their respective references to reflect the full reference below in "1" and "2".

1. 1989 Annual, Arizona Southern Baptist Convention, 61st Annual Session, November 14-15, 1989, North Phoenix Baptist Church, Phoenix, AZ.
2. A Time For Every Matter. 1989 Executive Director's Annual Report of the Arizona Baptist Children's Services, Phoenix, AZ.

The Barnicle Family Service Center was dedicated on June 2, 1989, at Little Canyon Campus (A Time For Every Matter).

May 17. The Bell Group Home in Mesa, Arizona, was opened for six special-needs youth (Resolution 88-PRO-6, approved by the Board March 17, 1989; *Footprints* 1989, Fall, 2).

ABCS was licensed by the Arizona Department of Health Services, Behavioral Health Division, qualifying ABCS to accept Medicaid clients (A Time For Every Matter).

Counseling was relocated to the Careb Professional Center at 2412 W. Greenway, Bldg. B, Phoenix, Arizona, (Executive Director's Quarterly Report to the Board, July-September 1989).

1990

The following two sources will be abbreviated in their respective references to reflect the full reference below in "1" and "2".

1. 1990 Annual. Arizona Southern Baptist Convention, 62nd Annual Session, November 13-14, 1990, North Phoenix Baptist Church, Phoenix, AZ.

2. Journey To Excellence. 1990 Executive Director's Annual Report of the Arizona Baptist Children's Services.

The Nancy Spann property, which adjoins the Glendale Property in Phoenix, was purchased to allow enlargement of the Glendale Campus and provide for additional storage space ("Journey," 3).

The Church Representative Network was started (Journey).

A Church and Community Relations Department began with Karen Merick as the first coordinator (Journey).

Counseling and Foster Care programs were moved to new offices at 6122 N. Seventh Street in Phoenix, and a new counseling office was opened at 2412 W. Greenway (Journey).

First Annual ABCS Volunteers Appreciation luncheon was held (Journey).

1991

The following two sources will be abbreviated in their respective references to reflect the full reference below in "1" and "2".

1. 1991 Annual. Arizona Southern Baptist Convention, November 12-13, 1991, North Phoenix Baptist Church, Phoenix, AZ.
2. Keys To Success. 1991 Executive Director's Annual Report of the Arizona Baptist Children's Services; Annual, 129-131.

The thirtieth anniversary of ABCS was celebrated February 15, 1991, at the Hilton Pavilion in Mesa, Arizona. A twelve-minute video, *ABCS: Making a Difference*, was premiered at the dinner. Marlene Klotz, a local television person, narrated the production. Two hundred thirty-nine were present including forty-five staff (Annual, 129-131).

Corporate restructuring of Arizona Baptist Children's Services was developed following the business model. Subcorporations under the ABCS Holding Corporation were ABCS Little Canyon Center, ABCS Behavioral Health Services, ABCS Endowment Corp, and ABCS Thrift World (Keys to Success).

April 1. Journey Group Home for five troubled boys ages eight to twelve was opened across the street from the Little Canyon Campus at 3118 W. Missouri (Annual 1991).

The Tucson counseling center was closed; and Marvin Humble, former trustee, was employed part-time as Southern Regional coordinator, which included supervision of Sunglow Ranch (ibid.).

ABCS purchased its own administrative and foster-care offices located at 8920 N. Twenty-third Avenue in Phoenix at a cost of $375,000. (Annual 1991, 129).

The Mothers' Day offering reached a record thirty thousand dollars. There were now 221 members of the Circle of Champions who have pledged $38,305 (Keys To Success).

The counseling offices were moved to larger quarters at 15650 N. Black Canyon, suite 210, Phoenix, Arizona (President's Quarterly Report to the Board, July-September 1991).

May 17. The Children's Center, a day care program at First Southern Baptist Church, Phoenix, was dedicated. The program resulted from a gift from Dr. Virginia Furrow of Tucson (Annual 1991).

The counseling office in Show Low is closed in the fall, 1991 (Keys To Success 1991, 37).

1992

The following two sources will be abbreviated in their respective references to reflect the full reference below in "1" and "2".

1. 1992 Annual, Arizona Southern Baptist Convention, 64th Annual Session, November 10-11, 1992, North Phoenix Baptist Church, Phoenix, AZ, 145-147.
2. Our Best in the Worst of Times. 1992 Executive Director's Annual Report of the Arizona Baptist Children's Services.

The Little Canyon Residential Treatment Center again received full accreditation by the Joint Commission on Accreditation of Health Organizations (Our Best).

The first ABCS Legislature Appreciation Dinner was held at the Tucson Doubletree to honor Tucson area state legislators. Ninety-seven guests and five legislators were present (President's Quarterly Report to the Board, July-September 1992).

1993

The following two sources will be abbreviated in their respective references to reflect the full reference below in "1" and "2".

1. 1993 Annual, Arizona Southern Baptist Convention, 65th Annual Session, November 9-10, 1993, North Phoenix Baptist Church, Phoenix, AZ.
2. A Winner in the West, 1993 Executive Director's Annual Report of the Arizona Baptist Children's Services.

On September11, ABCS began its first major successful three-year financial campaign, "For the Children," assisted by financial consultants, Cargill Associates of Ft. Worth. (A Winner)

1994

The following two sources will be abbreviated in their respective references to reflect the full reference below in "1" and "2".

1. 1994 Annual, Arizona Southern Baptist Convention, 66th Annual Session, November 1-2, 1994, North Phoenix Baptist Church, Phoenix, AZ.
2. For the Children. 1994 Executive Director's Annual Report of the Arizona Baptist Children's Services.

October 27, 1994. Mary Jo West, popular local television personality, was mistress of ceremonies for "For the Children" fund-raising campaign dinner attended by over two hundred people at the Crescent Hotel, Phoenix, Arizona; $121,000 was raised in pledges (For the Children).

The first annual board planning retreat was held at Sunglow Ranch (*Insider*, the ABCS in-house monthly staff newsletter, August-September 1994).

ABCS and two other Phoenix child- and family-services agencies join in a partnership, called AcurCare Group Arizona, to provide employment assistance programs to other similar agencies both inside and outside of Arizona (Minutes, ABCS Board, Resolution 94-ADM-1, approved March 26, 1994).

School-based counseling groups were started in elementary schools in the Phoenix area. Seventy-seven children and their parents were served (President's Quarterly Report to the Board, April-June 1994).

September 15. ABCS Children's Center, located in the First Southern Baptist Church, Phoenix, is closed due to underutilization and cost overruns (President's Quarterly Report to the Board, July-September 1994).

The new kitchen-dining room building is completed on the Little Canyon Campus and dedicated on May 15, 1994 (Annual, 158).

1995

The following two sources will be abbreviated in their respective references to reflect the full reference below in "1" and "2".

1. 1995 Annual, Arizona Southern Baptist Convention, 67th Annual Session, November 14-15, 1995, North Phoenix Baptist Church, Phoenix, AZ.
2. Transitions. 1995 Executive Director's Annual Report of the Arizona Baptist Children's Services filed in the Agency archives.

ABCS receives its largest gift to date. John F. Long, donated $2.3 million in property, which would fund the John F. Long Family Development Institute (*Baptist Beacon* 1995, 56:10, May 11, 1; *Footprints* 1995, Summer, 8-9).

On June 30, the "For the Children" campaign was completed with 289 people and 21 businesses or corporations giving and pledging $3,617,318. This exceeded both the basic and challenge goals. A gift of four hundred thousand dollars was given by Mr. and Mrs. Jerry Smithey for a chapel and educational building on Little Canyon Campus (Transitions, 1-2).

A five-year strategic plan, "Building a Future For Children," was adopted by the board. The focus of the plan was to shift program emphasis from residential care only to family and home-based services through six statewide regional centers (Transitions).

One thousand five hundred and eleven children and families were served in the year. Ten made professions of faith, and five were baptized by Chaplain Mike Ransbottom (Transitions).

June 9, 1995. The thrift industry opened a second and much larger facility at 8933 N. Seventh Street in Phoenix (Jennings, "1994/95 Annual Facilities Report," Transitions).

One hundred forty-five children were served in 87 ABCS foster homes during the year (The President's Quarterly Report to the Board of Trustees, ABCS, for October 1, 1995 to December 31, 1995).

May. The Glendale Bunkhouse emergency shelter for boys was converted into two group homes for boys (The President's Fourth Quarter Report to the Board, April-June 1995).

Counseling offices were opened in the First Southern Baptist Church, Avondale, Arizona (President's Quarterly Report to the Board, July-September 1995).

1996

The following two sources will be abbreviated in their respective references to reflect the full reference below in "1" and "2".

1. 1996 Annual, Arizona Southern Baptist Convention, 67th Annual Session, November 12-13, 1996, North Phoenix Baptist Church, Phoenix, AZ.
2. Building a Future For Children. 1996 President's Annual Report of the Arizona Baptist Children's Services.

This was the first year of a five-year strategic plan, "Building A Future For Children" (Minutes, ABCS Board, March 15, 1996).

March. Jack Willis retired as vice president for Administration on March 31, 1996 (Annual, 1996, 88).

ABCS purchased all the shares from their AzCare partners and became sole owner of the employee assistance program (Building a Future; Minutes, ABCS Board Resolution 96-ADM-4 approved by the Board).

Total children in care for the year was 1,511. Fourteen young people make professions of faith, and eight were baptized (Building a Future).

Sunglow Ranch hosted 1,669 guests during the year (ibid.).

The "Focus Groups Network," was developed as a method for agency management and planning (*The Insider* 1996, January -February, 9).

April. The original thrift store on Nineteenth Avenue was closed (President's Quarterly Report to the Board, January-March, 1996).

August 15. Groundbreaking took place for the eight-thousand-square-foot chapel and educational center on Little Canyon Campus, (*Baptist Beacon* 1996, 57:19, September 12, 3).

School-based counseling was conducted in ten schools and five school districts, serving 904 students and parents (President's Quarterly Report to the Board, January-March 1996).

Sunglow Ranch was sold in September (Seeds of Crisis; Minutes, ABCS Executive Committee, September 5, 1996).

ABCS begins a Quality Management Program following Joint Commission guidelines (President's Second Quarter Report to the Board of Trustees, October-December 1996).

The only girls unit at Little Canyon Center is closed due to underutilization, making the campus all-boys (President's Quarterly Report to the Board, October-December 1996).

December 11, 1996. The Journey Group Home occupied a new facility at Thirty-ninth Avenue (Jennings, "Facilities Report," in The President's Quarterly Report to the Board, October-December 1996).

The boys in the Journey Group Home, located at 3118 W. Missouri in Phoenix, were moved December 11, 1996 to a larger house at Thirty-ninth Avenue and Campo Bello. The Bell Group Home property for boys in Mesa was sold April 25, 1997; and the residents were transferred February 24, 1997, to the former Journey Group Home at 3118 W. Missouri, across from the Little Canyon Center (Seeds of Crisis).

1997

The following two sources will be abbreviated in their respective references to reflect the full reference below in "1" and "2".

1. 1997 Annual, Arizona Southern Baptist Convention, 69th Annual Session, November 11-12, 1997, First Southern Baptist Church, Tucson.
2. Seeds of Crisis and Fruits of Success. 1997 President's Annual Report of the Arizona Baptist Children's Services.

The Glendale Campus at 5115-5133 W. Myrtle was closed. The Wrangler House was closed in January and the Bunkhouse closed in March. (Seeds of Crisis; Also, Board Resolution 97-ADM-1).

The first agency-wide Spiritual Emphasis Week was led by Chaplains Mike Ransbottom and Bill Gifford (The President's Third Quarter Report to the Board of Trustees, January-March 1997).

Total children served during the year were 1,938. Twenty children made professions of faith and thirteen were baptized (Seeds of Crisis).

Growth in counseling services leads to opening new offices at Thirty-fifth Avenue and Cheryl Drive, near Metro Center, Phoenix, Arizona, (*Footprints* 1997, Spring, 2).

All properties in Phoenix, which were donated to ABCS by Mr. John F. Long, were sold resulting in two hundred thousand dollars in cash and nine hundred thousand dollars in notes, to be paid off in five years (President's Quarterly Report to the ABCS Board, January 1-March 31, 1998).

A one-hundred-thousand-dollar gift was made by Chimiarra Investments Limited to provide furnishing and equipment for the new chapel/ educational building and other upgrades on the Little Canyon Campus (*Footprints* 1997, Fall, 2).

The forty-bed residential treatment center on Little Canyon Campus was reduced to thirty beds by closing one of the four units. The closed unit was converted into a ten-bed therapeutic group home for the boys in the Bell Group home across the street at 3118 W. Missouri (President's Quarterly Report to the Board, July-September 1977).

1998

The following two sources will be abbreviated in their respective references to reflect the full reference below in "1" and "2".

1. 1998 Annual, Arizona Southern Baptist Convention, 70th Annual Session, November 10-11, 1998, First Southern Baptist Church, Phoenix, AZ.
2. Reaching Out, 1998. The President's Annual Report of the Arizona Baptist Children's Services filed in the Agency archives.

January 1. The "Family Builders" Program was started in Northwest Phoenix. This was a joint family-based project with a coalition of other agencies working with Child Protective Services(CPS) Division of Arizona DES (Reaching Out; President's Quarterly Report to the Board, January-March 1998).

January. The ABCS Southern Regional Family Service Center opened in Tucson, January 1, 1998 (Reaching Out).

March 27. The Smithey Chapel/Educational Building was dedicated (*Footprints* 1998, Summer, 4-6).

P. David Jakes was retained as a consultant in business and administration (ibid.).

The Little Canyon Residential Treatment Center was reaccredited with "commendation" by the Joint Commission on Accreditation of Health Care Organizations. In addition, all ABCS programs were accredited by JCAHO (ibid.).

The Little Canyon School was accredited by the North Central Association, following several years of preparation (ibid.).

August. ABCS Thrift World was closed after ten years of operation (Minutes, ABCS Board, Board Resolution 98-P&F-3 approved June 5, 1998).

The second ABCS Regional Center was dedicated and opened in Yuma, Arizona, October 3, 1998. Rev. Charles Wesner, former ABCS trustee, was named the director. A satellite office also was opened in Parker, Arizona (*The Yuma Daily Sun* 1998, October 2, 4).

ABCS president, C. Truett Baker, announced his retirement to be effective in September 1999 (Reaching Out).

1999

P. David Jakes was elected as the fourth president of Arizona Baptist Children's Services beginning January 1, 1999. Former president Truett Baker continued as a consultant assisting with the transition in presidency and serving as interim director of the foster care and adoption departments (President's Report to the Board of Trustees, March 19, 1999).

ABCS begins the process of meeting qualifications for being licensed to do adoptions (President's Report to the Board of Trustees, March 19, 1999).

February 4. First annual Trustee Assessment of the Board. Nine participated (Minutes of the Executive Committee of ABCS Board of Trustees, 8-20).

March 6. An open house and dedication was held for the ABCS Eastern Regional Office in Show Low, Arizona. The First Baptist Church there provided office space (Minutes, ABCS Board of Trustees, April 5, 1999).

March 18. ABCS receives its adoption license (Minutes, ABCS Board of Trustees, June 4, 1999).

March. A Spiritual Renewal Week was conducted under the leadership of Chaplain Mike Ransbottom ("Chaplaincy Services Report," President's Quarterly Report to the Board, January-March 1999).

AzCare stock is sold July 1, 1999 ("Transitions and Change," ABCS President, David P. Jakes; Minutes, Executive Committee, ABCS Board, August 12, 1999).

The budget for ABCS in 1999-2000 was $7,392,908 (Minutes, ABCS Board of Trustees, June 4, 1999).

ABCS is awarded the Restoring Arizona Family Traditions (RAFT) contracts from the Administrative Office of the Courts (juvenile) for Maricopa, Yuma, and La Paz Counties (Minutes, ABCS Board of Trustees, June 4, 1999).

The Southern Regional Office of ABCS in Tucson moved to a more central location and began partnering with Crosspointe Counseling, Christian Family Care, and Crisis Pregnancy Center (Minutes, ABCS Board of Trustees, June 4, 1999).

ABCS now has 129 children in eighty-five licensed foster homes (Minutes, ABCS Board of Trustees, June 4, 1999).

The "Family Builder's" program served an average of over six hundred lives per month (Minutes, ABCS Board of Trustees, June 4, 1999).

The programs of ABCS will be conducted through six regional centers, including the Central Region in Maricopa County (Minutes, ABCS Board of Trustees, March 24, 2000).

The strategic plan for 2000-2004 was approved by the Board (Minutes, ABCS Board of Trustees, March 24, 2000).

The chaplaincy program was extended to provide chaplaincy services at the Buckeye Correctional Facility. Rev. David Garza was the chaplain (Minutes, ABCS Board of Trustees, April 5, 1999).

The computer system is expanded to include the UniCare System Software for clinical and medical services (Minutes, ABCS Board of Trustees, April 5, 1999).

August 10. The Arizona Corporation Commission issued a cease and desist order to the Baptist Foundation of Arizona. All foundation funds were subsequently frozen, and Chapter 11 bankruptcy was later filed (Board Memo from ABCS President, David Jakes. "Impact of BFA Cease and Desist Order on ABCS," to the ABCS Board of Trustees, September 14, 1999).

September. C. Truett Baker, ABCS's third president, retires (*Footprints* 1994, Winter:4).

ABCS joins "Full Circle" Network for providing behavioral health services (Minutes, ABCS Board, Resolution 98-P&F-4, March 19, 1999).

ABCS provided foster care for ten children from one family prior to their legal adoption by one of its foster parent. (*Portraits* 3:10, December 1999-January 2000, 8-10; *Dallas Morning News* 1999, August 9, 15A; *Footprints* 1999, Winter: 6-9).

2000

ABCS received Joint Commission Accreditation for three more years (Minutes, ABCS Board, December 1, 2000).

ABCS observes Fortieth Anniversary but cancels celebration (*Footprints* 2000, Winter, 2).

The Charter Hospital (59,700 s/f) and its eight-acre campus at 6015 W. Peoria in Glendale is purchased for the future site of all ABCS services in Maricopa County, Arizona (Minutes, ABCS Board, Resolution 00-ADMIN-07, December 1, 2000).

The Sydney R. Browning Memorial Library Fund is established (Minutes, Board of Trustees, September 22, 2000; Board Resolution 00-C&CD-1 approved June 9, 2000).

The first child was placed for adoption by ABCS (Minutes, Board of Trustees, September 22, 2000).

ABCS Northwest Regional Center is opened with offices in Kingman, Bullhead City, and Lake Havasu. Bill Greco is appointed director (Minutes, Board of Trustees, September 22, 2000).

Mother's Day offering of $75,798 from the ASBC churches sets a new record (Minutes, ABCS Board of Trustees, September 22, 2000).

September 18. Thirty youths are baptized at the Southwest Juvenile Correctional Facility in Buckeye. A portable baptism tank was donated for this purpose (Minutes, Board of Trustees).

2001

December 20-21. ABCS Administrative offices, adoption, foster care, and outpatient programs were moved into the new John F. and Mary P. Long Family Life Development Center at 6015 W. Peoria, Glendale (*Footprints* 2001, March).

"Caring for Kids," an affiliated corporation of ABCS, is established. (Minutes, ABCS Board, Board Resolution 01-C&CD-04, approved December 7, 2001).

The Eastern Region, which began in Show Low, is moved to Snowflake with satellite stations in Winslow, Springerville, and Show Low (Board Minutes, ABCS Board, March 16, 2001).

The ownership of Arizona Baptist Children's Services was transferred from the Arizona Southern Baptist Convention to the ABCS Board of Trustees. A "cooperative agreement" will continue to link the two organizations for support and fellowship (Key, Memo to Board, "Arizona Baptist Children's Services," March 26, 2001; ABCS Board Resolution 01-EXEC-01, "Approval of Revised Articles of Incorporation," effective July 1, 2001, March 16, 2001).

Little Canyon Campus, site of the original Children's Home, is sold to Grand Canyon University (Minutes, ABCS Board, December 7, 2001).

Foster care and outpatient (counseling) programs in Maricopa County are closed effective September 30, 2001 by ABCS for economic reasons (Minutes, ABCS Board, October 30, 2001; *Baptist Beacon* 2001, October, 1-2).

2002

The Dedication of the John F. and Mary P. Long Family Life Development Center was held April 14 (*Footprints* 2001, October, 1).

June. Children in Little Canyon Center and Bell Group Home are moved into their new home in the John F. and Mary P. Long Family Life Development Center in Glendale (*Portraits* 2001, July-August, 4).

Arizona Southern Baptist Convention Agencies—Baptist Senior Life Ministeries, and the Historical Commission-move into leased space at the ABCS John F. and Mary P. Long Building (Minutes, ABCS Board, June 7, 2002).

An open house and dedication are held for the Smithey-Link Educational Center November 20.

APPENDIX B

Board Of Trustees

ABCS Board of Trustees

F

Everett, J. Herbert, 1977-82, 86-89
Ferguson, Ralph, 1964-1968
Fielding, Bethea, 1983-84
Frederick, Joe, Jr., 1981-83
Fuller, Louise, 1987-91
Fuller, Stan, 1997-2001

G

Gammage, Uva, 1985-88
Garrett, Malcom, 1980-82
George, Jay, 1983-1988
Gillham, Frank, 1966-68
Godfrey, C. W., 1960-66
Goins, Jim, 1964-65
Goodman, Brian, 1995-99
Grantham, Les, 1974-1980
Green, Gordon, 1970-72
Groves, Mary, 1966-73
Gunn, David, 1987-93
Gurule, Martha, 1992-93

H

Hall, Barry, 1976-81, 1995-2001
Hanna, Steve, 1993-97
Hansen, Doug, 1991-93
Hart, Keith, 1959
Henderson, Fay, 1995-96
Henry, Jim, 1970-73
Henton, Mrs. Wiley, 1959-61
Hibbard, Clovis, 1983
Hill, Ennis, 1969-74
Hill, Wilma, 1975-80
Hoffpauir, Sandy, 1984
Holloman, Jim, 1985-87
Hoover, Beva, 1987 -92
Howell, J. D., 1970-76
Huff, Barbara, 1993-98

Huff, Richard, 1974-76, 82-87
Hull, George, 1979-85
Humble, Marvin, 1984-1990

J

Jackson, Lee, 1960-65
Jackson, Wanda, 1985-92
Jacques, George, 1984-86
Jenkins, Robert, 1960-65
Jennings, Les, Jr., 1971-77, 1990-93
Jennings, Lester, Sr., 1959-64, 1966-71
Jewett, Barbara, 1979-84
Jewett, Bill, 1976-78, 85-90
Johnson, E. W., 1959-60
Johnson, Pat, 1983-84
Jones, Lona, 1995-2001
Jones, Wesley, 1989
Jordan, Lillian, 1981-82
Jude, Kima, 1998-2000

K

Key, Sandra, 1997-2001
Kinney, Mrs. R. Q., 1962-64
Kinney, R. Q., 1967-69
Kinnison, Paul, 1998-2001

L

LaBeet, Terre, 1997-2001
Lamb, Bill, 1968
Langdon, Ray, 1983-88
Lawhon, Pete, 1989-93
Lawson, Glenn, 1994-97
Lee, Karlene, 1994-99
Lewis, Evelyn, 1992-99
Little, Curtis, 1981-82
Lindy, Fred, 1998-2001
Loving, Don, 1976-78
Lows, Melissa, 1990-98

M

Maben, Jack, 1959
Martin, Lena, 1960-63
Mathis, Quincy, 1964-67
Mauldin, Joe, 1962-65
McCreigh, Penny, 1990
McCroskey, Bob, 1987-88
McDaniel, Don, 1995-2000
McDaniel, Doug, 1994-99
McKown, Steve, 1995-2000
McNeal, Jack, 1966-72
Meeks, Vernon, 1962-64
Miller, Del, 1987
Miller, Jack, 1980-81

Minard, A. E., 1989-94, 1996-2000
Minefee, Hugh, 1999-2000
Monroe, Jerry, 1983-85
Moseley, Mrs W. I., 1960-65
Myers, Jim, 1999-2001

N

Nagle, Mrs. George, 1959-60
Nimmo, Louis, 1968-71
North, Wayne, 1973-74

O

Ogston, Rick, 1999
O'Neil, Bill, 1989-91
Ong, Henry, 1973-1979
Ong, Roxanne, 1993-98
Osborn, Carolyn, 1992-98

P

Packwood, Ed J., 1960-63
Pardue, Bill, 1985-88
Parrish, Jim, 1990-93
Phillips, I. B., 1965

Podleski, Ted, 1976-77
Pollvogt, Ron, 1999-2001
Porter, Jim, 1983-89
Preston, James, 1999-2001
Pugh, Lloyd, 1964-68
Pyfrom, Randall, 1964-70

R

Ramer, Gary, 1966
Ray, James, 1959
Reeder, Mark, 1989-94
Reel, Claude, 1971-74
Rhodes, R. D., 1967
Rich, Bob, 1979-80
Richardson, Jack, 1966-70
Ridenhour, Garnett, 1992-96
Riemer, Ron, 1983-89
Risinger, W. A., 1959-60
Roberts, James, Sr., 1969-70
Robinson, Kitty, 1995-2001
Robinson, Robert, 1989-90
Roden, Paul, 1960-63
Rogers, William, 1990-92
Rucker, L. F., 1959-60

S

Scism, Sherrell, 1984-86
Seymour, Linda, 1994
Sixkiller, Sam, 1973-75
Sledge, Linda, 1983-85
Smith, Richard, 1968-71
Spillers, Ronnie, 1990-91
Spillman, Clair, 1965-67
Stensrud, Carol, 1999-2001
Stephens, Archie, 1968-72, 1993-98
Sterling, John, 1993
Stevens, LeRoy, 1978-80
Storie, Martha Jane, 1986-90, 1998-2001
Street, John, 1960-62
Sutton, Frank, 1971-78

Index

Gambrell Memorial Association, 30
Garland, Diana, 282, 342-43
  Church Agencies, 341
Garrett, Robert "Bob," xvii, 85-86, 144, 147, 263
Garza, David, 218
Gaston, Matt, 265
Geeting, Doug, 121
Gifford, Bill, 216, 379
Gilliland, Edna, 155
Gilliland, Ron, 155
Gladding, Bob, 149
Gladding, Debbie, 149
Glasco, Dean, 122, 153, 195, 220
Glendale Bunkhouse, 85-86, 93, 143-44, 289, 365, 367, 377, 379
Godejohn, Fred, 173
Goncher-Cardenas, Kerri, 235, 249
Goodrich, Alice, 159
Goot, David, 159
Goot Pharmacy, 159
Graham, Velma, 262-63
Grand Canyon College, 34-35, 60, 69, 74, 116, 139, 149, 184
Great Awakening, 4-5
Greco, Bill, 268, 300, 385
Greco-Roman world, 2
Green, Gordon, 75
Grosskopf, Jenean, 182
group homes, 91-93, 361-62, 370, 377
Gunn, David, 190, 197
Gutierrez, Kaye, 210

H

Hall, Barry, 268
Hanna, Steve, xvii, 259-61
Hansen, Debbie, 182
Harris, Selwyn, 161-62
Hart, Keith, 40
Hart, Thomas B., 30
Harvie, Carolyn, 149
Hayes, S. T., 30
Health Care Finance Administration (HCFA), 206-7

Heath, Mike, 209
Hebrew Orphan Asylum, 7
Hedgcock, David, 199-200
Heintz, Morrisa, 263
Heke, Brenda, 263
Helm, Bill, 156, 212, 216
Henricksen, Kristin, 308
Henton, Wiley, 40
Hill, Pam, 195
Hill, Samuel, Jr., 278
History of the Arizona Southern Baptist Convention, A (Pair), 36
History of the Baptists, A (Torbet), 15
His Word Is Light (Baker), 198
Hite, Jim, 96
Hoffman, Maria, 200
Holohan, William, 82, 84
Hood, Charles, 41
Hoover, Beva, 218, 226
Hoover, Dwain, 218, 226
hotels de Dieu, 3
houseparents, 56, 96-97, 113, 119
Huff, Barbara, 154, 227, 260
Huff, Richard, 104, 154, 227-28, 370
Huffman, Maria, 211
Hughes, Shirley, 310-11
Hughes, Van, 310-11
Humble, Ginny, 155
Humble, Marvin, 155, 190, 260, 373
Hunter, Barbara, 239

I

Industrial Revolution, 3-4

J

Jakes, David, xi, xv-xvi, 226, 242, 244, 267, 289-91, 293, 296-98, 308, 313-14, 324, 326, 381-82, 384
Jefferson, Thomas, 276
Jennings, Les, Jr., xvii, 38, 74-75, 115, 123, 162, 231, 362-63, 377, 379
Jennings, Lester E., Sr., 38-40, 51, 74-75, 115-17, 153, 162, 361-63, 377, 379

Mills, John, 17
Mills Home, 17
Miltenberger, Mayola, 53, 102
Mims, Vernon, 74
Minard, A. E., 169
Minard, Charlotte, 169
Mississippi Southern Baptist, 16
Mother's Aid, 18
"Mother's Day Offering" (*Love in Action*), 68
Mouser, Marvin, 20

N

Nagel, George, 40
Nelson Garrison, 266
Newell, Wendell, 64
New Mexico Baptist Children's Home, 30-34, 341
New Mexico Baptist Convention, 18, 29-31
New Mexico Baptist Orphanage, 18, 30, 353
New York Catholic Protectory, 8
New York Children's Aid Society, 9
New York Society for the Prevention of Cruelty to Children, 10
Nilsson, Joel, 204
North American Mission Board, 147, 221, 317
North Carolina Baptist Homes for Children, 17
North Central Accreditation, 270
North Central Association, 101, 299, 381
Northern Regional Center, 268-69, 300-301
Northwest Regional Center, 266, 300, 385
Norton, Mary Beth, 9
Norwood, Aaron, 216
Nugent, Lillian, 167

O

offerings
  birthday, 33-34, 63, 65, 117, 354

Mother's Day, 68, 112
Ogston, Rick, 261
Ohio Baptist Foundation, 20
Oklahoma Baptists, 18
Oliver Twist (Dickens), 5
Olson, Tina, 236
Omnibus Budget Reconciliation Act of 1993, 246
Orphanage, 5-9, 11-12, 14-15, 17-18, 25, 31, 33, 47-48, 58, 81, 120, 125, 131, 245, 279, 332
orphan trains, 9
Osterle, Rachel, 307
Owen, Dennis, 278

P

Packwood, Ed, 40, 61
Pair, C. L.
  History of the Arizona Southern Baptist Convention, A, 36
Papago Indian Children's Home, 94, 104
Paradise Valley Conference Center, 222
Paral, Robert, 228
Pate, Cyril, 33
Patton, June, 87
Paul (apostle), 2, 283
People Places, 337
permanency, 19, 243, 246-47, 305, 309, 324, 334
Perrin, Gayle, 205
Peter (apostle), 283
Peterson, Mike, 311-12
Peterson, Tami, 311-12
Pitts, Mark, 154
Pitts, Nancy, 154
placing-out, 9-10
Porter, Valerie, 159
Preston, Jim, 106, 108
prevention, 19, 342
Priest, Andrew J., 33
Protestant Reformation, 3-4
Pudoka, Janie, 159
Purkaple, Jerry, 264-65

Sunglow Mission Ranch, 138, 154, 168, 227, 260, 290, 375, 378
Sunny Crest Children's Home, 20
Suttill, Betty Jean, 169
Sutton, Roy, 68, 115
Swan, Mrs. D., 121
Swickle, Mort, 182

T

Taeger, Gilbert, 263
Taeger, Mary, 263
Taylor, Eric, 210
Temple, Paul, 267
Texas Baptist, The, 16
Texas Baptist Children's Home, 20
Thomas, Tommy, xvi, 267, 300
Thomasville Baptist Orphanage, 17
Thornton, Alice Hardy, 149, 192-93, 308
Thornwell Children's Home, 24
Title XIX, 98, 166, 202-5
Tommy (resident of ABCS), 162
Torbet, Robert
    History of the Baptists, A, 15
Total Quality Management (TQM), 236, 239
Tripote, Jim, 169
Tsoi, Simon, 133-34
Turnagain Children's Home, 21
Tyson, Charles, 190, 263

U

Ursuline nuns, 7
Ussery, Wayne, 189

V

VanderHaar, Darryl, 319
Varner, Victor, 218
Vercher, Paul, 33
VerHoeve, Wayne, 173, 190
Virginia Baptist Children's Home and Family Services, 18, 133, 340
Virginia Company, 5

W

Wagnon, Lloyd, 165, 171, 182, 186
Walker, Bob, 101
Wallis, Jim, xii, 285
Walnut Street Baptist Church, 16
Walz v. Tax Commission, 278
Welch, Byron, 117
Welch Associates, 116-17
Wesner, Charles, 262, 264, 299, 381
Wesolowski, Kurt, 299
West Missouri Campus, 122-23, 141, 150
Westmoreland, Timothy, 152
Wheeler, Etta, 10
White, Charlotte, 171
Whiteaker, Robert R., 96, 119-21, 135
Whitfield, George, 5-6, 332
Wiles, Tom, 190, 220
Wilkins, Dennis, 204, 218-19
Wilkins, Marsha, 218
Willcoxon, Dr. Ronald, xvii, 142-43, 179, 321
Willett, J. O., 29
Williams, Sam, 133-34
Williford, Darryl, 143-44
Willis, Jack, xvii, 133, 137-38, 147, 153, 161, 163-64, 190, 209, 289, 366, 377
Willis, Joyce, 251
Willis, Sarah, 138
Willis, Tim, 224
Wilson, George, ix, 32, 40, 47, 49-50, 53-54, 60, 62-63, 68, 75, 77-78, 93, 102, 110, 115, 323
Wilson, Mary Ellen, 10
Women's Missionary Union (WMU), 31, 33-34, 51, 63, 112, 116
Wood, Ruth, xvi, 195
Woodson, Mariah Louise, 17
World War II, 12, 19
Wrangler Program, xvii, 86, 143-47, 231
Wright, Charles, 75, 78

X

xenodocheion, 2

Y

Yeary, Dan, 225
Yost, Russ, 248-49

Z

Zwingli (Protestant leader), 3

Edwards Brothers,Inc!
Thorofare, NJ 08086
21 October, 2010
BA2010295